LONG STANDING AMBITION

The first solo round Britain windsurf

Jono Dunnett

First published 2017

ISBN: 978-0-9957782-0-7

A CIP catalogue record for this title is available from the British Library.

Photographs: author's own unless stated
Maps: author's own from Ordnance Survey coastal outlines
Cover (front): Sail shelter - St. Andrew's beach, photo by Steve MacDougall, *The Courier* Newspaper
Cover (back): Bass Rock - Firth of Forth, photo by Paul Rigg
Cover designs: Edwin Bozo

To those who are curious

Dream is not that which you see while sleeping it is something that does not let you sleep.'

— A. P. J. Abdul Kalam

1

Exhausted, I pull the sail up again, I sail at breakneck speed crashing into lumps of sea for another few hundred metres until wiping out in a ball of spray. I haul myself back on to the board with water cascading from drysuit and rucksack, and consider my options. This is still the best option. Get breath back. Repeat.

I've no idea how many times I repeat. A dozen at least. Sufficient to get within sight of Dover.

Some background.

Three days ago I set off from Clacton-on-sea, looking to fulfil a dream I'd carried - mostly secretly - for nearly 20 years. A dream that had niggled and gnawed away at me, that had created a sense of unease and unrest.

The dream had made me dislike myself. It was pointless and selfish and deluded. It embarrassed me. Had my family been aware of it - it would have concerned them. Even now, thinking about it, I screw up my face. I didn't consider it a dream so much as a guiltily held desire.

I wanted to solo windsurf round Britain.

For years I ignored and belittled the single true and consistent ambition I held in life. Until one day - in the midst of what might euphemistically be called a 'rough patch' - I listened to myself. At 40 years of age, I stopped trying to suppress the desire, and set about achieving the dream.

So the above situation - being swept down towards a concrete wall being pounded by the waves of a near gale - was entirely of my own making. Not for the last time on this adventure I reminded myself "be careful what you wish for, Jono".

2

At times during my life I have come to think that I am a little bit different. At other times, I have forgotten this. Lately, I have come to realise that it does not matter.

* * *

As kids, we - my brother and I - had been fortunate enough to have parents who allowed us to roam. Gregg and I would head deep into Epping Forest. We'd climb trees, crash bikes, make weapons and generally drink freedom. The forest attracted all sorts, and as the elder brother I made the calls on staying safe. We never split up, usually had a dog, never talked to anyone and maintained a significant distance between ourselves and other forest users. We never had problems with strangers but did on occasion witness curious behaviour, and were once tracked for a while by a police helicopter until we left the forest.

Academically, I was a reasonably bright kid and a good student. I got picked on a bit at primary (Caroline Wright, you are forgiven) and secondary (Paul Palmer, likewise) school, which I put down to being tongue tied under stress and completely lacking the ability to come back with a repost, witty or otherwise. This definitely contributed to a dislike of school.

I enjoyed sports (except rugby) and was good at running, which was handy when Palmer was around. My favourite school project *ever* was designing and building a papier-mâché island. It goes without saying that my island would have been a special place to sail.

At weekends the family would jump in the car and head to Clacton. Gregg and I loved the sea so were always keen to go. We sailed Topper dinghies at the local sailing club which at the time was as permissive as our parents. If it was windy we'd sail two-up for extra ballast. Windier and we'd borrow a parent to help stay upright. Launch and landing on the ramp was hazardous, and the rescue boat was more so, so we learnt to self-rescue and stay out of trouble. I disliked having the rescue boat near and even at that age considered myself more able than those who were crewing it.

Highlight of the sailing year was the cruise to the Gunfleet Sands - a sand bar that only dries on very low tides, that lies about 8 miles diagonally offshore from The Club. The cruise was usually cancelled on safety grounds and no longer forms part of the calendar, but somehow one year Gregg and I - aged 10 and 11 - were allowed to tag along 'two-up' in a Topper. That return sail from the sands is my earliest memory of an epic sail! The wind had increased and it was a gloomy early evening when the rising tide released the boats from the offshore sandbank. The faster boats streaked away and the slower ones like our Topper were left behind, so we were essentially sailing alone. Land was barely visible as we ploughed through the waves and the salt water spray stung our eyes.

Conditions were exhilarating, yet I felt a deep sense of calm and very comfortable in the situation. Boundaries between self and environment were blurred, and everyday worries were far from mind.

Then Gregg, who was helming, changed course. My altered state shattered, I protested! We needed to sail a true beat to get back, not just head inshore! We fought. Gregg wanted inshore, I wanted to finish where we'd started from - if in the dark then so be it. I threatened to jump out of the boat unless Gregg took a direct upwind course or let me helm. Gregg started crying but would not oblige or shift. Gregg's will prevailed and my threat was a bluff. To my disappointment the final leg of our sail was made by road.

I loved the freedom of being on the water, and sailing and windsurfing would continue to, and still do - occasionally - gift me moments when I truly do disconnect from life's mundane concerns.

Nowadays, this tends to happen in challenging sailing conditions. The task at hand occupies but does not overwhelm. When it happens, there is an expanded awareness of the present, and this can be literal in that vision becomes tunnelled and magnified. There is a simple joy derived from doing something that has taken a great deal of learning to do, and doing it well. On my windsurf round Britain I would occasionally find myself in this agreeable place. I would also find myself pushed to places far beyond.

As young kids, we would take family holidays to Scotland, and I would never want to leave. The emptiness and majesty of the west coast was indelibly marked on my psyche. Sorry England, and Wales, but you can't quite match your northern neighbour. I learned to windsurf in Scotland and can still vividly remember a seal swimming under my board, and the jelly-legged sensation of fear that produced. Accustomed to the murky Clacton sea, I was fascinated by, and petrified of, the clear water and all the life to be observed under the surface. As I sailed, I would scan the world beneath. As the depths increased, a sense of vertigo would set in. The wildness of Scotland had me hooked.

Windsurfing replaced sailing as our pastime of choice. Four of us grew up sailing together - Gregg, Tim, Clyde and myself - and we would sail whenever the opportunity allowed. We would crave strong winds. Later on, all of us would work for at least a few years in windsurfing connected roles.

Clyde and I also competed on the Raceboard circuits, largely thanks to Clyde's parents also being keen to travel around the country in their campervan. Most weekends for a few years, we would head off with Clyde and family to race. I rose up the rankings to be top of the pile locally and threatening-to-break-through-but-not-quite-getting-there nationally.

I loved the sailing, the racing and the travelling of the bigger regattas. We got around the country, becoming acquainted with the coastlines of Bridlington, Abersoch, Weymouth, Menai Straits and more. There are plenty of days I can vividly remember. I think it likely that the seed of wanting to windsurf round Britain came during these years. Apparently, on the long post-event journeys back to Essex I would not-so-subtly - and without success - attempt to convince Clyde of the merits of such an endeavour.

The flip side of the big windsurfing events were the socials, either planned evening gatherings or informally hanging around waiting for wind. I hated both. My strategy was to stick close to

Clyde and then slide away for a solitary wander when I could no longer do that without appearing odd.

This seems as good an opportunity as any to apologise to Clyde for being such a pain in the arse.

One day - out of the blue - I received a phone call from the Royal Yachting Association team coach to say that I had qualified to represent Britain at the Youth World championships to be held in Italy. At the regatta I was ill and missed some of the racing, but I was proud to have come in 'under the radar' and made the team as an outsider.

Tuition fees had yet to really bite, so we drifted into university without much thought (or as a post A-level afterthought, in my case). Tim, Gregg and I ended up in Swansea; Clyde in Bangor. On the exposed west coasts we became far more proficient wavesailors. With formulaic predictability, we also learned to surf. We learned to read the waves and the weather forecasts as surfers do. For the long summer holidays we would head to the French Atlantic coast, and surf some more.

In my final year at university I had a serious injury from a surfing wipeout. I was surfing well this day, taking some late drops. I was most definitely in a *zone* type state. Brimming with overconfidence I took a wave I couldn't make and this time fell. My board hit me on side of my head, fracturing my skull and causing a bleed on the brain. I had an operation to remove the clot and was 4 weeks in hospital. I was very fortunate to have not lost consciousness in the water, and to have had no resulting long term damage. I assume this – to my knowledge no-one has seriously suggested otherwise.

I became a more cautious surfer as a result. A year later I had another accident - this time caused by a lack of confidence. I tried to back out of a wave I was already too committed to, and went *over the falls* straddling my board. I ended up under the surgeon's knife again. The pain this time was *much* worse.

After graduating I did what I was encouraged to do without knowing why, and embarked upon a Master's degree. It wasn't the right thing for me to do then. To this day I regret not handing in the dissertation, but at least I don't wake up in a panic about that now.

I came within a hair's breadth of becoming a medical research writer, which would have set me on an entirely different trajectory - how entire lives hinge on what is essentially luck! Instead, I headed out to Menorca to work my first of many seasons as a windsurfing instructor.

In Menorca I met a pretty local girl who became my girlfriend, and for a number of years was happier than I had ever been. The day job suited me down to the ground. I worked hard and was good at my job to the extent that when I didn't show for the obligatory evening social, nothing was said. Having been around people all day I would need a break and discreetly head off for some solitude.

Over the years I came to know the Bay of Fornells as well as anyone. On light wind days I would lead groups exploring its indented coastline (and, of course, circumnavigating its islands). I especially loved the peace and seclusion of the south of The Bay where - away from the irritating rescue boats and noisy Catalans - osprey would sometimes fish.

There is something about exploring your *home island*, and Menorca felt like home from day one. To sail around the island soon became an ambition. Menorca, being just a little bit smaller than the Isle of Wight, is a perfect size for a challenging one-day circumnavigation. Working for a sailing centre meant that I had access to good equipment and a seaworthy safety boat. I had been in Menorca less than a year when I completed that trip. It was a difficult and hugely rewarding sail, taking 9½ hours to complete.

When I return to any of the headlands sailed past (or even eat the same brand of biscuit consumed that day!) I still experience a sense of satisfaction. There is the satisfaction of having done it (perhaps first, perhaps fastest) - which I think is a little bit vain, and the much deeper satisfaction of *getting to know* the place you live. Having windsurfed around Menorca I feel like I know the island in a way few other people will know it. The island let me round and we became friends. That we had a bit of a battle and a few difficulties along the way increases the strength of our connection.

There is no denying that having windsurfed around Menorca my focus shifted, and locked onto, the idea of windsurfing around

Britain. That was the point of no return. Getting to know my *home* home-island, by windsurfing around it, re-established itself as my confirmed ambition.

Flush from the success of windsurfing around Menorca, I wasted no time in putting a plan into action. I ordered a book.

3

Round Britain Windsurf

It was Bill Dawes from *Boards Magazine* who put me on to the trail. I'd emailed Bill and asked some questions about windsurfing around Britain, and he'd explained that this had already been done, and the chap in question had written a book. This didn't come as a disappointment. Quite the contrary! It had been done? Great! That means it's possible and I can do it too!

The book in question wasn't in Clacton library, or even in Colchester's Waterstones. Fortunately for me, a web search later and in an early *I-love-technology* moment, I was able to locate and buy a copy from a library sale in Seattle. Round Britain Windsurf, by Tim Batstone, became my first ever internet purchase! The internet - that was to be the facilitator for my own windsurf round Britain - was already fuelling the dream.

The book is a first-hand account of Tim Batstone's pioneering 1984 adventure.

I was gripped, and devoured the book in no time. Batstone had considerable support, including a yacht and an inflatable boat accompanying him on his journey. The team effort approach was quick. Tim could change sails and board according to the wind strength, as well as carry all supplies, rest and sleep on the boat. Having the inflatable on the water allowed him to sail to his limits without this becoming a safety issue, as if he did push it a bit too far, become exhausted, break something become becalmed or find conditions too challenging - his support team could pick him up. At the start of a day's sailing the inflatable boat would deliver Tim where he had sailed to the day before, and at the end of the day it would deliver him back to the mothership.

At the start of his Round Britain Windsurf, Tim was - by his own admission - not an expert windsurfer. His 'preparation' included a rather risky solo sail around the Scilly Isles that must have scared him, and most certainly would have provided a useful wakeup call to the scale of the challenge he was taking on. Windsurfing equipment from that era was also heavy, difficult to use and prone to breakage. By today's standards - terrible. In easier to comprehend cycling terms: this was the penny farthing era. Windsurfing Round Britain in 1984 was a remarkable achievement, and several times during my own rounding I reflected upon this fact.

However, despite my admiration, I knew back then that I was not looking to replicate Tim's feat. For a number of reasons his was not an approach that appealed to me.

First, the inevitable tensions of a team challenge would detract from my enjoyment of the experience. There are people who would enjoy the people management aspect of such an endeavour, but I am not among them.

Second, I would dislike having a support boat present. It would be like a fly buzzing around my face.

Third, the idea of 'chunking' passages - 'banking' progress by GPS waypoint position and then returning to the location under motor - to finish the job another time - seems contrived. I think this is fine for a first attempt, and if you are looking for records and that is the precedent that has been set then that is fine also. But a new record was never my motivation. For me, I wanted to do things the way seafarers of old would have done them, thinking in terms of passages and consolidating progress by making safe havens on the way round.

Fourth, the cost of doing a trip with a support crew would have been prohibitive.

So, not only did doing things the same way not appeal, it was also non-viable.

* * *

The post round Menorca enthusiasm lasted a while. I wrote a few letters enquiring about sponsorship and secured…wait for it: a hydration backpack. Useful, but not exactly sufficient to get any momentum for a Round Britain campaign. More critically, I also hadn't mentally accepted that this challenge was going to have to be a solo effort. Instead, I'd been persisting with trying to convince Clyde that he also wanted to windsurf round Britain. It definitely made sense to sail with Clyde. His parents had the campervan and are alternative enough to consider lending support. And the safety in numbers thought was comforting. Unfortunately, Clyde just wasn't up for it.

As for Gregg, I wasn't keen on having him as a sailing partner. This was possibly a reflection on his relative lack of raceboard experience, and also possibly a protective response to close kin accompanying me on a journey that might have a few dangers (sorry Clyde, that didn't kick in for you). Maybe it was just that Gregg didn't come with a campervan.

So nothing came of it. Clyde, Gregg and myself drifted along doing the things most people do as they get older. But you can't pretend to be young forever and eventually we all grew up a bit.

The dream I harboured became buried. There, but not voiced. Completely incompatible with the life I was leading working at a sailing centre. I could get one week off in the summer, not the 2 or 3 months I would need.

I became embarrassed about having an unrealistic dream so kept it to myself. I'd always kept it fairly low profile, but it now went under the radar, and I didn't mention it even to Clyde or Gregg. I didn't share it with my partner, thinking that would demonstrate a lack of commitment to her. I didn't share it with family, thinking it would concern them. In the intervening years I mentioned it just once - much later - to a friend who was concerned enough about my low mood at that time to enquire what I really wanted out of life. I immediately glossed over my admission and portrayed it as something I wasn't really serious about. The unfulfilled ambition became at least slightly repressed. I am sure it contributed to a general sense of restlessness that bothered me.

Then in 2012 I left Menorca for a new relationship and way of life in Scotland. After 15 years of Mediterranean island living, the contrast was quite extreme. It would be fair to say that I struggled to adjust. I tried hard to make myself fit the new situation in which I found myself, an exercise destined to fail. With a little more wisdom - rather than try to make myself fit - I might have revealed more of my true nature and talked at this time about my dream to windsurf round Britain, which had returned with a vengeance to intrude upon my thoughts.

These were difficult times, but their legacy was positive. I became more self-accepting, and repaired damaged family ties.

Eventually my partner and I split, and I returned to my native Essex. I found myself living between my parent's houses and spare rooms. I was more unsettled than ever, and warded off the blues by frequently moving on. I enrolled on a training course to become an electrician. It was 'OK', as pretty much everything was 'OK' at that time, and I made progress without difficulty or enthusiasm. I paid my modest overheads through working on websites.

Despite my glumness, hindsight suggests that my subconscious was well aware of the bigger picture. I was keeping myself fit through running and cycling, and was doing long distance sailing. I also entered and competed in the 2014 Raceboard World Championships (finishing twenty something in a hundred-strong fleet, and sleeping on a carefully selected blow up mattress that would later be my bed for the expedition). Long before I admitted to myself that Round Britain was my goal, I was ramping up the preparation. The 'training' sails I did seem laughably short to me now, but they were out of the ordinary and testing my comfort zone at the time: from Clacton to Harwich, up to Mersea, or offshore to the local wind farm. The bouts of exercise and excitement of being offshore were a tonic to my low mood.

Towards the end of 2014, the electrician training company I was enrolled with went into receivership and a large number of students, myself included, were left in limbo. It didn't particularly surprise or upset me that things weren't working out again. In truth, I had only been going through the motions anyway.

But my remoteness at this time - a clear cause of concern for my family - was not as a result of this or other disappointments. It stemmed from a shift in my own attention, which had become completely absorbed with the task of working out just *how* I was going to windsurf round Britain. These were no longer speculative musings, and the adrenaline pumped as I considered the details. The fear of my imaginings gripped me.

It would be a while yet before I felt ready to publicly declare my intent but I did at last tell family. First off I told my Mum. She knows - has learned - better than to wave a flag to a bull, so did not expressly say she thought it was a bad idea, but understandably she was more concerned than enthusiastic. When I told my Dad he was interested in the details of my plan, which he thought were reasonable. Both parents seemed pleased that for once I was animated about something.

Gregg was quite surprised. We have always been close, but he had been unaware of my long-standing ambition. I guess I had lived with it for so long that I just imagined that he knew. He came across as supportive of the idea.

4

A Masterpiece of Design

Before I go into further detail, I need to introduce the reader to a masterpiece of design: the Raceboard windsurfer. A basic understanding of this board will make it easier to follow this story.

Raceboards are long and thin and much more buoyant than the typical windsurfer you might see blasting in and out from a beach on a windy day. They are not the fastest style of board in all wind and sea states, but they cope extremely well over a variety of conditions. In light wind trim they glide through the water with the elegance of a canoe. As the wind picks up these boards change 'mode', elegantly transitioning from being craft that sit *in* the water to craft that skim along *on top of* the water's surface.

This is a slight oversimplification, and does not reflect the nuances of sailing these craft, and of sailing in general. In reality each of the numerous possible 'points of sail' - courses relative to the wind direction - will have a different corresponding mode. An added twist is that the mode for a particular point of sail may be completely different in different winds strengths. The varied repertoire of modes in which raceboards can be sailed is what makes them so well suited to such a range of wind and water states.

The ability to sail in multiple modes is made possible by features not found on other styles of board. Specifically, raceboards benefit from a sliding mast track and a pivoting centreboard, both of which can be adjusted whilst sailing.

All these variables mean that raceboards are a little bit more complicated to sail than standard windsurfers. Specific knowledge and practice is required to get the best out of them. But they are a joy to sail. and for all-round performance are unequalled. They are really the *only* choice of board for long distance windsurfing.

The round Britain raceboard kit, here sailing upwind in
breezy conditions. Photo: Gregg Dunnett

5

Planning

Having incubated the idea of windsurfing round Britain for so long, my unconscious had done a lot of the background thinking for how it *might* work. A significant part of this was built upon the recollection that someone had at some point solo windsurfed around Ireland, with camping gear strapped to the front of their board - a raceboard, naturally. This I believe I read in a one-paragraph mention in *Boards* magazine, many years ago. Now that I wanted to find out more about this person, I couldn't. I asked some of the wise old men of windsurfing, and some of these seemed to have a similar recollection, but no amount of googling would reveal a name or more information. Despite their being a risk that my inspiration source was apocryphal, I took the round Ireland sail as evidence that round Britain by similar means was also possible.[1]

Around this time I also found the book *Land on my Right* by Ron Pattenden. In 2004, the author had solo sailed Britain on a Laser dinghy, carrying some of his gear inside and some strapped onto his boat. Predictably, I was gripped by his account. Pattenden was clearly another unexceptional sailor who was particularly unfazed by the 'rules' of what could and what couldn't be achieved. His preparation was basic, and it is true he needed rescuing a couple of times - notably off Cape Wrath - the northwest tip of Scotland. But he got round. I knew I was a more experienced sailor than Ron Pattenden, and - during preparation and the event proper - many times I told myself that *if he got round in a Laser, I can get round on a windsurf board*. It was particularly useful to read Pattenden's account because his was a

---

[1] I was thrilled to hear from the round Ireland windsurfer – whose name is Robert Henshall – at the end of the expedition. We eventually met up to compare experiences at a fine pub in Ardara, South Donegal.

solo sail. In relation to my own ambition, Pattenden's achievement was more motivationally inspiring than the previous roundings of Britain by windsurfer.

So, I reasoned, carrying equipment on my board would work.

The most obvious place to carry extra gear on a windsurf board is the front. The deck is clear and luggage would not interfere with normal sailing. However, repeated thought experiments revealed that front of board storage would be very problematic in stronger winds. In these conditions the nose of the board is being continually driven into, over, or through waves. It is bouncy, frequently submerged and also liable to being hit quite hard by the rig and/or sailor in the event of a fall. If this was how the Ireland guy did it (on the assumption he existed) he must have sat out or gone very slowly in stronger winds.

The issue of waves hitting the gear also troubled me. A bag would have far too much resistance and water would be slow to drain. Some sort of solid container would work better. Better still, the container should be held elevated off the deck, so that water can flow around the container on all sides, thereby letting waves wash through. Perhaps the most elegant solution would be for storage within the board, but this I rejected on grounds of difficulty of construction.

I doodled and played around with dead-end ideas for a while before satisfying myself that the front of the board approach just wouldn't work for me. The performance compromise of carrying gear on the front is too great and would sacrifice the simple joy of windsurfing. I also reasoned that I would also need some sort of barrel as my container.

With the front of the board ruled out, and the middle of the board too 'busy', the only place to carry kit is at the back. Would this work? I guessed it could, but really didn't know. There was only one way to find out and that was to get testing.

So straight after Christmas I headed out to Minorca - ostensibly to help my friend John replace our mutual friends' kitchen - although that was a secondary agenda. Over a couple of evenings, I explained to John and his wife Sarah my plans to windsurf round Britain. As big boat sailors with round Britain and round the world experience, and also windsurfers, I knew that John and Sarah were key allies in my quest, and I was keen to pick their brains and get them on-side.

Sarah would not be engaged and gave no encouragement whatsoever. She understood the scale of the challenge and did not think I would succeed. I was left in no doubt about her opinion, and - given the nature of that opinion - consider her response to have been appropriate and responsible.

John's response was initially similar. As I explained how it could work I watched him. John was gazing into space, uncharacteristically silent. I could see him contemplating the challenge ahead, mentally taking himself to the headlands that would have to be negotiated, returning to angry seas, reliving battles with currents. He's done all this before.

Casting his mind back must have triggered the emotions experienced on his own voyages, and he would have relived the loneliness and occasional fear of those seafaring years. Imagining the challenge of Britain, alone, on a windsurf board, would have been sobering indeed. He was having a battle in his own head about whether I could do this.

It took him a few days, but fortunately for me, he decided I could.

John's internal struggle settled, he pulled out charts and pointed out what seemed like every single headland, constriction, tide race and eddy in the United Kingdom. He drilled into me the importance of tides on sea-state, pointed out numerous locations where it was very important I pass on slack water, talked about the danger of getting hit by shipping, or hitting rocks, identified complicated passages - including, tellingly, the rounding Land's End passage - and generally made the whole idea sound pretty terrifying and astonishingly complicated.

During these evenings of complete information overload, I listened intently. Some key messages stuck in my mind and these would later become mantras that I would use to bolster my courage and steel my nerve.

Next, we set about designing and building a barrel carrier to trial. The design brief was for a carrier for the back of the board that would not hinder sailing, that is light and strong, not too difficult to make, and that wouldn't ruin the board it was fitted to.

We sawed, bent, drilled and riveted a few bits of aluminium and - voila! - version 1 was born. The design is basically a slightly elevated bar, with a 'saddle' upon which the barrel sits. The bar is fixed at the rear by the fin bolts and at the front by a 'plug' that fits snugly into the centreboard casing.[2]

The first sea trial was conducted in February 2015, during some local club racing in Menorca. Wind conditions were light and the barrel was only minimally loaded. Pleasingly, the barrel proved less of a hindrance to my own sailing than it was a distraction to the other sailors, to the extent that I won the first race. Between races the barrel fell off, so a better securing system obviously needed to be found, but - in these winds at least - the system appeared to work extremely well.

My return flight to the UK was looming and I was anxious to do a more thorough barrel test before heading back. Conditions stayed very light for days and then - boom! - the Menorcan Tramontana wind was in and conditions were far too extreme to head out on raceboard. Eventually, on the morning of the day of my return flight, the wind eased sufficiently to test the carrier system in some livelier conditions. I loaded barrel with a hefty rock wrapped in a coat and headed out. John took up position with his camera.

It was still overly windy and very much a struggle to be sailing a raceboard in these conditions. Perfect. Upwind sailing was still fine - the barrel did interfere slightly with the foot of the sail - but nothing too bothersome. And downwind sailing was comfortable despite the extra weight being much more noticeable. Gybing was more difficult but I could muddle round the corners OK. I sailed the board up into the mouth of the bay where some sizeable but messy swells were rolling in, then freed off for a downwind blast. Board speed downwind in windy conditions is up around 20 knots

---

[2] The 'plug' is the clever part of the design and was entirely John's idea. It fits into the board's centreboard case thereby increasing lateral stability of the carrier. This is important as when waves hit the barrel on the side the forces trying to 'roll' the carrier are considerable. Version 1 had a pivoting bar to allow on-water access to barrel, but this feature was dropped in later versions.

- fine when flat but jarringly bumpy in a confused sea. I bounced into and submarined through some big lumps of water. It was only a short test, but it was realistic, and nothing failed. Coat and rock emerged shaken but dry.

As I relaxed into my aeroplane seat that evening, I reflected upon the significance of the day. The barrel carrying system - critical to the whole project - worked. John had got some great shots. I narrowed my eyes and exhaled, and a flush of adrenaline confirmed my dream a stride closer.

6

windsurfroundbritain.co.uk

For a few weeks, in between barrel and kitchen, I had also been developing the website that would be central to the round Britain adventure. I had crafted the text that would hopefully persuade people to offer their support, and I had built the functionality that enabled people to become Local Contacts by putting their virtual pin on the map. I had put into words my reasons for choosing the charities that I would be raising funds for.

I knew with clarity that I wanted to raise funds for pancreatic cancer research. A close friend in Menorca, Paco, had died of the disease, leaving behind his wife and their 2 young daughters. The daughters are now grown up but the haunted look in Paco's eyes remains with me, as does my own sense of powerlessness to intervene or even help in any way as the cancer took its brutal and inevitable course. I wanted to sail for Paco, and for his girls.

I also considered it important to acknowledge that cancer is a very western worry, and I wanted to recognise this by offering people the opportunity to donate to a charity that looked beyond our own comfortable worlds. I chose a charity that supported education for Tanzanian orphans and widows.

Before the website was ready, it needed a little bit more content. I populated the blog section with some news about the barrel carrier development and a few write ups of training sails, including two failed attempts to get round the Isle of Wight from earlier in the year.

The first of these attempts was with Clyde and Gregg - both by now family men with inflexible timetables - and consequently from the outset it was pretty obvious the tides and the wind (not to mention our late morning departure from Avon beach, a few miles west of the Island) weren't going to allow time to get round before dark. Camping - sleeping under sails - was mentioned.

It was a great adventure rounding the iconic Needles, then bouncing over the disturbed water off St Catherine's Point on the south of the island, then becoming becalmed, before finally rounding the eastern tip and making it back into the Solent in fading light. But in the dying evening breeze I couldn't understand why Gregg and Clyde were pointing so low! We needed to sail higher, on a true beat. Where were they going? We'd agreed to spend the night under our sails, hadn't we? They were heading to the mainland. It was like the Gunfleet Sands Topper episode all over again. Slightly disappointed - but without threats to jump off - I undid an hour's worth of upwind sailing to join them. We made landfall in the twilight and were rescued by road.

The second attempt was just Gregg and I. This time we started in the Solent with good wind, and only slightly late. We made good upwind progress to Yarmouth and went through the Hurst Narrows at fairly slack tide. Already acquainted with the Needles, this time they seemed much friendlier as we passed close by before turning east on a dying breeze. Concerned about our chances of completing the rounding, Gregg was having a change of heart. A few wobbly miles later we aborted the attempt. It took a while to beat the tide back to the Needles - them and us practically 'mates' by now – and once around and on to the Solent side, the tide ran with remarkable speed. We passed Hurst on a conveyer belt of water that carried us through the constriction like pooh sticks down a river.

Both IOW attempts will go down in history as failures, but the experience of sailing unfamiliar waters and employing a 'sail it as you see it' strategy was exhilarating and useful. I was also confident that we *could* have got round both times by stopping on the island overnight, so the official track record of failure did not concern me. In a mischievous way I enjoyed the silliness of failing on the IOW but continuing with Britain.

Next website tweak was the addition of John's photographs from the windy barrel trial in Minorca. These really brought the website to life visually, and by early March 2015 I was ready to gamble that it was presenting a credible enough plan to be taken seriously.

Before 'coming out' to a wider audience I emailed Roger Tushingham, founder of Tushingham Sails and contact from my sailing school days. I sent Roger a preview link of the website, explained the plan and politely asked for some equipment to use for the expedition. To my relief and excitement Roger confirmed that Tushingham would like to be involved. This was a clenched fist moment that boosted my confidence and added credibility to the expedition.

Roger said that they would be able to help with the sails, masts and booms that I would need, but that supplying a board would be problematic, as there were none available. I glossed over the board issue at this stage, knowing that as a last resort I could use the old board I had used for barrel testing in Menorca. In any case, I thought that Starboard - the biggest board manufacturer in the World -might step in to help out.

Next I emailed Gul, another UK company, with a similar pitch for help. Again, a no quibble response - total support. In a matter of days new drysuit and clothing accessories arrived through the post. Throughout the trip, the willingness to help of both Gul and Tushingham was fantastic.

The whole project was suddenly gathering momentum. Kit was arriving on my doorstep. Busy people were going out of their way to support my bid. No longer was I in a situation where I could abandon the plan without consequence. I monitored my reactions: "I am comfortable with this. I am not getting cold feet. OK then, let's continue." It felt good that exciting things were happening, and it was shoring up my self-esteem that it was me who was making them happen.

Although there is never truly a point of *no* return, commitment became (effectively) total with the public announcement of my intention. On 8th March 2015 I copied the now live website address into my Facebook status, and raised my finger ready to click 'post'.

And there I paused - allowing myself one last opportunity to save face. Ahead, I feared - lay humiliating lack of interest, or incomprehension. Would people really want to help me out? Would they glance at it and think "tosser" before deleting me from their friends list? Am I deluding myself that I am up to this? As is often the case with our fears, they lose their potency when confronted.

I clicked the 'post' button:

"I hesitate only slightly to announce...

www.windsurfroundbritain.co.uk"

And that was that. The cat was out of the bag. Almost immediately I started receiving supportive messages. Ex-colleagues from Minorca Sailing, friends from Menorca, and university friends who I'd lost touch with were coming out of the ether to offer their support and encouragement. People were enthusiastic, this was something that was capturing their imagination! The website local contact map started receiving its first sign-ups. Also encouraging was that these weren't all people who I knew (although almost all did have *some* link to the sea or sailing). Over the course of the expedition, there would be more than 150 sign-ups, and a few dozen more would offer support through social media. I'd always been a rather ambivalent Facebook user; and also a timid user - but as a tool for spreading word of the expedition it proved invaluable.

Buoyed by my initial success with expedition sponsors I sent a second tranche of emails for the bits and pieces I would need. The companies I approached were often receptive. Standard Horizon were happy to supply a waterproof handheld VHF radio (that could be charged by USB, so no need to take a charging dock), a fantastically upbeat guy called Tim from Mobilesolarchargers called me up upon receipt of my email and bellowed down the telephone "RESPECT JONATHAN! RESPECT!", before offering to supply a solar charger and battery for charging USB devices on the go.

Richard Brook, an ex-Minorca colleague got in touch and arranged for his current employer – Viking Renewables Ltd – to support the expedition with cash that would keep me in fish and chips until halfway round. Richard remained supportive throughout the expedition.

Phil Holman, another ex-colleague offered help organising the planned London start.

* * *

The excitement post website launch was tempered by some sad news. A family friend since my childhood, Dennis London, had died. He had finally succumbing to Pancreatic Cancer. Now I knew I would be sailing for both Paco and Dennis.

7

Testing

I was acutely aware of my extremely limited luggage carrying capacity, and obsessively researched the weight and volume of every item I might take. I put in a frankly ridiculous number of hours researching things like the pack size of sleeping bags and the merits of the "beer can stove" versus other stove-fuel alternatives.

Helpful as this was, it was the test sails and training that delivered real insight into *what* I needed to find solutions for, and *how practical* the solutions I was finding really were.

On one sail, I ended up beating back upwind in breezy conditions when it was effectively dark. This was on my 'home' patch but there were sea defence works going on and it was high tide, so there was no landing for the last couple of miles. It was an eye-opener to the difficulties of windsurfing at night. Just reading the water and the waves was extremely difficult. Even a trivial gear problem would have been very difficult to fix in the dark. Also, I realised, I was completely invisible to other craft in the vicinity. It wasn't very nice. Waterproof head-torch went on to my shopping list.

My training sails up to now had been with an older raceboard that I couldn't easily adapt to carry a barrel. These sails had been useful, but I was aware that I was overdue practising with a fully laden expedition ready board. Would this be more difficult? Would the barrel be too heavy? Would I be able to carry all the kit?

I gave up hope of Starboard helping out and moved with some haste to get my own board over from Menorca. The board I was to use was also a Starboard - I would have preferred one of their more recent and voluminous models but seeing as one wasn't forthcoming - my 2009 model would have to do. Tushingham donated a Starboard-branded sun visor instead – which I wore and became very fond of, despite not really wanting to!

With the board-in-wrong-country problem John once again came to the rescue, and helped load it into a UK bound furniture removal van. I picked the board up from Portsmouth and with 7 weeks to the off was all set to do some proper sailing in full expedition trim.

8

Lundy Island Test Sail

This was the first real expedition simulation. The idea had been Ian Leonard's, a friend from Boards magazine testing days who lives on the North Devon coast, and who can see Lundy Island from his lookout tower next to his converted barn. Lundy has been tempting Ian for the last 15 years and he was very much on the lookout for a chump (or two) to sail out there with him. Gregg and I agreed without hesitation.

It was my first experience of a very satisfying crossing achieved. And when you complete a crossing there is - believe me - a very deep sense of satisfaction.

The write up from this micro-expedition is available on the windsurfroundbritain blog.

Lundy was a special place to stop, very beautiful and inhabited by kind and warm people. Not lost on me was that Tim Batstone also stopped here, and that I also might choose to stop here on my Round Britain journey. For an unsupported sailor it is an ambitious crossing from here to Wales, but that is my plan.

On our trip, Ian and I walked to the north end of the Island. From our vantage point on the cliffs above the lighthouse I scanned north, wondering if I might be able to spot Wales. Visibility was good, but there was just empty sea ahead. It had looked a lonely place to launch in to.

9

Final Preparations

Back in Essex summer was with us, and sea conditions were typically benign. Sailing around here is quite flattering to your skills and possibilities. After Lundy, it seemed very easy and non-intimidating. I went on a few more test sails which were not really testing my sailing but were helpful to refine the contents of my barrel to make for comfortable camping.

I didn't have room for a tent, so instead used the rigged sail as a makeshift shelter for protection from wind and rain. By propping up the end of the boom with a 'handy stick' and orientating the sail so that the wind was pushing down on the end of the boom I had an effective and cosy bothy. It worked well with a couple of provisos. One, if the wind changed direction during the night you might need to re-orientate. Two, a suitable stick was required.

The bigger problem was the stick. You'd think finding a stick would be easy, but my testing was suggesting this wouldn't always be the case. Accordingly, I decided to adapt the barrel carrier to take a paddle. The long shaft of the paddle would be an ideal stick, plus, I reasoned, if I found myself becalmed I would be thankful to have a paddle.

I repeatedly experimented trying to find a practical method of paddling the board with the rigged sail attached. Paddling a raceboard windsurfer is easy, but paddling with a large sail attached that catches and drags in the water is surprisingly difficult. I failed to find a good solution. Still, the paddle was useful as a stick, and it demonstrated that I was thinking about safety, so it was coming with me.

I thought a lot about safety, particularly about personal buoyancy. Windsurfers don't typically wear life jackets or buoyancy aids. But then they also don't typically sail alone and miles offshore, like I would be doing. In a genuine fix, a lifejacket would be a nice thing to have. But I was already fully loaded with harness, backpack, safety and navigation kit. Carrying *more* gear, and making myself *more* cumbersome and prone to getting caught up under my sail didn't seem like a wise move. My board would be my buoyancy, and in a rescue situation I would tie myself to my board. I considered the ways that a sailor can become separated from their board at sea, and the difficulty of swimming in a baggy drysuit with backpack. There are situations in which the board could be lost and these are very serious. Do everything possible to not lose the board was the best strategy. And if I do lose the board, I *must* be able to send a distress signal.

I'd previously announced that I would be starting from London Bridge, in my mind to follow in the footsteps of Tim Batstone and Ron Patterson.[3] I sought the required permission from Port of London Authority - presenting them with a passage plan and explaining that Docklands Sailing Centre would be helping out. Thanks go to Phil Holman from DSC for his efforts to secure the London start. Unfortunately though, despite our efforts, permission was not forthcoming. Had I been in a boat I would have been welcome, but as a windsurfer my application and appeal were both directed downriver to a potential start at Crossness, site of an iconic sewage works... Oh well, rather than get indignant about the injustice of the decision I changed plans to a Clacton start. Much simpler, and really I wouldn't have enjoyed the fanfare and hassle of a London start anyway. That also allowed me to shift the start forward a week as I wouldn't be dependent upon the outgoing London tide.

---

[3] A closer reading of these accounts would have revealed the London Bridge photoshoots to have been ceremonial, rather than official starts

Day 1 - 7th June 2015 - Expedition Start

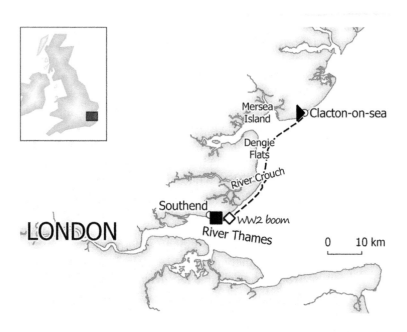

In the week leading up to the off I scan the weather forecasts. They look very promising. It looks like there's going to be a run of easterly winds that will help me make progress along the south coast, once I get there.

That would be ideal. Really though, I just hope to get off without incident. Press are going to be there, friends and family are turning up to see me off. I need enough wind to move, but not so much so that it is a battle, or worse still I am forced to postpone.

I pack my barrel on my last evening at home. My 3-year-old niece stands in the barrel and I pretend to her that she'll be coming with me too. She giggles a no that elicits a broad smile in her uncle. She wouldn't fit anyway, but her reaction is a nice memory to take with me. I appreciate Gregg being around too, someone who understands and I don't have to explain things to. Gregg doesn't ask for details he knows I can't provide. I'll be leaving tomorrow and I'll see where I get to. Hopefully, Southend, as I have a Local Contact there who I know to be friendly. The forecasts are now for light winds though, so if I don't make Southend I'll look to camp somewhere on the Essex marshes. I stay up late until I am tired, and sleep a last night in my bed.

Saturday 7ᵗʰ of June dawns. There is no panic or rush. I drive to the beach in good time and get rigged up. It is a beautiful sunny day. Friends and family turn up as I prepare, Denis's family too - it has only been a short time since he passed away, and I sense that my challenge has become symbolically important for them at this time. Out of the blue I see an old codger I recognise from my Minorca Sailing days: Keith! Out of normal context (without knotted handkerchief and faded fluorescent wetsuit) he seems more reserved than normal, but I am touched that he's made the effort to come along. People who had seen me grow up at the sailing club are on the beach. All well-wishers are very sincere. There are strong undertones of *be careful*.

I don't know when I'll be back and I suspect some people are questioning *whether* I'll be coming back. These are good lucks rather than see you soons.

With impeccable timing Maria, Gregg's partner, comes to say goodbye. "See you in Bournemouth, probably next week!" I hear. Gregg and María live in Bournemouth. I smile - grateful to think of this as a sail round the southeast corner - rather than the complete circumnavigation - of Britain.

A short delay as the coastguard has got wind of my intentions and wants a chat. Bugger. I'd forgotten to let them know. I phone them and explain the expedition. They seem satisfied, and say I should call again to check in at the end of the day.

I fulfil my duties as centre of attention: making sure I thank everyone for turning up, helping stage photographs, a polite chat to a guy from the council who had arranged the free teas and coffees, liaising with the Beach Patrol guys who are going to help out with on-water photographs.

Now I focus on my routine. The abridged version follows:

Drysuit on. Check zips fully closed. Shoes on. Harness on. Close waterproof backpack according to procedure: three folds, toggles, clip. Backpack on. Ensure phone and GPS are in their waterproof pouches and seals are correctly closed. Activate tracker and position in barrel. Firmly close barrel lid. Place barrel on carrier and rotate to make sure tracker is at top. Secure barrel by tightening line and finish with three knots. Test tension of line. Fit secondary stabilising strap over barrel. Tie additional security line between barrel and board. Clip board and sail together. Visual check of all components.

It takes a while. I'm not yet practised.

I look up. People have moved away, watching from further up the beach. They seem to know that I have gone already.

I sail out and go past the pier the wrong way, before turning back to cross again from east to west. The official start-finish line, crossed. Gregg follows in the Beach Patrol boat and takes some pictures. After a while there is no reason to follow any longer. Gregg says an apologetic goodbye. We both - I sense - realise this is a significant departure. Best to just get on with it. Another "see you in Bournemouth!" restores stiff upper lip.

I focus on sailing for a few minutes and - when I look back - I am alone. The wind is from an offshore direction so I am facing out to sea. Safe in the knowledge that I won't be seen, I let the emotion rise in me and cry a few tears through my broad smile. Finally, I am on the path I need to be on.

* * *

Despite my training sails in this area, it is only an hour or so before I am in unfamiliar waters - heading south, with the Dengie flats (mud flats, not housing) to my right. It is very easy sailing. I don't yet know it, but there will be very few days as easy as this. The wind goes very light but progress is still acceptable as I am carried by the tide up the Thames estuary. I nibble on fruit and chocolate bars, and fiddle with gadgets which still have novelty appeal. I experiment with clipping the GPS to the boom, where I can read it. Both phone and GPS are secured by elastics to their designated pockets of my drysuit. There is no boat traffic around, and in the very calm and easy conditions I half-listen to the radio through my phone. When the wind swings and freshens I feel the

Farewells on Clacton's Pier Beach. Photo: Gregg Dunnett

need to concentrate. I stash the tangle of wire from the headphones and get on with the business of sailing.

I am now beating upwind in zigzags, but slightly perplexed by the effect of the current, which seems determined to take me up the River Crouch. As I get closer to the estuary mouth I realise why - a huge spit of sand is channelling all the water from this bit of sea into the river. The sheltered water next to the spit is absolutely flat. I sail further out and try a few times to sail over what looks like navigable water, but each time ground the fin in acres of ankle deep water. Eventually I learn my lesson: I can't sail over sand. The required detour is considerable.

The next obstacle I come across is the Shoeburyness boom. I'd had a tip-off about this from the shop owner at Wet'n'Dry Watersports. The boom was constructed in 1944 to prevent enemy shipping and submarines from entering the River Thames. It is smaller than it used to be, but still protrudes over 2km into the sea. Fortunately there is a small gap half way along which saves a longer detour. The gap is roughly level with Birdshit Island, which is as easy to recognise as it sounds. Once through the boom it really does feel like sailing on a river. Kent is clearly visible on the other side and the water is very obviously warmer, and dirtier. Ships are in the main channel. The riverbanks are in full-summer weekend mode with crowded beaches and plenty of folk out on sailing craft. I land on a beach used by the dinghies of Thorpe Bay Yacht Club. I've covered a good distance and the tide has just turned and will soon gather strength going in the opposite direction. I'm well pleased with progress and when the Commodore of TBYC introduces himself and invites me to their balcony for refreshment, I am happy to accept. I am more tired and dehydrated than I realise and gratefully gulp down 2 pints of Coke as I dry out in my thermals in the late afternoon sun. I don't yet feel like someone who is windsurfing round Britain, but I do feel like someone who is doing something a little bit different, and that feels good.

* * *

My contact here - Richard - locates me at the Yacht Club. Richard is the most regular windsurfer I know. He sails from the second Saturday in May until the following Friday, and has done for the last twenty years. I know this because I met Richard two weeks in to my first season at Minorca Sailing, and then again for the same week at yearly intervals for every year that I worked there. It was always a real pleasure to sail in groups that Richard was part of, and never felt like work. In lighter winds we'd do plenty of cruising and *exploring* of the bay's islands, most likely going round the main island at least once. In stronger winds we'd have some good sailing. Richard is one of the gentlest and least pushy people I know.

Richard had registered on the website probably expecting to be the last port of call on the round Britain trip, but due to the late change of start location had become first stop. I'd called him a week before the off, and we'd pre-arranged a meeting place. He'd also contacted TBYC which explains their preparedness for my arrival.

It is getting late - and we both have a passing interest in the soon-to-start Canadian Grand Prix - so we make our move. I de-rig the sail and we car-top the gear back to Richard's house. I wonder where Richard got the roof rack from - he may have bought it for this function alone, and it would be just like him to do so quietly and without letting on. Dinner is an enormous and delicious Chinese takeaway. The Grand Prix is, predictably, completely forgettable. We agree a 4:30am start, ready for 5:00am at the waterfront the next day. 3am would be no bother for Richard, but I manage to negotiate a lie in, then hit the sack exhausted.

Day 2 - 8ᵗʰ June

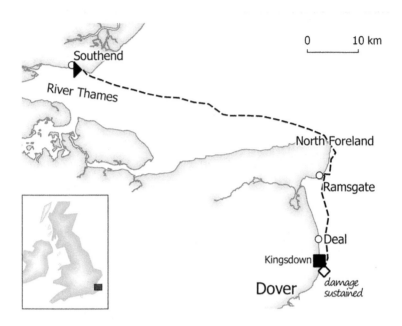

The day starts with a gentle breeze and I am sailing by 5am as planned. There is a nice bit of tide-assist heading down the middle of the Thames estuary. I go close by the navigational marks which are themselves the size of small boats and observe the Thames broth streaming past. The wind settles in and freshens from the northeast. I am sailing close-hauled and can maintain the angle I need without having to zigzag. There is a small short chop and the sailing feels familiar - like on my training sails. My course takes me through the Kentish Flats wind farm. I am 10km from the land, but with the wind having an onshore component I feel relatively comfortable despite this separation from shore.

Progress is better than I had expected. The plan had been to head for Minnis Bay, where I would perhaps link up with local windsurfers who had contacted me through the website and offered some help if required. I would like to link up with these people in some way to acknowledge their generosity, but given the conditions I know it makes no sense to do this. The forecast is for a strengthening wind and the longer it takes to get around the tip of Kent - North Foreland - the more difficult conditions will become. Indecisive and against my better judgement, I put the board in reaching mode, adjust GPS waypoint, and free-off towards land. I'm now on the back section of the board and travelling at speed. But I can see the tip of Kent! Sacrificing my upwind position like this is madness! If I continue inshore to Minnis Bay I will then have a true beat and a real slog to get round North Foreland. I change plan: progress must come before politeness. People will understand that. I stop, lay my sail in the water, and phone my contact to inform him of my decision to sail straight past.

Dilemma resolved I put the board back in upwind mode - daggerboard down and mast track forward - and power on toward the headland in the distance. It is exhilarating sailing. A few miles before North Foreland I find myself sailing towards breaking waves. Sand banks - how bizarre! I find a channel through, occasionally scraping the fin in shallow water.

The wind increases as I draw close to my first headland of the expedition. On the final approach are some ships at anchor. I pass to leeward of the first and fall in as a result of misjudging the extent of the wind shadow, and underestimating my own fatigue. I make a late decision to head-up and pass to windward of the next ship, and do so close enough to see the faces of the crew on the bridge. They watch me pass with expressions that remain distant.

North Foreland is a rounded rather than a jutting headland. The tide is out and there is flat and rocky reef at the bottom of the cliffs. When I judge the angle to be right for passing the corner I adjust for downwind mode and change course. Within seconds the board responds and is powering along at around 20 knots. For a few kilometres I am sailing parallel to the coast. I try to pick a smooth line but every now and then receive a faceful of spray as the board ploughs into a wave. As the coast bends round further I cannot sail any deeper and the angle being sailed starts to take me away from the coast. After a while I gybe so that the angle takes me back closer to shore. With the wind directly behind me I make progress in zigzags – broad reaching and gybing my way down the coast.

The following wind and sea offer welcome relief after the long beat to North Foreland. The frequent zigzagging also helps unwind my neck, which had been craned left the whole way. For the moment, the sailing is lively but comfortable, but I am aware that the forecast is for stronger wind. I've eaten a couple of chocolate bars but am tired after the early start, and could do with a second breakfast. I'd also like to check the map. I sail close in to a beach with a town behind - later identified as Broadstairs - but at low tide the beach looks quite rocky so I continue. A few miles further on I spot an easy landing and put in on Ramsgate beach.

I sit outside the *Belgium Café*. I'm wet under my drysuit so strip off to my thermals for a coffee and bowl of euro porridge. The wetness is from sweat but also from seawater that has been forced up past the suit's ankle seals. The annoyance is of my own making, as the drysuit I requested from Gul is a size too big. Oh well, the warm sun will soon dry my shorts. I check Facebook and am pleased to see a few positive comments about progress so far. Social media is something I am going to have to get my head round how and when to use. Gregg has posted an update about the start for the website and that seems fine for now. The porridge is piping hot and delicious. And there is a lot of it: I eat for nearly an hour.

A break was needed but I also need to get on. The internet weather maps show the wind increasing and remaining strong for the next few days. The north-easterly winds will funnel through the gap between England and France. Where the gap is narrowest - the Dover Straits - the wind will be strongest. It is a stretch of water I am nervous about: partly because I assume stopping options under the White Cliffs will be non-existent, and partly because I must negotiate my way past Port of Dover - the world's busiest passenger port where there will be a constant stream of fast moving ferries toing and froing. A windsurfer here is the equivalent of a hedgehog crossing a busy road. I sense that today it is important to go for it: get past this corner. Focussed and restored I head back out for more.

I stay well out to sea. There is a nice swell developing and the board is getting thrown around, but I am coping with the exhilarating conditions for the moment. Ahead are the White Cliffs. An hour's sailing and I reach their start, where shingle beach merges into ascending cliff. I press on - the effect of the wind acceleration in this area is evident and conditions are livelier. *Hurry up Jono!* I urge myself. Another 15 miles and I'll be through the gap and into more sheltered waters.

Over the wind noise I hear a muffled crack. *Fuck! What was that?* I look behind me to check on the barrel. *Shit!* The barrel is still secured to the cradle but the whole cradle has ripped off the arm. I'm very close to losing the whole lot. *What are my options?* If I continue, I have little idea of what to expect other than at some point Dover. But sailing fast downwind is bumpy and the barrel will be shaken off. Turn back and within a mile I will reach the beach before the cliffs. And sailing upwind I can chug along slowly and smooth out the ride. Not much of a choice. I elect to turn back.

The barrel and cradle assembly flops around as I gingerly sail through the oncoming sea to Kingsdown. I have to pick my moment for a landing on to the steep shingle beach. I'm well aware that it's not going to be easy getting off from here. I assess the damage: confirm that the rivets have pulled out. *Fuck it!* I am annoyed with myself for the oversight - it would have been easy to beef up the cradle-arm connection. But because it had never shown signs of being an issue I'd overlooked it. Still, it is only a minor setback. Surely I'll be able to borrow a few tools to get the barrel carrier fixed and strengthened. I try the pub, which seems to be Kingsdown's only commercial offering. No luck there, although they are happy to look after my barrel whilst I go further back up the coast. Apparently there is a sailing club at Deal.

The launch is now distinctly difficult, but without the barrel the board is easier to carry and I pick my moment to run at the waves and beachstart quickly away. It is windy now. I slog upwind the few miles to Deal where again timing and full commitment are required to make a safe landing. The sailing club is open but no sailors are to be found, it appears that the building is used by tea drinking pensioners too. In town I get lucky and find a bike shop who will do the repair. Instructions are left to over-engineer and I agree to return in 40 minutes. Deal is a handy little place and I make use of the shops and conveniences whilst waiting.

The repair is wonky and looks flimsy. I take control - instructing and supervising the fitting of additional and larger rivets. Eventually the dog's dinner of a repair is complete. But it will do. Beggars - after all - cannot be choosers.

I look at the sea for a while before heading back to Kingsdown. *What kit would I choose to be on out there?* Definitely a waveboard. It's windy. Windy enough to be a toss-up between a 4.2m and a 4.7m sail. My 9.5m sail is way too big for this, but I need to get back to the barrel. I downhaul and outhaul to maximum settings to depower the sail as much as possible and again risk a - now very risky - launch through the shorebreak. Tenths of a second separate my rig getting trashed in the dumping waves from making it out. That was very close, and my heart is racing. There is an adrenaline high at having negotiated near disaster.

I tear off downwind for a few hundred metres before giving up on proper sailing. This is too risky. The likelihood of catapulting and breaking myself or equipment is too high. I don't hook in and have the sail open in front of me to catch as little wind as possible. I try to fit between the waves rather than plough into them. It doesn't feel unsafe sailing like this but it is exhausting. I am shattered by the time I escape for a third time up the shingle bank of this exposed stretch of Kent coast.

I know that is *it* for the day, but don't want to admit it. The forecast has me very uneasy. I'm stuck just the wrong side of where I needed to get to. It is unusual to get easterly winds. If I were past the southeast corner of Britain already, then in the next few days I would be able to benefit from these winds and make good progress heading down the English Channel. The really strong winds are only in the short stretch of the Dover Straits. But stuck where I am I'll be going nowhere. I'm also acutely aware that I'm only two days in to a very public adventure, and that the southeast corner of England is hardly Cape Horn. Two days in doesn't count as a Round Britain attempt and I don't want to be holed up here.

I console myself with the thought that this wasn't meant to be easy, and find a sheltered spot to set up my sail shelter. My first home brewed coffee of the trip restores me. Without this misfortune I never would have stopped here, and it really is a very picturesque little place, Kingsdown.

* * *

In the evening I take a walk up on top of the White Cliffs, hoping to spot Dover. I reach a war memorial, still no Dover in sight. It is howling on top of the cliffs, but as the coast bends round the wind becomes more offshore, and the wind on the water close to the cliffs is not as fierce. If I can get far enough round, it will get easier, I reason. I also reason that the wind in the morning will be less strong. The wishful thinking becomes a plan to bust out of here tomorrow.

Back at Kingsdown's pub I am too late for food. Beer and crisps make a good substitute. I then return to camp and cook a first couscous meal of the expedition. The wind is cold, but it has been a long day and sleep comes easily.

Day 3 - 9th June

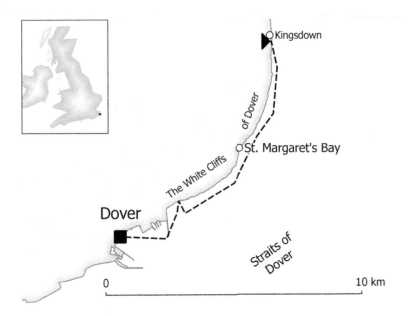

I breakfast coffee and porridge which warms my insides. Out to sea white horses are marching from left to right and then disappearing from view as the White Cliffs block line of sight. My eyes narrow involuntarily as I assess the situation. I am under no illusions - sailing in these conditions will be a battle and I need to stack the odds in my favour as much as I can. This includes going *now* - before the wind picks up even further. My focus is intense as I prepare. Boom and mast extension settings are given an extra notch so that the sail can be tensioned yet more, helpful to dump as much power as possible. I assume I will be swimming and suit up in preparation for a wet day.

To placate my parents and Gregg, I had said that I would set Beaufort force five as my upper wind limit - effectively cherry picking nice conditions for quick and safe progress. This was part of a risk analysis exercise suggested by Gregg to allay the concerns that my Mum had about the trip. In reality though, that risk analysis was usually far from my mind, and it was my own internal risk assessment - based on a lifetime of accumulated sailing knowledge – that guided my decisions to sail.

Influencing the decision today was a pressing desire to get round this corner of Britain whilst I could. To not get stuck this early on in the trip when there was still so far left to go. My approach to what constituted an acceptable level of risk changed as the expedition progressed but, for now, my priority was progress. Whilst it looked like I *could* sail there really was no question that I *would* sail.

The shingle beach is composed of stones rounded by the action of the shorebreak. I slide down the bank. It is a complicated launch but I get out unscathed. No sense of relief this time though - just the beginning of a bigger adventure. I move my feet into the footstraps and point the board downwind, keeping my body compact to control the immediate excess of power. The straps help keep me on the board as the sail tries to lift me up. A wide grip on the boom helps provide sufficient leverage to muscle the sail under control. The board is flying. I'm overtaking the waves - which are tightly enough packed to make it a jarring ride. I try to in vain to pick a smooth line. The board slams into the waves in explosions of spray - the resulting deceleration serving to further increase the pull from the rig. It is difficult and exhausting sailing and before long my muscles are burning. The harness helps to take some of the strain, but hooked in there is the risk of a heavy fall - getting thrown by the rig and perhaps breaking something or injuring myself. After about a mile I plough into a particularly square wave. The board submarines and decelerates in an instant. My arms and legs only have reserves to partially compensate, and I crumple on top of the sail. It isn't a violent fall this one, but in these conditions the next could be.

I haul myself out of the water and sit on the board to regain my breath. The water drains from my drysuit and backpack. I am back to about level with where I'd got to yesterday, before the barrel carrier breakage. It's not pleasant but it is progress. Still no Dover in sight.

I proceed along the cliff-lined coast in short bursts punctuated by falls when I can hold on no longer. The wind is really funnelling and I get repeatedly flattened by strong gusts. On one fall I temporarily lose contact with the board for a second or so. Swimming with all my gear on is slower and more energy sapping than normal, and I recognise my good fortune that a wave did not carry the board away from me in this instant. I sail closer inshore as I pass a beach - St. Margaret's Bay. I elect not to stop – I need to get further. The cliffs are bending round and there are signs that ahead - inshore - there will be some protection for the worst of the wind. Progress is challenging but unrelenting as I sail and drift downwind. Inshore, the gusts of wind are fierce. Further out, away from the shelter of the cliffs, I am unable to sail. If I manage a minute between falls I am doing well. To sail, concentration has to be total, and it is only when sat on the board recovering that I am able to shift my attention beyond the waves in my immediate path to review progress. First, I see ferries. After a subsequent fall these become bigger Ferries. Eventually - many falls later - I see Dover itself, and realise I have a problem.

The problem is about a mile long, extending out into the sea, protecting the Port of Dover from exactly these sorts of conditions. Waves pile up against the wall to create a confused and angry sea in its vicinity. Further out, a two-way stream of fast moving ferries emerge from or dive into a break in the wall.

The only way I can get past this monster today is to battle my way a long way out, then fall and drift past. This 'strategy' is deeply unpalatable. I'll need to somehow make it well over a mile out to safely clear the port. The wind will be far too strong that far out. The only way of making progress downwind will be drifting. And I very strongly suspect that I won't manage to drift past the world's busiest passenger port without provoking a major rescue response.

I am out of ideas so hold position, inshore, a few hundred metres short of the wall, for a few minutes. Suddenly I see a double sized gap between the ferries and go for it. I charge out to sea - sailing as broad as I can manage. As soon as I lose the shelter of the cliffs I am flattened by a monster gust. I've made no distance at all. This isn't going to work. That established, and with the ferries bearing down on me, I lose no time in reverting to plan B - an entirely spontaneous change of plan. Previously I had spotted a narrow strip of shingle beach at the base of the cliffs, half a kilometre back, and it is to there that I sail.

I slump on the stones and suck dry an energy gel. Water pours out of anywhere water can get to, including the legs of my drysuit. The beach will be covered at high tide. At a push perhaps I could scramble a short way up the cliffs? But then what? Certainly there is no way of getting to the top. How many days would I have to stay here?

I am pleasantly surprised to see that I have mobile coverage, and decide to phone Gregg. We chat for a while as he tries to be useful by explaining that once round past the wall there should be some stopping options. Gregg gets a rough deal here - I'm asking him to make better a situation he has no control over. His role on this occasion is just to hear that I'm having a rough time. Some rain starts to blow through and it looks as though it has taken the edge off the wind. Hurriedly, I explain this to Gregg and hang up. Again, the decision is totally spur of the moment.

I pull out my handheld VHF which has spent a good proportion of the day underwater and radio Dover Port Control. I've been practising my radio call for the past few days and try to sound breezy and confident: "Dover Port Control, Dover Port Control this is Windsurfer Phantom, over". Communication is established and I matter-of-factly state my intention and request permission to sail past the port, east to west. There is a long delay and then a short exchange during which the essential information is confirmed beyond doubt: Windsurfer Phantom is not a yacht, current position is out of sight on the strip of shingle under the cliffs to the east of the port, permission is sought to cross from east to west.

Again a long delay, before:

"Stand by Windsurfer Phantom. We want to keep an eye on you and are sending a launch. Await further instructions."

Fifteen minutes later the launch is powering through the waves towards my position, and when close enough to communicate with hand signals indicates that I should proceed. It is a big pilot boat, with enclosed cabin, and windscreen wipers, working hard to clear the spray. Unfortunately, the rain has now cleared and the wind is back up to uber-strong. Oh well, too late to change my mind now.

I head out and fall four or five times in the first few hundred metres. It is very difficult to sail broad enough, and with the angle I'm making I'll need to head at least two miles out to clear the wall on the other tack. The launch is trying to coax me further downwind - they probably don't quite understand the problems involved in taking the line they suggest. I hold it together for a longer run before falling again. Still miles to go and it is just getting windier and windier. The guys on the launch are wearing serious expressions - they can see I am struggling and recognise that any sort of intervention in these conditions will be difficult. I run through my options, none of which work. As I am doing this I am looking at the ferry port entrance, the angle now 'makeable' in one very broad and very scary reach. The entrance is officially for shipping and ferries only, but I'm beyond worrying about that. I sign my idea to the crew of the launch: I point at me, then I point at the gap in the wall. The guys on the launch almost nod their heads off in agreement.

I haul the sail up and hook into the footstraps before bearing the board deeper and deeper off the wind. I don't dare hook in but only need to hold it together like this for about a kilometre. The distance to the wall halves and then halves again. The water in the final approach to the gap is chaotic with steep peaks and spikes travelling in all directions. My eyes are nearly bumped out of their sockets. And then, incredibly, I've made it through. The wind swirls and I fall in behind eight storeys of blue painted steel. The guys on the launch shoo me away from the manoeuvring shipping. They don't realise that my energy has gone. I make it to the beach within the port. The launch guys depart with a friendly wave. I haul myself and gear up the shingle bank.

I'm tired and dazed. Someone from Dover Port Control comes over for a chat. I'm expecting a ticking off but he says that he and his colleagues were impressed that I followed correct protocol and had a passage plan. It means a lot to hear that, even though the passage plan bit may be being a little over generous. He is a kitesurfer and offers a place to warm up and sleep, but I am away with my thoughts and nothing is really registering now. I forget where he points to and don't know where to find him later. Right now, I'm just so relieved to have averted a disastrous start to the trip. I could so easily have ended up receiving or perhaps requiring a rescue today. That would have been a personal humiliation and would have dragged the names of all windsurfers though the mud - something I desperately want to avoid. It crosses my mind that I am only on day three. That this is only the south east of England. That it doesn't get any easier than this.

It's only early but the wind is already smoking even inside the port. There will be no more sailing today. I de-rig to prevent the sail getting buffeted and store the kit in Dover Seasports' lockup. It is a cold wind, and the hot shower at the centre is very welcome. To the staff at the centre I am clearly a bit of a nutter, but I suspect the jury is still out on whether I am an expedition windsurfer. I don't really feel one yet. Their kindness seems to come from pity.

I take a walk in the afternoon. Dover castle seems like a good idea until I am quoted the £18 entry fee. I was only really planning on finding a sunny grass bank to go to sleep on, and am able to do this outside of the castle grounds instead. I sleep for several hours.

In the evening I have fish and chips at Wetherspoon's, far better value than the castle. I'm fairly shattered. Having lost my good offer of a place to sleep I will be under the boats at the sailing centre, but it is an exposed spot on a cold and windy evening. Before bed I let escape a fart that isn't a fart and realise that I am a little bit ill - a present from Rafa or Alba at the start, most likely. So day three finishes with a skinny dip in the sea to clean myself up, before crawling into a bivvy bag to warm up and sleep under a boat. Dover really isn't rough sleeping friendly.

Inside the shelter of Dover harbour. Photo: Paul Boland | doverforum.com

Beach inside Dover Harbour – signing off with the Harbour Patrol boat crew. Photo: Paul Boland | doverforum.com

Day 4 – 10th June

As predicted, it is howling. A horrendously windy day. Only narrow glimpses of the sea outside are visible through the harbour entrances, each over a mile away. Even from this distance, big white-crested swells are visible rolling past. Today clearly isn't a day for raceboard sailing, but the difficulty of monitoring conditions unsettles me nonetheless. From the shore, it is hard to know what is going on out there. Dover is a well-appointed lay-by, but I would rather not be here.

Breakfast is in McDonalds, the earliest open establishment that would have me. A hotel initially claimed to be open for coffee but changed their mind upon closer inspection. My odd looking fingered shoes also draw comments from the local youth. Later I do some website admin. I want to reply personally to each offer of support. I buy a needle and thread to repair the non-functional chest strap on my back pack. I'm still not feeling great, so an enforced day-off maybe isn't such a bad thing.

There is a small group of *Team-15* (youth) windsurfers at the Seasports centre today. One of them sails but the conditions are really unpleasant so most are just hanging around. I am a subject of curiosity. When a talk about the expedition is requested I am happy - although a little bit shy - to oblige. The contents of the barrel are used to kick off a discussion. It is nice that the kids seem genuinely interested and ask questions. I enjoy the talk and it takes my mind off being stuck in Dover.

One of the kids Mum has a sister who died of pancreatic cancer earlier this year. Most people you meet know or know of someone affected by the disease. When people talk of their lost loved ones the humanity within them is so evident. Listening to this lady brings a lump to my throat.

For the second evening running dinner is in Wetherspoon's, followed by a night under the boats. No swim required this time.

With some of the Dover 'Team 15' windsurfers

Day 5 - 11th June

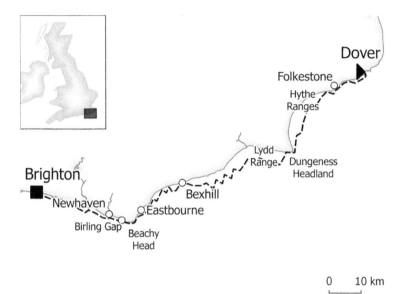

I check the forecast at 7am and see that slightly less wind is now forecast for today. From what I can make out - through the distant gaps in the harbour wall - it seems as if the sea state has also calmed down. I can't see enough to be sure though, and am tense as I breakfast on home-brewed coffee and porridge. The last time I launched into the unknown it was quite a harrowing experience and here I am two days later about to do something rather similar, or at least it feels that way. Stopping options until past Folkestone are probably none and I really don't know what I'll find until I sail out of the harbour.

I delay my start until after the Dover Seasports team have arrived: partly to say cheerio and partly because Dover doesn't do public conveniences. Feeling more prepared for a day on the water I suit up and then radio DPC requesting permission to leave. No pilot is dispatched this time - I am free to go.

The preceding days have shaken me and I am nervous as I make final preparations - fumbling the knots to secure the barrel to board. Finally on the water, the 10 minute sail to the gap in the harbour wall settles me a little. The water around the gap itself is choppy and outside there is a swell running, but it is nothing like the panorama of the last few days. Wind and tide are also going in the same direction, which contributes to a more settled sea state. I set up on a broad reach and in a few short minutes Dover is behind me. The sailing is still quite physical, and I bury the nose and fall on one occasion - but compared to two days ago this is definitely within my comfort zone. Confidence returns as I pass Folkestone and an inviting sand beach, confirmation that the Straits of Dover are behind me. What a relief that is. I feel like I am on my way again.

Close in to Folkestone beach the fin of my board catches an unmarked floating line and sends me flying around the front. Fortunately no damage is sustained. I take the opportunity to sit and gather myself. The next obstacle is Hythe ranges - a Ministry of Defence training area with an exclusion zone of 1.5 miles out to sea. The range boundary is marked by buoys and the curve of the coast means that it can be respected without inconvenience.

Conditions are now ideal. The wind has dropped a little and its north-easterly direction means that I am able to maintain speeds between 15 and 20 knots. I zigzag my way downwind in glorious sunshine. Clearly visible is my next target - Dungeness headland. Ness apparently means headland in old Norse - so perhaps more correctly I was sailing to Dunge headland.

Even at these speeds it takes a while to close down on the 'Ness. It is a significant geographical feature and despite being low lying there is noticeable wind acceleration on the approach. Tide and wind are working together and the sea state around the headland is livelier, but not problematic. The flat water in the lee of the headland makes for easy stopping and I set foot on land for the first time since leaving Dover.

Behind me is Dungeness nuclear power station. Initially it seems that this huge building and I are alone on this oversized shingle spit, but company arrives within minutes. My landing site is just short of the eastern boundary of Lydd range and a MOD patrol boat has parked up on the boundary with its bows facing directly towards me. I'm aware that Lydd range has an exclusion zone of 3 miles and ponder the best way to approach this obstacle. I eat my sandwiches hoping the boat will go away, but it doesn't.

As a delaying tactic I try to phone anyone who I have a number for but no-one picks up. I consult my road map. The irksome boat holds position.

I studiously avoid looking in the direction of the craft and surreptitiously prepare for launch. I reason that I am very much on the MOD radar, so won't be accidentally shot or bombed, and that I am probably not worth the political fallout of being deliberately taken out, so reckon a dash across the range is my best option. I wonder if by disrupting their bombing practice I will be saving the taxpayer money or increasing costs.

I've been here long enough and it is time to go. I jump on my board and the flat water behind the headland means I am straight away blasting at over 20 knots. I'm heading out cutting across the corner of the range. The boat is a bit slow to respond but soon gives chase. This is fun - up until now I've been sailing prudently but now I'm just going as fast as I can - this is like the windsurfing equivalent of joy-riding - although I suppose I would have to be on stolen kit to make it genuinely authentic. It surprises me that the chase boat is closing on me. *Damn - they're quick!* Then, all of a sudden they stop. I realise I must have passed the state boundary, err, sorry, I mean 3-mile limit.

I sail a bit further to re-establish a useful gap between myself and the boat, and then gybe to sail along the outer limit. The boat follows a few hundred metres shoreward. I'm soon out of their territory and am once again alone. Not long after come the explosions from resumed range activity.

I am navigationally lost but conditions are really ideal and progress is fast. The only annoyance is the paddle which I am carrying. The blade hangs over the back of the board and catches in the waves as I clatter over the lumpy sea. It twists round and drags in the water - which slows me down - and somehow manages to bend the aluminium supports it sits on, causing it to painfully pinch my toes. I stop occasionally to bend the supports back in to place and relieve the pressure on my squashed digits. Do I really want this damned paddle? I remain unconvinced of its benefit and swear at it throughout the day.

I spot what looks like a nice place for refreshments and appears to have an easy landing. Partly because it amuses me to ask, and partly because it is a complete faff to operate my phone within its waterproof bag, I enquire as to my whereabouts. Apparently I'm at Bexhill. Very nice too. I make for where all passing windsurfers must make for: the Colonnade - an attractive semi-circular Edwardian building, and perfect sun trap, with an excellent little café. I'm soaked from sweat, and seawater that has found its way in through leaky ankle seals, so strip-off my drysuit. The warm sun is blissful and dries me out whilst I eat, and drink coffee, twice. I check my carefully selected roadmap - and see that the next landmark - already visible in the distance - is Beachy Head. Dover seems *so* far behind me it is difficult to believe I was there just this morning.

When I return to my board the water is lapping at its chines - the tide has turned and is now coming in. Literally - for the next 6 hours - a large bulge of water will make its way up the English Channel. This will make for slower progress this afternoon - as the knot or two of foul tide will be actively *pulling me back* the way I don't want to go. Furthermore, I'll also be in for a bumpier ride. With the direction of the current and the direction of the wind now in disagreement, they'll scrape against each other to fold the surface of the sea into bigger, steeper and more crenelated forms. This *wind against tide* effect can be very significant, and has the potential to create dangerous sea states for small craft. This is particularly the case around headlands - where currents flow stronger.

I'm aware from the map that Beachy Head is a fairly significant protrusion, but confidence is high and... well... this is only summer on the south coast and progress has got to be made. By the time I am passing Eastbourne the sea is indeed quite significantly larger. It catches on the paddle repeatedly, bending its supports into my already bruised toes. The wind is also increasing and the shoreline looks hostile for landing. Now to my right is a cliff-line ascending to Beachy Head in the distance. I tension the sail up to maximum flop - as depowered as I can make it. Mentally, too, I batten down the hatches.

The sailing is high octane. Excitement tinged with fear. The wind is being accelerated by the coastline - a good force 5 now and more ahead. The distant sea is a spectacular blue with myriad white horses: a mass of them gathered off the headland itself, and beyond many more racing away far out to sea. The near cliffs are a brilliant white, the water below a fantastic turquoise. Everything is *so* vivid! I stay close inshore approaching the headland. It is flatter and there is less current. I sail a hundred metres past the lighthouse then gybe to avoid sailing into rougher water. Fully planing, I head over a wave - a crumbling hump literally a stone's throw from the lighthouse, now towering above me. I'm flying along - but not crashing through waves as before - now everything is strangely smooth - like skiing in powder. And then I realise that the wave beneath me is still there, and that I am not flying past - but rather creeping along - this wave, that extends all the way to the shore and is stationary. The wave is forming where the currents from each side of the headland meet. It allows me to hold station without effort, but even fully planing my speed is insufficient to cross. To be suspended in motion by the natural forces of wind and tide is completely absorbing, and it feels as if time slows down as I register every detail. I am able to tilt my head back and take in my surroundings - awesome in both horizontal and vertical planes - as I inch along the tidal treadmill.

A few seconds later I pop over the wave and am battling the strong current beyond. The water is flat. But then suddenly I sail out of the wind. A minute's break and then *bang!* - a huge gust. Then nothing then *bang!* - another huge gust. This one slams me in under the sail. Suddenly I'm feeling very tired - these gusts are violent and the next two miles take a lot out of me. It is with some relief that I see there is a beach ahead. I gratefully put in to Birling Gap.

There is an odd structure: it appears to be an elevator down to the beach from the cliff top, but on closer inspection they are steps. I ascend out of curiosity, and the scene is as popular as National Trust locations are countrywide: middle-class and pleasant.

I forego the walnut cake to rescue my equipment from the incoming tide. The violent gusts off the headland have almost completely ripped the stickers from the sail. I finish the job then stash the crumpled sticker ball in my bag. Today I will push on to Brighton - where I have support from friends Rod and Louise.

Winds in the lee of Beachy Head are blowing from over the land, making for a flatter sea but gusty conditions. Leaving the headland behind, the gusts are thankfully less strong and once again I settle into a rhythm of sorts. I recognise and pass Newhaven, and reel in a foreign yacht heading in the same direction. I am grateful for the company and the distraction as fatigue is really setting in now.

The coastline becomes more built-up and a distance further on becomes semi-industrialised. Further still a skyline emerges with tall buildings, resembling a modest city - Brighton. Progress the last few miles is slower - against the tide and with only intermittent planing. And if earlier I was fatigued then now I am shattered. I've been sailing 9 hours. The exertion and the elements, plus dear Alba's stomach bug have left me drained. I don't know it yet but I've sailed over 100 miles today.

I beach at King's Esplanade, on Brighton Seafront. Rod and Louise, and numerous others, are enjoying the afternoon sun. It is a different world here on the beach: entirely benign and offering no hint of the tougher conditions earlier in the day.

"You've come from Dover? Well done, that's nice." says someone from my hosts' group.

We find a spot for board and sail in Rod's garage and a mutual friend of ours, Helen, joins us. Helen and Rod are both knowledgeable windsurfers and it is nice to be with people who understand what I am doing and the difficulties involved.

Birling Gap, where cliffs start their rise to Beachy Head

Contented after today's achievement, I enjoy their company and hospitality.

Rod and Louise make me feel at home, despite being packed up and ready to change theirs. They are moving to a flat one storey higher, trading up sea views. We find a spot for board and sail in the garage. I shower, eat, and borrow some clean clothes whilst mine are laundered. Rod has a dry sense of humour and the ability to keep a straight face when winding people up. His specialism is intolerant people, and he tells a great story. Often several times.

So as to not disrupt Rod and Louise's move preparations any further I accept Helen's offer of a futon bed for the night. I sink into the soft mattress and am soon asleep.

Day 6 - 12th June

I wake up tired. Yesterday evening I took some Imodium but it hasn't worked its magic yet. I force down some porridge and with Helen we walk down to the seafront for 8:30am. The wind is an almost non-existent offshore, and it is a grey and brooding day. The atmosphere feels heavy, and I wonder if there will be thunder and lightning today. The conditions and above all my tiredness have drained my motivation to sail.

Helen is more upbeat, and offers me use of her flat whilst she is at work. She helps me to appreciate that I need to get well and that there is little point sailing today. It is a sensible and welcome suggestion, and I take little convincing.

During the day I catch up on admin. Yesterday, in my agitated state before leaving Dover, I had failed to start the tracker, so was not tracked on the website. Those following progress online have been complaining! Fortunately, not only had the tracker not tracked, but I'd also *failed to turn off* my handheld GPS - which to save battery is normally only turned on for short periods. These double oversights now cancel out: the track from the handheld can be used to repair the track on the website.

I am grateful for - and scratch my head at - this unlikely piece of good fortune. Google Earth shows that the crow flies distance from Dover to Dungeness to Beachy Head to Brighton is 75 miles. The GPS track shows the distance sailed as I zigzagged downwind to be 112 miles. One of my unstated targets for the expedition had been to sail 100 miles in a single day, so I am rather proud with this achievement. It also makes it seem altogether reasonable to be rather tired! Things seem to be working out, my mood is lifting, and energy is returning.

Later on Helen and I head over to Rod and Louise's for a delicious lasagne that Louise has prepared. There is plenty more catching up to do. The day off has done me good and we enjoy a pleasant and relaxed evening.

Day 7 - 13ᵗʰ June

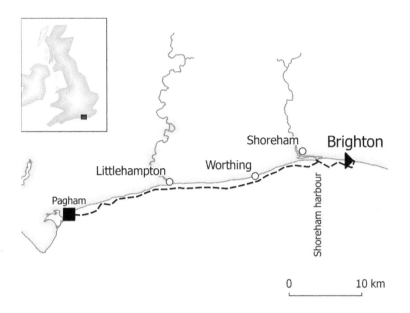

I am down at the seafront by 8:30am. I'd really like a nice easy day to just get comfortable, but am disappointed. Conditions once again look to be bruising. It is high tide and there is a solid force 5 blowing from the southwest. The shorebreak is going to make for a touch and go launch.

Not keen, but wanting to move on from Brighton I enlist Helen's help to bring board and sail to the beach. The wind is tearing around the buildings and manoeuvring the gear is a two-person job. Nervously, I prepare to sail.

I congratulate myself on a successful but sketchy launch and head further out to see what I find. Unfortunately, it is every bit as windy as it looks. Although I can sail, it is a battle. I tack upwind and the board takes a battering from the waves. Each time I come in near enough to the beach to observe the crunching shorebreak I wonder how I'll ever be able to stop in this. The word for this morning is *harrowing*.

Just 3 miles up the coast I spot Shoreham harbour and decide to put in. Perhaps conditions will improve later. The harbour has high walls protecting it from the swell outside and stopping is easy.

I counsel myself against despair. I never intended to sail every day and I should enjoy the times when I am unable to. The experience is about more than just the sailing.

The reality is that I am finding this difficult, mentally. One week in and I've only had one sailable day that hasn't been at least in some way traumatic. I'm still doing the easy bit, what might lie ahead?

I put this out of my mind and walk into Shoreham. I'm not expecting much so am surprised to find an attractive little town centre, next to a river replete with craft. There is an Italian market so I take the opportunity to eat some tasty food and observe goings on whilst sat on a nearby bench. It all helps to take my mind off that lonely and hostile sea.

I give it two hours then check back. Now colourful windsurf sails and kites are everywhere, the tide is dropping and the shorebreak is less destructive. Nice conditions on small kit. I'm not familiar with the South Coast but Gregg had told me that this was the pattern. I didn't really believe him but he might have been right. I spend an extra hour undoing an experiment to shorten my drysuit legs, which I thought might have helped with the water ingress problem. It hadn't really helped and the modified legs rubbed at the inside of my knees. Not a success.

When I can procrastinate no longer I head back out. The swim-launch takes 20 minutes since the harbour walls are now well above the water level causing the wind to swirl devilishly, and swells are periodically surging in. It is hard and wet work to get out. I ponder the minds of the fishermen, who don't seem to twig that it might be a good idea to cast somewhere other than at me.

I am comparatively happy this time as I start upwind on what will prove to be the longest directly upwind leg of the expedition. My target is Pagham - 25 miles west, as the crow flies. I have friends there. For most of the way I will be against the tide, so 50 miles to sail is a realistic estimate.

I am slightly disappointed that no-one says hello as I sail through the mass of sails off Shoreham. I thought *someone* might have altered their line to come and wish me luck. The sailors buzz in and out, gazes intently locked onto the bit of water immediately in front of them. I weave through them anonymously. Next time, maybe if I wear a giraffe outfit...

The sails recede into the distance. There is an enjoyment to the challenge of this long upwind leg. I use the GPS to monitor speed and progress, concluding that water state rather than wind strength is the major determinant of speed - flatter being faster. Thumping into the waves this morning I was going much more slowly than I am now, despite it having been much windier earlier. I am also battling the tide so I keep my tacks short and frequent to avoid the stronger current offshore. Changing tacks often also helps delay the onset of fatigue.

I pass Worthing Pier early on. I almost got a job at Worthing once. Would I still be doing *this* had I landed that job? I doubt I'd have had the necessary preparation. Probably a narrow escape then. I'm feeling very fortunate and getting luckier by the day.

I keep pressing on: past Goring, Littlehampton, Bognor. I've never been to these places and although I've now gone past them, I'm none the wiser having sailed straight past. I frequently drink - plain water from the bladder in my backpack - no hands required for this once the tube is in my mouth. I periodically eat from the assortment of gels, chocolate and cereal bars in my drysuit pockets - a one handed operation. Peeing on the move is more conditions dependant - hooked in whilst sailing upwind is the preferred technique - again, a one-handed operation.

The wind moderates towards the evening and eventually becomes overly light. From Bognor progress is slow. There are also lobster pots and lines everywhere along this stretch of coast. At least it keeps it interesting - *anything* that distracts is welcome to take my mind off how tired I am.

I worry that the wind will completely desert me. How frustrating it would be to be so close yet not make it. I needn't have worried. A few tacks and a few thousand lobster pots later and I am making my final approach to Pagham Yacht Club, where a small and unexpected welcoming party awaits. It is shortly before 9pm.

Tim, Rhona, Kat and dog are on the beach, as are several Pagham YC members. It is a nice-looking club and the representatives are friendly and welcoming. Chips and Guinness follow a minute or so later. A lady called Viv, and her husband, offer their beach house for board storage overnight. This is working out great, no need to derig either. Very convenient. Viv is enthusiastic about the expedition and offers to become involved in the publicity and social media side of things. I'll think about it. I know that promotion isn't my favourite activity, but recognise there is a need to generate interest if my sponsors and chosen charities are to benefit from the project. I do think about it. I'm sure that Viv would do a good job, she certainly takes good pictures, and has bags of energy, but I prefer an understated approach, and I'm pretty sure that Viv is a superlatives girl.

I sink into the car seat on the way back to Tim and Rhona's house. I enjoy the drive, or rather *being driven*. Sat in a comfortable car being driven down tree lined country roads is my new luxury. The ultimate pleasure.

Tim and Rhona know how to look after a weary windsurfer. It's lasagne again. Perfect after the chips and Guinness appetizer. I accept seconds then thirds. Tim encourages me to make use of the oversized bath which I like to think he reserves for people who have made a real effort to visit. That too is excellent. It ends up a late night but has been a day of excellent progress. The Isle of Wight is just round the corner.

Day 8 - 14ᵗʰ June

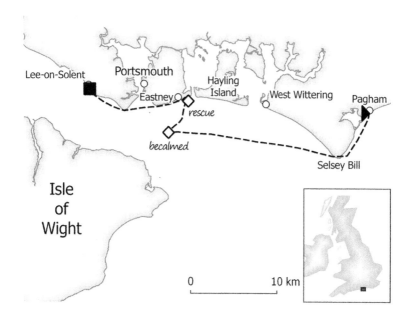

A later start today in easy conditions. How nice to have an easy launch - no breakers to deal with, and enough puff to cruise along. First on the local agenda is Selsey Bill - a promontory with a tidal race that in lively weather would kick up quite a sea.

Today the race is benign. I reach it towards the end of ebb (outgoing) tide and am carried past the low headland without issue. Somewhere on this peninsula is Dee Caldwell's house. Dee was one of the pioneers of windsurfing back in the 60's and he signed up on the website. I'd have liked to have stopped and met the man, but the summer is short and I must get on - if I were to stop at every contact I have on this stretch of coast, I'd be delayed for weeks.

I sail straight past three or four more contacts at West Wittering. I don't like doing this - it feels like poor manners. I feel a pang of guilt and wish I could more easily thank everyone who has offered support. Further round the coast, where contacts are spread thinner, I imagine that I'll be stopping more often.

I sail close hauled, sailing as close to the wind as I can, which is taking me straight up the Solent - equidistant from the Isle of Wight and the mainland. Then, an hour beyond Selsey Bill, the wind switches off.

There are worse places to be stuck, and it is for just such occurrences that I have a paddle. I am becalmed, in flat water, 3km from the shore. Surely, if the paddle is going to prove its worth, it is here. I give it a determined effort, and try several different methods attempting to prevent the sail dragging in the water: sail balanced on the back of the board, supported by guy lines, disconnecting from the board and sat on, stood upon. Sworn at is the most satisfying. An hour later I have made 500 metres, am dripping with sweat, and have managed to attract the attention of the RNLI, who are cruising over ready for the rescue.

The lifeboat crew look a bit overdressed for the occasion. It is a fine and hot day. I'm evidently looking a bit cooked too, and am offered a bottle of water. I congratulate myself on a good catch, and am soon gulping down at a rate only the thirsty drink at. Seconds later I slightly regret doing this: I have plenty of my own water, and I wonder if I have compromised my attempt at an *unsupported* rounding.

We have an agreeable chat. I am cheerful and relaxed and enquire about tide times. It seems to me that I have now sailed far enough to demonstrate that I am not a complete whacko. I examine the faces of the half-dozen men opposite me, searching their expressions - in vain - for evidence to support this conjecture. After a pleasant chat I apologise for not being in distress. My new friends zoom away. The Baywatch theme tune plays in my head.

A few feeble puffs are visible on the water a few hundred metres away and I use the sail to row through the air towards them. The advantage of zero wind is that you can go in any direction using this technique. As soon as a breeze of sorts is present, it is back to zigzagging to claw my way upwind. *Any* sort of sailing is better than paddling, I conclude. Forty minutes later I beach at Eastney. There is little point trying to sail in this, particularly as the tide is now against me, so I set up temporary camp on the pebbles and prepare for a brew.

I look up and something *wrong* catches the corner of my eye. A few hundred metres offshore there is a conical shape, the sort of shape that could be the bow of a sinking boat, proudly standing tall in its final moments. Yes! It really is a sinking boat, I realise, as I spot two heads in the water nearby. Having studied bystander apathy and similar effects as a student, I decide the responsible thing to do now is immediately alert the authorities: 999, then coastguard gets me through to the right people. Disappointingly – for me - I'm not even their first call. Engaged bystanders at Eastney. I suggest to the operator that it might be nice for me to go and keep the bobbing heads company, but am snapped at and told twice and in no uncertain terms that I should not become involved in any way. Right you are. I hang up, then sail over anyway to get a better view as the two guys drown.

When I arrive on scene one of the guys is very keen to hold onto my board. The other one seems a strong swimmer and capable of reaching the beach, but stops for a rest anyway. I piece together the details of what has happened: small boat with too much engine, line hanging out back of boat, propeller catches on line and whips engine to full lock on one side, boat flips, our boys swimming. An unfortunate mistake, but if you are going to make it - then a sunny June afternoon in the Solent is a good time and place to do so.

I think the boys would be happy to get to shore and forget the whole episode has ever happened, but minutes later a helicopter is hovering above us and I break it to the shipwrecked pair that such a low-key resolution seems unlikely. I give the thumbs up for the winchman to descend, but this may be misinterpreted as "all accounted for and no casualties". Pity.

Next, lifeboats are powering towards us, but not my friends from earlier. Just how many lifeboats *are there* around here, I wonder? I've seen 4 and a helicopter today already. Before they arrive, our heroes resume their swim for shore, perhaps wondering if they can pretend the upturned cone not 100m away is nothing to do with them. *Oh yeah, we're just out for a swim. Fully clothed, that's right! We'll be off now. Bye!*

The lifeboat crews home in on the swimmers and I slide away from the drama to an emptier bit of sea, and then the beach. Relieved to find that the whole episode has not been an elaborate scam to make off with my expedition gear, I put the water back on for that brew.

There's not much wind for the rest of the day but I do eventually put afloat, hugging the shore to cheat the tide. At Southsea someone swims past me going in the opposite direction. Very fit no doubt - but also very vulnerable in such a busy bit of sea. At Portsmouth harbour, I patiently wait for a decent gap between the ships and ferries before crossing. A bit farther along I beach on the pebbles at Lee-on-Solent, at exactly the spot Gregg Clyde and I stopped at on our first failed Isle-of-White rounding. It isn't a great spot for camping under the sail, but sometimes known is a better bet than a gamble, so I decide it will do.

I leave my board and sail in a dinghy compound, and head to a pub that must be the worst that Lee-on-Solent has to offer. The food is really poor. My worst decision yet in eight days of expedition. Never mind - although of doubtful nutritious value, the food is at least fuel. I return to the beach and crawl under my sail that is nestled in a pebble-lined dip. Fishermen are nearby and my sleeping arrangement is a bit public, but when darkness descends I can put that out of my mind. It is not quiet, but is peaceful. I narrow my awareness to only the lapping of the wavelets, and fall asleep.

Day 9 - 15th June

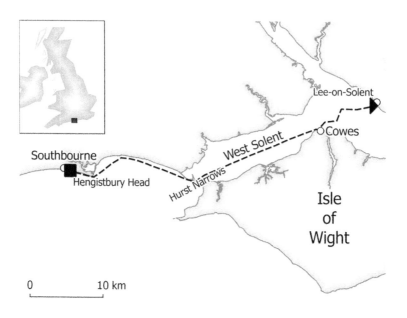

I'm on the water by 8am after a breakfast of porridge and coffee. There is a pleasant following breeze as I broad reach and gybe my way over to Cowes, on the Isle-of-Wight, where I have arranged to meet my friend Amanda. The final part of the crossing is busy with yachts, ferries and hovercraft, all contributing to a choppy sea. It is busy like an airport, with the harbour entrance being the runway. I wait my turn next to a yacht headed in the same direction - a yacht is unlikely to get mown down, I figure, so I'll stick with them. During a lull in activity we both cross without incident.

The road is adjacent to the narrow strip of beach and before I have time to doff my backpack Amanda pulls up. I don't know how we've managed to coordinate that so well. There is a hotel opposite and Amanda is respectable enough to be taken seriously. We have coffee and toast in the most pleasant of surroundings - china cups and saucers in the morning lounge - how civilised this windsurfing round Britain can be. It is great to see Amanda - I'm really enjoying crossing paths with seldom seen friends on this trip.

Time and tide wait for no man, as the androcentric proverb correctly states, and after polishing off Amanda's uneaten toast it is time to zip up and head back out. I feel in fine form as I gently ride the tide down the west Solent, and less than two hours later am being swept through Hurst Narrows. I'd have been nervous about this constriction with its fast-flowing currents before our Isle-of-Wight attempts, but knowing them well now I enjoy negotiating the rapids this time. It helps to rationalise my concerns about the notorious navigational challenges ahead to remind myself that fear of the unknown is the real terror.

The wind is exceptionally light and I don't want to end up becalmed and far from shore again, so for the broad sweep of Christchurch Bay I stay close inshore. Conditions are entirely non-threatening and for comfort I take my backpack off and strap it to the board. I am not entirely happy with this arrangement though: even in these very calm conditions the bag is permanently being dunked, and - more critically - I have separated myself from my Personal Locator Beacon, which is secured to the shoulder strap of my backpack. The PLB is registered to my name and I carry it as a last resort safety measure. When all else fails, or – for example - in the nightmare situation of separation from board in open sea, I could push a button to activate the beacon and my position would pop up on a screen at the Falmouth Coastguard Operations Centre. The telephone numbers I supplied at the time of registration would likely be called first to discount the possibility of a false alarm, and then a search and rescue operation would be launched. I certainly don't intend to be in a position where I would need to activate the beacon, but it is hugely reassuring to have this technology at hand. Today I am on familiar ground in easy conditions, but even so - sailing with the link between myself and beacon compromised seems wrong.

In the scorching heat I am also sailing with my drysuit unzipped: more pleasant, but foolhardy too. If I were to fall, the open drysuit would fill with water in seconds and I would struggle to pull myself back onto the board.

I decide that both these risks, however controlled they may seem, are simply unnecessary. Ten minutes later I am back to my standard configuration - feeling hotter and more uncomfortable - but no longer vulnerable.

The light winds today are giving me the opportunity to review my systems and mull over changes that need to be made when I reach Bournemouth. I am increasingly appreciating the value of simple. This is a virtue that John had emphasised too: *Keep it Simple Stupid*, he had said. No offence was taken.

I have decided to ditch the paddle. It makes sailing more complicated which is potentially a safety critical issue. The inconvenience of not carrying a sail prop for camping is *not* safety critical. My experience in the East Solent yesterday also (re-)confirmed that paddling with a rigged sail is practically impossible. And in any case, the mast itself is also a paddle of sorts that could be used if the sail were broken or derigged. I also know that I want to simplify and beef up the barrel support. It contributes to a settled mind to have these decisions made.

The hot day is setting up some thermal air currents and I benefit from an unexpected puff of breeze that takes me straight to Hengistbury Head. In the lee of the headland it is calm again and I resort to pumping the sail to make progress. Gregg had offered to pick me up from anywhere nearby, but I am determined to make it to their local beach at Southbourne. Anything else would seem like a job half done.

I crawl the last half mile in the non-existent breeze. Rafa and Alba are perched on a wooden groyne with Gregg behind. They, and I, are all smiles, assuming 18-month old Rafa is given benefit of the doubt. Grubby - the family hound - is also there, thrusting his big head seaward as if to sniff the sea air or establish whether it is really me. Not much needs to be said when I land - it's great to see the kids, and Gregg and I know that a milestone has been reached. We can talk more later. For now we'll just be happy.

Clyde and other friends pop round in the evening. It's normal to see Clyde but to have other visitors is, I think significant. I have become - temporarily, obviously - interesting.

Day 10 - 16th June

Today the plan is for maintenance, repairs, processing new sign-ups to the windsurfroundbritain website, re-applying sail stickers (replacement 'high tack' versions arrived this morning), applying security updates to some other websites that I maintain, buying expedition food, entering waypoints into my GPS and 101 other things I can't fully remember.

Consequently, I start the day on a mission and my stress levels gradually rise as it becomes increasingly evident that there just isn't time to get everything done.

The interest the expedition is receiving through social media and website is exciting and welcome, but it is also stressful. I don't yet have a consistent strategy for how to keep people informed of what is going on. People are sharing things, messaging me, leaving voicemail, and when I do attempt to respond I'm already out of date, things have moved on, or worse I find myself on the wrong timeline or twitter account. I know I need to get on top of this.

The online attention also leads to an imagined expectation to be back sailing as soon as possible. This too weighs on my mind.

By late afternoon all I have really managed to do is repair the barrel carrier. It is now, at least, rock solid and I am happy with my work. I've replaced all the rivets for beefier marine grade examples, and added plenty more for good measure; the nylon clips on the secondary strap have been exchanged for dependable stainless steel. A few extra grams is an insignificant price for a properly secured barrel.

Finally, I see the light and admit to myself that I need another day to finish my jobs. With this decision made I am happier and become able to relax, smile, and enjoy the company of my brother's family.

Day 11 - 17th June

Most of the remaining jobs get done. The new stickier sail stickers are applied. I buy reserves of Cuppa-porridge and Snickers. I study the *Reed's Nautical Almanac* - a birthday present from my Dad that is far too big to carry with me - and write down slack water times for Portland Bill: a major headland to round in the coming days. I devise a way to carry my strobe safety light and spare mastfoot on the board, rather than in my backpack. The benefits of this are twofold: a lighter pack, and easier access to these items that I hope I won't need; but if I *do* need – then being able to easily access them will be important.

I feel happier and better prepared, ready for a reasonably early start the next morning.

Day 12 - 18th June

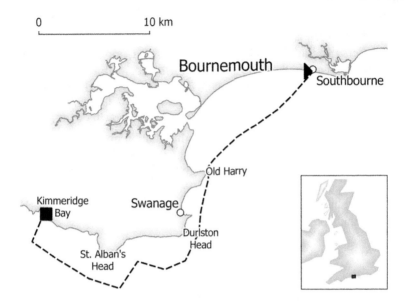

I wake early as planned to find my email inbox populated with new "Security updates available" notifications. *Crap!* A load of websites needing updating isn't a great start to the day. I decide the sensible thing to do is to apply the updates now and delay heading off. As it turns out I am lucky: it is a windless morning, the updates go without a hitch, and I am left with a clear conscience to resume expedition.

By 10:30 I am sailing, cutting across Poole Bay towards Old Harry Rocks. Old Harry is a chalk stack with the same geological heritage as the Needles, though more modest renown. The plan is to get some photos as I sail past. Gregg is on his way there now, driving with Alba, Rafa, and mutual friend Colin as childcare backup. The straight-line route takes me a few miles out to sea and it is reassuring to draw closer to land - in these light airs the possibility of becoming becalmed is a continual concern.

I decide to sail between Harry and one of his wives, of which polygamous Harry has a few. When I emerge from the gap Gregg and helpers come into sight on the cliff top. Alba wails an excited "Hello Jono!", and I return the greeting. Harry has other visitors too, and in the light winds under the cliffs I bump into a friendly group in a rubber boat. They are having a tasty looking picnic and before I know it I have accepted a strawberry. As I bite into the red juiciness I catch the glint of the long lenses on the cliff - the paparazzi caregivers have snapped the strawberry handover. This is my second slip up. If I complete the rounding will it still count as unsupported, I only half joke with myself.

I put the strawberry incident behind me. Blackmail on grounds of dereliction of childminding duty should be sufficient to have the images deleted.

Next up is Durlston Head, by Swanage. A fishing boat comes and asks me if I'm OK. I'm in a strong tidal stream and there certainly isn't enough wind to go anywhere other than where the current is taking me. It is fine, but commitment is total. These are the first significant overfalls of the expedition. Not far away there is a canoeist playing in the standing waves.

The tide shoots me out beyond the headland and suddenly I am into a feisty wind - a solid force 4 on the nose, wind against tide conditions. The coastline has become empty and impressive. This feels much more like serious sailing. I tension the sail to cope with the increasing wind and punch through the oncoming waves during a series of long upwind legs. Ahead more overfalls come in to view - these are off St Alban's Head. I sail out to sea to avoid what looks like the area of roughest water, but find that the farther I sail the farther the rough water area extends.

A mile and a half out the breaking waves don't look too bad, so I decide to cross the lumpy patch. It isn't a place to fall in, but it is OK if upright, and the solid pull in the sail and upwind angle both contribute to stability. The pointed nose of the board spears through the lumps with accuracy and poise. The 10-kilogramme barrel provides additional momentum and contributes to a clean line through the melee. The sensation is of riding a torpedo.

Past St. Albans Head an MOD boat joins me. I'm upbeat after the excitement of the headland and the crewmember who emerges on deck is interested, enthusiastic and helpful. We have a nice chat, the range ahead is closed but I am fine for sailing as far as Kimmeridge Bay, and then moving on early tomorrow morning before firing begins. That was my plan anyway but confirmation of timings is welcome. I bid my friend goodbye and continue powering along upwind, revelling in the ideal conditions, scanning the coastline ahead for recognisable features.

Twenty minutes later my friend's launch comes alongside once again.

Where am I going? I replay the question to make sure I've heard it right over the background noise of sea and wind. "Kimmeridge!" I holler back, wondering why we are repeating our previous conversation.

"Kimmeridge is over there!"

I follow the extended arm which is pointed back at the coastline downwind of me. The MOD man is right. I've managed to sail straight past a bay I know well and have sailed from on several occasions. I'm much further out to sea than I appreciate and have misjudged distance and scale. Kimmeridge is a decent size, but from out here it is no more than a stitch or two on a much more extensive tapestry.

I apologise to and thank my interceptors, before setting off on a series of broad reaches to make land. The episode brings home to me that I am typically sailing in the band of sea where yachts might sail, but windsurfers rarely venture.

I spend an agreeable afternoon at Kimmeridge. Clyde and his little boy Casey show up in the evening and we have a barbecue.

After Clyde leaves I set up camp in the failing light. There is a strict no camping policy at Kimmeridge, and a warden doing his rounds comes to move me on. He is only really interested in the people with vehicles or tents though, and having established that I have neither, wishes me a peaceful night.

Day 13 - 19th June

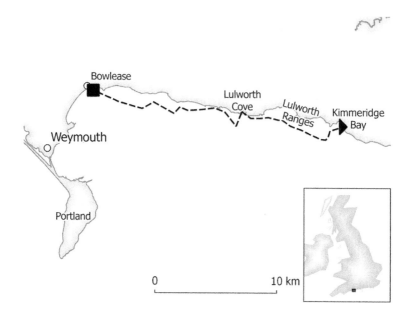

I am on the water by 7am, which gives me two and a half hours to sail through the Lulworth Ranges. The schedule has forced me afloat, but the wind has not yet stirred. For ninety minutes I pump the sail to generate my own wind, but there is minimal reward for considerable effort. Mercifully, a light westerly breeze eventually fills in. My jagged zigzag course decompresses, and at last I start to make progress against tide and wind. The same range boat I saw yesterday comes over. My cheery friend seems to think I'll clear the range just before it opens.

That prediction is a bit too optimistic - by 9:30 I still have a little way to go. A different range boat comes over and tells me that I am in a dangerous area and that I should move on. I explain that I have been trying to do that since 7 o'clock. I am instructed to stay close in - presumably so that any stray munitions pass overhead - and 30 minutes later I'm beyond the lookout post that marks the range boundary.

Just beyond here there is a break in the limestone shoreline - the entrance to Lulworth Cove. I decide to head in for a break and am glad I do - for inside it is spectacularly pretty. The sheltered turquoise pool and dry brightness of the rocks remind me of Mediterranean shores. I stroll the length of the well-kept village and buy a coffee and bacon roll. To my surprise I am identified by the lady serving, who seems to know that someone is windsurfing round Britain. I imagine my fame has spread but perhaps she just saw me sail in. I chat to a few people and generally enjoy the stop.

The next few miles are slow. Portland Bill is only 10 miles away but I won't make it to the headland in time to catch the tide today. I stop at Bowleaze Cove, in the broad sweep of Weymouth Bay, to assess options. *Bacon sandwich or tuna roll?* I am grappling with the decision when I get a tap on the shoulder and am pleasantly surprised to see Colin again, and to meet his partner - Donna.

Colin explains that they have been trying to intercept me by chasing the tracker. They just missed me at Lulworth Cove. Tracker update lag and patchy mobile internet coverage in rural Dorset apparently make this game more fun.

I am slightly bemused at how animatedly Colin describes *the hunt*, but his subsequent apologies for stalking are unnecessary, and there is no indication he is dangerous. As far as I am concerned, the more eyes on the tracker the better: definitely safer to be watched. Donna and Colin suggest a drive round to Portland Bill for a closer look at the tidal race off the headland.

The fear of the unknown is most unsettling, particularly when the unknown has a fearsome reputation, so I welcome the chance to reccy the Portland race before sailing it tomorrow. I'm relieved to see that - despite the sea further out spilling over itself and looking generally unpleasant - there is an inside track close to the rocks looking much more in control. Donna then produces a picnic of epic proportions and variety that totally eclipses the lunch offerings of Bowlease café.

I am dropped off at my board later in the afternoon, and find a note tucked into the footstrap. A couple I know from Minorca -

Portland Bill

Pat and John - also chased the tracker to Bowlease. Their note wishes me luck for the expedition. That's very nice, you certainly can't have too much luck.

I call some old uni friends who have ended up living down here, and end up staying with Matt and Helen, who I haven't seen for about 20 years.

Their lives are a bit more constrained now - two kids have seen to that - but other than that they are essentially unchanged. I don't think our underlying nature ever does change, although at times in our life we might try - or find ourselves - living in a way that conflicts with how we really are.

Day 14 - 20th June

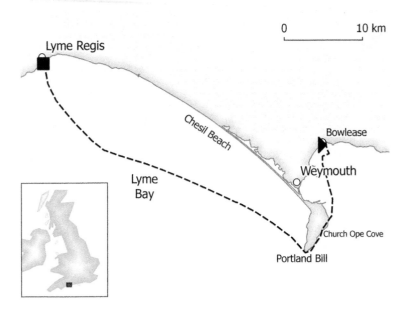

Before heading off in the morning I briefly cross with more friends from years back - Mark and Catherine, who now have three kids in tow. It is great to see Mark, a super positive guy. His enthusiasm betrays an easily recognisable yearning for adventure.

I'm anxious to be in position for rounding Portland Bill on slack water, so bid farewells. The wind starts light and I head towards Weymouth hoping for a back eddy in the current behind the headland. It seems to work, and with the wind filling-in I make excellent progress. Ahead of schedule I beach at Church Ope Cove a very nice spot - just a mile or so from the tip of the peninsula.

Here I have a nice conversation with some ladies who seem most thrilled to have met an *explorer*. Apparently last week they had just missed Colin Firth, but they are generous enough to consider me a worthy substitute.

Just before high tide I set off once again, tacking upwind in a light breeze. I stay close inshore, wary of stronger currents that might drag me into more turbulent waters. Speed and upwind angle are measured by GPS and feed into my awareness of conditions.

The sea around me is gently flowing south towards the tip of the Bill. At the moment it is very flat. Soon the low cliffs give way to boulders and the lighthouse comes into view. I see that - today – for now - the Bill is dormant. Good timing and good luck with the weather mean that I will be allowed to sail round unchallenged.

It is flattest and I feel more secure on the inside track, so continue with the short tacking. On the cliffs I notice someone running and then stopping to take pictures. It is Colin again, who is evidently out for another day's stalking. The attention seems bizarre and exaggerated - the notoriety of Portland Bill had made me fearful but sailing round today is pleasant, interesting and easy. A bit further round I see Mark who is waving from the rocks and beckoning me over. Conditions are such that I can manoeuvre in close enough to be handed a piece of cake. That sums up the rounding. Today at least, it really is that easy.

Past the lighthouse the vast expanse of Lyme Bay stretches out. It would be more comforting to continue following the coast but to do so would trade my relatively upwind position for marginal return. By sailing close hauled from the tip of the Bill I can make... well... I don't know where, but definitely further west. There is a better breeze on the upwind side of the headland. I tuck my feet into the footstraps, let the board lift to an angle where it cuts through the water with minimal resistance, and set my target on empty sea. I double check GPS compass bearing. Land, I am confident - although below the horizon - is somewhere ahead.

I sail continually and cover 30km in two hours. Then, as if a switch has been flipped, the wind drops and eventually peters out altogether. I can see land to my right and adjust my course accordingly, but progress towards the dry stuff is painfully slow. A trickle of breeze returns, enough for me to pump my way in from 10km out.

The coastline starts off a uniform grey. As the separation narrows, distinct colours and features become discernible: fields, forests, towns. I pick a town to head for. Later, I can make out what appears to be a harbour. Pleased to be much further inshore, next I notice a pair of model boats outside the harbour. Their rapid pitching movement reminds me of the way wading birds busily pick at shoreline morsels. Another twenty minutes and I realise the model boats are real boats - their pitching caused by a thermal breeze operating near to land which is producing a short chop. I eventually draw near enough to pick up this breeze too. No longer feeling exposed, I savour the last mile into the beach.

I've been alone with my thoughts and a single overriding goal - to get back to land - for most of the day. Physically and mentally it has been tough. But it is an ordered world out there. Above all there is the order of the waves: patterns upon patterns. Around me now is normal life in all its glorious chaos: people on the beach, in cafes, on the phone: talking, laughing, moving in every direction. Where to direct the attention? The contrast is stark.

Usually I'd give myself at least a few minutes of quiet time to adjust to my new surroundings, but this time - immediately - the busyness is upon me. Bounding down the beach are Rod and Bernadette. I'm not too sure who they are at first but boy they sure do know me!

It's a lovely welcome. Bernadette is loopy and excitable in a crazy arty way. This Rod is a friend of Gregg's who I'd been introduced to at the beach once. He exudes warmth and enthusiasm too. I'm rushed off to a cafe for very welcome tea and mints (yep, mints). Later we roof top the board back to near Weymouth, and have a nice pub meal with Rod's mum.

Today has been a landmark day. Outside of the comfort zone of the south east, beyond the refuge of Bournemouth, into what for me is the unknown. I have a sense that the expedition proper has now begun.

Day 15 - 21st June

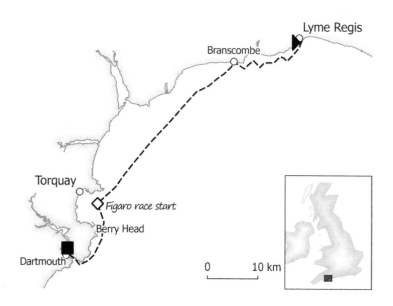

An inconsistent headwind makes for a slow start to the day.
Conditions are easy - not taxing physically - but there are voids in
the breeze and the wind direction is constantly wandering, so
gains can be made by sailing tactically. There doesn't seem to be
much current, so I'm mostly looking for and trying to predict
where I will find more wind and/or favourable changes in wind
direction. It is an inexact science but I claw myself 12km west in
two and a half hours, before stopping for a break at Branscombe.
Not bad progress considering the conditions.

The café is doing good business in the summer weather. A
cream tea goes down well. There doesn't seem any hurry to push
on in this wind. I talk to two sets of people who are curious about
what I am up to. It is nice that people are interested. As I sail off
a rogue puff of wind pulls me in on top of my sail. What a pro!

The wind is better now: freshening from the southwest. Once
again it makes sense to gamble sailing close hauled - which takes

me away from the coast - but further west. Provided the wind holds, I will eventually hit land ahead: Dartmouth - according to the waypoints I have programmed into my GPS.

Branscombe to Dartmouth is about 26 nautical miles, approximately 48km. That is well beyond the horizon - but conditions and progress are improving such that it is a reasonable target. I frequently check the GPS and make the simple calculation of time remaining. At 6 knots I'll cover the distance in 4 hours 20 minutes. I check again, now sailing at 8kn and with 24nm to go: just 3 hours at this pace! The sums provide comforting confirmation that all is well. I invent and count off the milestones: half way; an hour to go; mile count in single figures. At the milestones I sometimes reward myself, most likely with a Snickers bar. I make sure I drink enough. I stretch out as well as I can when I detect aches, pains or stiffness. The reading of the sea ahead is continual. I am not bored. The single-minded goal of reaching land provides little opportunity for wandering of the mind.

The heading to Dartmouth takes me towards an Island, behind is the sweep of a broad bay, but it doesn't match with what I was expecting Dartmouth to look like. In the bay is also a fleet of decent sized yachts sailing around, all leant over at forty-five degrees. I call Ben, my friend and contact at Dartmouth Naval College, to ask for directions, an excerpt of which goes something like:

"Alright mate! Yeah you're at Torquay then ha! ha! not far now just round the next headland into Dartmouth up the river past the town mind the chain ferries! yeah careful they won't stop ha! ha! wind'll be really shit yeah tide'll ha! ha! be interesting! yeah just keep going past everything else can't miss it turn left at the minesweeper see you in a bit wicked ha! ha! Clearance is sorted you won't get shot! barbecue tonight!"

Ben speaks like that.

As I sail closer to the boats I realise that this is the start of the final leg of the Figaro race - a solo offshore sailing race I had heard from a friend that I might see. The boats look spectacular and I'm keen to get in amongst them, but just miss the start, and then fall in behind a spectator boat. I'm more tired than I thought, and decide to leave the Figaro fleet to their race.

From the shelter of Torbay it is a fast beam reach to Berry Head, and then 8km more of gusty offshore winds to the mouth of the river Dart. The rocks and cliffs around the opening are uninviting and sailing up the channel may be a challenge. I vocally question my decision to sail up here, and Ben's decision to suggest it.

My grumpiness is short lived. The approach to Dartmouth is spectacular. Castles guard either side of the narrow entrance. Impressive residences are built into the cliffs lining the estuary. The wind *is* crap, but the water is so smooth compared to the perpetual lumpiness of exposed waters, that even in my fatigued state the sail up the Dart is pleasurable rather than problematic.

As I am now becoming accustomed to doing, I savour the final approach. That the run in to Dartmouth is longer that it need be is welcome. I am conscious that I'll never repeat this experience.

In my own world, I gently zigzag my way upriver. Past the town. Minding the chain ferries. To the minesweeper - where I turn left.

* * *

The minesweeper is at Sandquay, part of the Britannia Royal Naval College. Ben is on the quay. In uniform. Familiar grin. The board goes in a hanger and we climb the hundred and eighty-seven steps to the College.

There is a heavy sense of history here. The training of naval officers at Dartmouth dates from 1863 and the college building where we are now has been operative for over a hundred years. The wooden steps on the staircases are worn. I wonder what battles the feet that have trod these boards have seen, or perished in.

I have a cabin assigned. High ceilinged and spartan. The furniture is of the type you would find on a ferry - fibreglass and with rounded edges. It lends an art deco feel. Unlike ferry cabins there is a large window that opens, and the air smells fresh.

We barbecue in the evening outside the college grounds. The trainee officers are in their civvy gear: shirt, trousers and proper

With Ben, having turned left at the minesweeper

shoes. They seem like a good bunch, give them a year or so and I can imagine they'd be capable of doing a decent job in a conflict or a crisis. Good luck to them - they may have some important decisions to make in their careers.

It could easily be that I don't see Ben for another ten years. But I look forward to the time when we do next meet up.

Day 16 - 22nd June

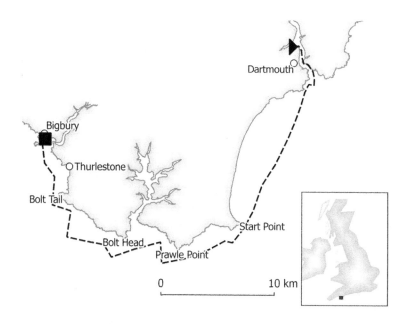

There is low cloud and misty drizzle hanging in the valley of the estuary. I creep past the boats and floating pontoons, occasionally pulling myself along next to them to aid progress. Out on the sea conditions are pretty hopeless - no real wind and a foul tide - but nonetheless I am pleased to be on my way again. After half an hour in which time I cover maybe 500m, I find a lobster pot buoy to tie on to, which at least allows me to have a rest without going backwards. It seems as good an office as any, so I take the opportunity to return a call to a journalist and text the contacts who I hope to reach later in the day.

A breeze fills in and I am able to sail directly towards Start Point. I admire the lighthouse on the promontory as I sail past. There is something about lighthouses that makes them *fit* in their landscape in a way that most manmade structures generally do not.

Going past this headland the wind builds. Tall cliffs for the next ten miles add to the sensation of exposure. Even though I am closer to land than I have been for most of the last two days, I feel like I am further out to sea. In a sense I am, for by their inherent jutted nature, all headlands force their navigators to detour into offshore waters.

There is a solid breeze and accompanying lumpy sea as I tack upwind past the next headlands. These come in quick succession: Prawle Point, Bolt Head, Bolt Tail. A zigzag course takes me alternately closer to land and further out to sea. Inshore feels unsafe for there is a sizeable swell crashing onto the rock-lined cliff base. Offshore feels unsafe too - the tether to shore insubstantial. I occasionally come close enough to a yacht, also heading west, to take in detail of the hull shape; grateful for the company it suggests.

Past Bolt Tail I recognise the coastline before me. Until this point I hadn't been sure where I was going to make for, but from here the coastline downwind looks rock strewn and hazardous, and I decide that I will consolidate what has been a tough sail by landing at Bigbury - where I know it will be simple to stop. Half an hour later I am on the beach.

Trish - a local contact and friend's mum - is first to intercept me, having seen me arrive from her flat overlooking the bay. She plies me with hot pasty and tea from the beach cafe. Next to turn up is John Hibbard, who works for locally based Tushingham Sails, and who has been super positive about the Round Britain project from initial contact. John explains that he spotted me rounding Bolt Tail, and has been running along the cliffs excitedly waving and explaining to bemused dog walkers the significance of the dot in the distance.

With two local contacts standing next to me I'm not quite sure what to do. Thankfully Trish and John are both models of niceness and their offers of support are made without any assumptions about what should happen next. I also don't like to assume, but understand that someone needs to take the bull by the horns here. I suggest that... maybe... I'll stay with Trish at Bigbury tonight, and tomorrow morning, maybe... visit Tushingham HQ with John, before sailing in the afternoon, if that sounds OK?

Of course, it is OK, in fact - nothing is too much bother. Every day of this journey, I'm receiving confirmation that the vast majority of people in life are fundamentally really nice.

We stash my windsurf gear at *Discovery Surf School* in Bigbury and I head back with Trish for what is, in effect, an afternoon off. I shower and get clean. Then enjoy cups of tea, the soft carpet between my toes, and a peaceful view out across Bigbury Bay - now bathed in afternoon sunshine.

My perception of what is *real sea* is changing. I've sailed at Bigbury on numerous occasions, always assuming it was the real sea. But for me now the real sea is to be found beyond the headlands. From the beaches where most of us sail, walk or build a sandcastle, the real sea is far away. It is *so* far away that when we look we cannot see it. We do not see its waves, hear its wind, or taste its isolation. When I sailed into the beach earlier today I had sailed through the real sea, yet when I arrived and turned to face it, it was gone.

Day 17 - 23rd June

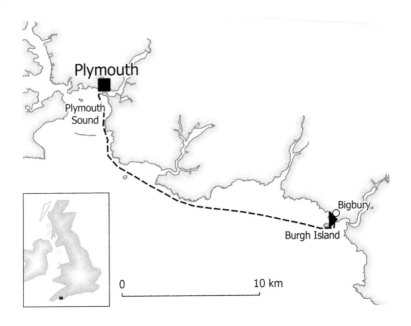

Conveniently, the morning is windless. I bid farewell to Trish - who has just loaded me up with two huge chunks of apple pie - ready to rendezvous with John.

John and I drive to Tushingham HQ - somewhere not too far away in the Devon countryside. I meet the rest of the team there and the visit is recorded with an official photograph. Their offers of support come across as very genuine and I am left in no doubt that if I do find myself in a fix then team Tushingham will do what they can to help.

John replaces a broken batten from my sail and provides a couple of spares.

He also has an idea to help prevent water finding its way into my drysuit via the ankle seals - a problem that I have whenever it is windy and that I could really do without for reasons of comfort and safety. John's idea is to wrap a surf leash cuff around each seal. It is a simple but brilliant suggestion, and perhaps a solution

Tushingham HQ

to the issue. On the way back to Bigbury we stop at a surf shop and the owners are happy to provide a couple of cuffs.

Shortly after midday I set off towards Plymouth in a gentle onshore breeze. I'm pleased with how the morning went, and also happy to be making progress now, but also a bit peckish. Hidden from view by Burgh island I stop for a quick break to polish off the first chunk of apple pie.

The wind is very light and the 22km to Plymouth take nearly four hours to complete. The south Devon coastline is really very pretty and the water beautifully clear. I see thousands of barrel jellyfish which are now so abundant that the fin of the board snags on them repeatedly. Despite the light winds the sea is still choppy and with no real power in the sail, balance requires effort.

Plymouth - like Dartmouth - is a bit of a detour. In fact, sailing to the town will add about 14km to my Round Britain journey. When I reach and turn left into Plymouth Sound I imagine friends of mine following the tracker path online and observing - incredulous and perhaps slightly annoyed - that I am going the *wrong way*. In particular I can imagine my good friend Ian shaking his head, watching in disbelief, despairing at this – this second! - inexplicable decision. "What *is* he doing?!" I can imagine Ian saying. I know and can later confirm that Ian's

Barrel jellyfish

frustration was real and was borne out of a very heartfelt desire for expedition success.

I am heading for Queen Anne's Battery, a marina in the centre of town, where Tamzine - who is Dennis's daughter - has said she will pick me up. To refresh readers' memories, Dennis died earlier in the year from Pancreatic Cancer. I was always going to stop at Plymouth.

In any case, the sailing inside the Sound is most pleasant. The coastline full of interest, of which the flat water allows for full appreciation. I park the board in a smooth forest of kelp and picnic on the second chunk of apple pie. My legs dangle in the clear water and I reflect that I've now come a long way from the muddy waters of Clacton.

Tam arrives soon after I land at QAB. We stash the gear at *Allspars* - a company that make yacht masts. Then it is back to the family home where I am well looked after.

Day 18 - 24th June

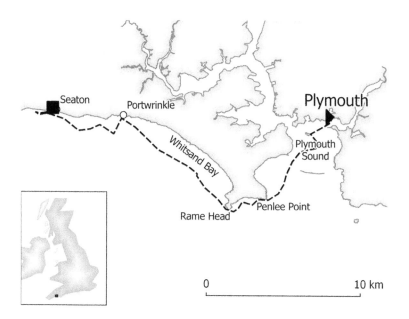

Today is a slow day. The sea is mirror flat - not a breath of wind. There is no point sailing just yet. I enjoy a few hours around the Plymouth coffee bars, using the time to catch up on overdue admin.

At midday there is a hint of a breeze: time to set off. In the Sound the wind is bang on the nose, but there is just enough to make reasonable progress. On my way to the breakwater that protects the sound I am checked out by a military launch which is inspecting and redirecting all craft in the vicinity. Conveniently they don't seem to consider me a threat and I alone am allowed to continue on my original course. Shortly afterwards a very curious bit of hardware passes by: armour plated, khaki camouflaged, gun turret. It kicks up a mist of spray as it passes. I take a picture of the craft, wonder if a windsurfer with a barrel could be a terrorist threat, half hope for a response to my espionage. Today, for the first time since leaving Clacton, the sailing itself is a little bit boring.

Outside the breakwater the sailing becomes a real slog. Multiple zigzags are required to get round Penlee Point and Rame Head. The challenge at least restores interest. The gentle conditions continue for a long but easy haul across Whitsand Bay. It is a glorious day, and I am able to listen to some podcasts to help pass the time. This is only the second time I do this, and also turns out to be the last. Not only is it awkward operating a device, but sailing with headphones I feel less aware of my surroundings. Often though, a repetitive tune bounces around my head.

From Portwrinkle the coast bends and the wind is again bang on the nose. I begin zigzagging up the coastline towards Looe where I have a friend - Joe - who has signed up as a contact. By early evening I am about two miles short when the wind drops off to near zero, and I am forced to retreat a short distance to Seaton.

No bother, Joe turns up with fish and chips, and we round off the evening with a Guinness in the local pub. It is a nice reunion. Joe has become more Cornish than ever and has just split up with his girlfriend because she wants to leave Cornwall, and he doesn't. I try to be philosophical with Joe about people sometimes wanting different things. Later I learn that Joe's ex only wanted a *weekend* away from Cornwall, and I realise just how native he has become.

Talk moves on to fishing and before departing Joe gifts me some line and a feather trace. In theory I can now catch mackerel.

For the first night since the Isle of Wight I sleep under the sail. I am on a patch of grass overlooking the sea. It is magical. This is how I imagined the expedition would be.

Day 19 - 25th June

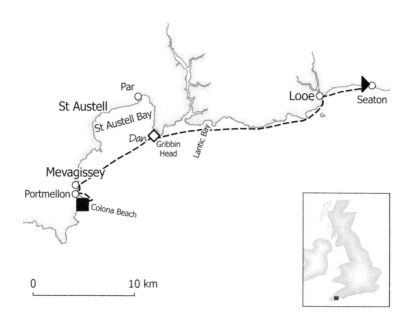

The morning dawns windless and I enjoy breakfast in bed from my top of sea wall vantage point.

When a gentle breeze fills in I sail the few miles that remain to Looe, by which time lunch is beckoning. I beach for half an hour for a quick hello and goodbye to Joe, who points me in the direction of a good pasty shop. On the beach I am recognised by a total stranger, who wishes me luck.

I don't stay long. The thought of how far I have to go, and the possibility of not getting past Scotland's north coast before the end of summer, is never far from my mind.

It is another day of slow sailing. The coastline however, is idyllic. Again, the water is crystal clear and big barrel jellyfish are everywhere. When I overheat I sit on my board with legs dangling in the sea to cool off. I'm fairly sure the Barrel Jellyfish don't sting but there also are a fair number of Lion's Mane - or as I record them in my notes *Messy Trifle* - jellyfish. These have long stingers which I am careful to avoid.

I pass and am tempted to stop at Lantic Bay. It seems nearly criminal not to stop at some of the bays I sail past. This one has a flat grassy area beyond the golden sand - picture postcard perfect for sleeping under the stars. But I've a long way to go, and the day has more miles in it.

I'm not far from Gribbin Head where I know I have a decision to make: turn right towards my contact - Dan - at Par, or straight line it across St Austell Bay towards Mevagissey. Dan was one of my first sign-ups on the website, and someone who also has dreams of windsurfing round Britain, so I feel bad about not linking up in some way. I decide to telephone, getting through to his wife.

"Dan's on the water"

At that moment I notice a sail in the distance. "Yes!" I say "I can see him!" Today, it is my turn to also experience the slightly inexplicable excitement of spotting a distant windsurfer. It reminds me of the childhood thrill I used to get upon chancing upon goldfish. *Look everyone! Goldfish!*

When I meet up with Dan we down sails, shake hands and have a sit down. I am very touched that he's sailed all the way out here. We have a brief chat. It makes sense for me to push on west and Dan points out places that might be good for stopping on the other side of St Austell Bay. We both know that the wind is likely to drop away to towards nothing in the evening, and both have a long sail ahead, so bid our farewells. Ten minutes later we are distant dots on each other's horizons.

The wind holds - just - for the five mile sail across open water to Mevagissey. It is difficult to consult any sort of map whilst at sea, and the mapping on my phone is very inadequate and awkward to read, so once again I don't really know what to expect. I poke the nose of my board into Mevagissey harbour. The water smells of trawler and prospects look poor for comfortable camping so I decide to try the next cove along.

That takes me to Port Mellon, which has a nice landing, but still no obvious camping location.

Third stop takes me round Chapel Head to Colona Beach, tucked into a small and secluded bay. Perfect.

I find a good stick to prop the sail and cook up a packet rice meal, made more palatable by sachets of mayonnaise and ketchup. Towards dusk lots of fish gather in the shallow water of the bay and I make a half-hearted attempt to catch one. Thankfully they're not tempted by Joe's mackerel feathers. I like fish, but don't really have the means to cook them.

Eventual camping spot at Colona Beach

Day 20 - 26th June

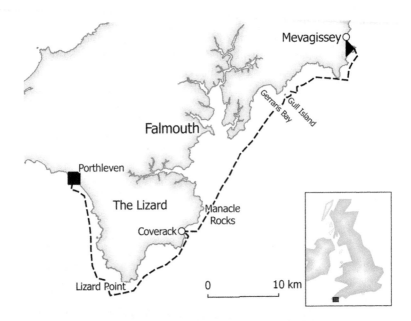

It is a drizzly morning, with a mist hanging over the sea that truncates the cliffs. The monochrome water is rougher today. It is difficult to make out what conditions will be like once I leave the shelter of my bay, the prospect of sailing into a world beyond view is unnerving.

I decide a full stomach will fortify my resolve, and after my own camp-porridge-breakfast walk the cliff path to Megavissey, for an excellent full English. I enjoy the walk. The mistiness is gentle and the freshwater wetness a welcome change from salt.

Back at camp the day appears to be on the mend. Time to head out.

The sailing provides a comfortable level of excitement and - despite yet another headwind - is enjoyable. Successive outcrops reveal themselves through the mist as I approach. Disappointingly though, the wind is dropping. I reach but struggle for an hour to pass Gull Island. Then the wind dies away completely, and I am becalmed.

The wind has stopped because the day is changing. The sun breaks through and when the breeze returns it is blowing from the west-northwest. This good fortune enables me to resume sailing parallel to the coast and on a flatter sea.

These are the first genuinely favourable conditions since Brighton, and all of a sudden I'm reeling in the miles. Gerrans Bay is soon behind me and I straight line across Falmouth Estuary too. I thread a path between Manacle Point and the actual Manacle rocks that lie beyond.

I hadn't expected to get this far today, and my recollection of the coastline ahead is hazy, so when Coverack Bay comes into view I take the opportunity to stop. After five hours on the water I could also do with a break. What a contrast from this morning! The harbour is filled with brightly coloured boats and the water is a stunning turquoise. I dump my board on the sand and race up the steps to reach the village shop before Cornish closing time.

I eat and check the map. I'm within striking distance of the Lizard Peninsula - Britain's most southerly point, and one of its most infamous headlands. The peninsula and its outlying rocks have claimed many ships and lives.

I have a childhood memory of sailing round the Lizard in a yacht, with Dennis. Conditions were glorious and the sailing exhilarating as we - relatively speaking - tore downwind amongst the swells. Sailing through an area of overfalls the bow crashed through the waves, water cascading over the deck. At one point dolphins joined in the party. It was the best yacht sailing I have known, though I say this with slight guilt - as I know that below decks Moira was struggling with seasickness. I can easily bring to mind Captain Dennis's approving expression as he masterminded our safe passage.

The seemingly reliable wind and imagined familiarity bolster my confidence about rounding the Lizard now. John's advice is also present in my decision: *when there is an opportunity, be bold.*

Food and adrenaline have made me strong as I leave Coverack and round the corner, to sail into a wilder sea. There are 11km – as the crow flies - to the tip of The Lizard. I sail upwind, well powered up, in mile long zigs and zags. The sea builds. Spray and wind whistle past my ears. And although I feel insignificant and exposed in these surroundings, I also feel good. I know that with this good breeze I can take any line required around this monster to keep me out of trouble.

I stay well offshore, south of and away from the shelter of the headland. The ocean breathes to a different rhythm out here. Atlantic swells are now the canvas of the sea upon which this morning's slop is now just detail. The march of the swells is effortless. Their scale – as wide as fields and as long as rivers, is sobering. From here the headland is a speck. I will be invisible from shore. I feel alone and vulnerable with such a weak connection to land. I tack. The new heading takes me closer in. But the waves soon stand tall and ahead of me they break on submerged rocks. There is no option but to tack back out to the relative safety of deep water. This is really quite a solid swell.

I round the Lizard with a mile to spare, far enough to stay out of trouble. I'm slightly surprised by the amount of swell but not particularly concerned at this moment. I keep sailing, keeping an eye out for somewhere to land.

As I beat along the coast I watch waves smashing into the cliffs. Ahead - far ahead - there appears to be a village on a hillside. Before there, it all looks pretty bleak. Will the village have a harbour I can get into on this swell? Time isn't on my side. If this wind drops - as is likely - I could struggle to make it that far in daylight anyway. I need a contact with Google Earth who understands the situation. I phone Gregg. No answer. Clyde. No answer. Fuck! Where's a mate when you need one? I phone Ian. Someone picks up! It is Bella, Ian's wife.

"I'm fine thanks Bel. No Ian? OK then. Could you find me on the tracker, please. Am I headed to Penzance?"
Bel does pretty well. "Jono, probably not. Penzance is twenty miles away. That could be Porthleven. There's a big long beach before you get there. Good luck love."

Big long beach sounds a lot better than big fuck off cliffs, but the whole coastline is fully exposed to this swell, meaning that a beach landing would be a desperate and last resort. I keep going for the Porthleven place. *Porth has got to mean port, right?* All the time the wind is dying. The roll of the swells moves me sideways, blocks the wind, robs me of upwind angle and power.

A few coves starts to punctuate the cliff line, but getting close enough to even check out whether they'd be viable options just looks too hazardous. At last I reach the long beach. There's not a lot of light left so I go in close for a look. It looks awful. 45 degree steep with a crunching shorebreak bouncing to double wave height on the beach. Fuck that. I tack out and continue. The town is only a few miles away now.

The town appears to have a wall. Breaking waves both sides. Any opening there? It doesn't look promising. There are two more headlands ahead. It could be better round those. I momentarily abandon Porthleven. *Jesus! You've no fucking light left!* Back for another look. That *is* an entrance. Viable at low tide? I make a snap decision to find out before it really is too dark to see.

I sail downwind a little to prepare my line, wait for a relative lull in the swells, then power up to sail full speed at a black wall. In the final metres I see that I have guessed right: the wall is two walls overlapped to conceal a harbour entrance. The mouth is only a few metres across, but it has a deep channel. I reach the shelter of the protective arm and am perfectly safe. I pause for a few moments to catch my breath and let the adrenaline subside. A body boarder paddles over, on his way in from the wave on the left. I look round to the right and there is another surfer looking for his last wave. And then I realise why the name Porthleven is familiar to me. The right where the surfer had been is perhaps the most famous surfing wave in Britain.

I drift into the harbour. The high walls shelter the wind, and there are steep steps to the hard, upon which sits a pub. I am spotted.

"Where have you come from mate?"

"Er, today from Mevagissey"

He takes a step closer. "Say again. Where've you come from?"

"Mevagissey."

A pause. "You've come from Mevagissey. *Mevagissey*? You've come from *Meva-fucking-gissey*?"

"Yep, any chance of a hand up these steps"

"Too fucking right mate. I'm Ian by the way and you need a

drink." and then to his compatriots "Here, we need a hand! This guy's just come on a fucking windsurfer. from *Meva-fucking-gissey.*"

Ian wades in to direct a board retrieval team and before I know it I am in the pub. Scampi and chips in one hand, Guinness in the other. I haven't had an opportunity to take my drysuit off, and we are both dripping seawater.

Ian is a seafarer. He sails with injured serviceman, helping them adjust to their changed lives. His warmth and humanity is obvious. We talk about my voyage so far, and about the challenge of Land's End that lies ahead. Ian knows the headland well, and his concern is evident. He wants me to be safe. "You want good puff for Land's End" he tells me.

I am also told that Porthleven beach is as hazardous as it looks. Swimmers were lost here earlier in the year, and dogs are drowned with sad regularity. With today's swell, that beach was never an option.

Porthleven is a village under siege from the sea. Literally, constructed as a fortress to withstand the Atlantic's onslaught. It is a hard place, and offers proof that the nicest of people live in the hardest of places. I meet more wonderful people in the village, including Ollie and Sophie who make me welcome in to their house, feed and clothe me.

Day 21 - 27th June

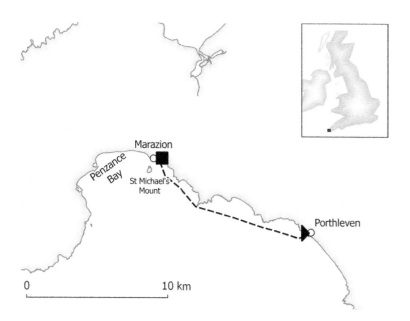

I start the day with porridge and freshly laundered clothes. The swell has dropped, giving Porthleven a picturesque rather than fearsome aspect this morning. I only have a short sail today - to Marazion - in the wide sweep of Penzance Bay, last definite stopping opportunity before Land's End.

There may be only a small amount of swell left over from yesterday, but it is rebounding off the low cliffs, creating a dog's dinner of a sea. This combined with the light winds make for uncomfortable, slow, tiring sailing. Every muscle works to maintain balance in these conditions. It is a relief to finally reach the flatter water within the curve of Penzance Bay. I sail to shore past St. Michael's Mount - an island connected to the mainland by a causeway at low tide. The Mount has a castle and summer flowers are out on the green borders.

On land I am approached by James, who has been painting the outside of his house and has observed my arrival. He is a

Porthleven

welcoming chap and we find a spot for my board next to his dinghy at the local sailing club, before heading to his house. Here I also meet Karen. They make a nice couple who are building a pleasant life for themselves in what is a lovely part of the world.

I am overcome by tiredness in the afternoon and attempt to sleep for a few hours, but the challenge of Land's End plays on my mind and if I do sleep it is fitful. I get up, study Google Earth, and enter what look like possible landing options as waypoints into my GPS.

The weather forecast suggests that overnight it will be breezy and rainy, with the wind moderating and a brighter day tomorrow. An improving forecast is certainly welcome, but nonetheless I am concerned about the wind and sea conditions I may encounter.

It would be easier to hear at this stage a *no bother if you need to stay an extra day* but James doesn't seem to pick up on my trepidation or consider that it might be problematic to move on. Today is, after all, a lovely day. Conditions for sailing in Penzance Bay look so easy.

I am sure James knows the sea. I wonder if he knows the *real sea*, the way the trawlermen across the Bay in Newlyn must know it. Possibly. And possibly he is just more fear tolerant than I.

Being a guest means I am more likely to set out tomorrow, for I do not want to overstay my welcome. But the real pressure to move lies deeper. The awareness of so many miles ahead, and the possibility of reaching Scotland when the summer weather is already turning, is never far from mind.

No, only if conditions are really bad can I back out. Windsurfing round Britain requires taking the opportunities when they arise. I would likely have to wait months for a perfect weather window to round Land's End. Good enough has to do. If it is good enough tomorrow I will sail.

Over dinner - lasagne, ideal - James tells a story of how he and a friend were left drifting for three days in a stricken yacht in the English Channel. The friend had bought the yacht for £600 on eBay, and assumed that James – a very able dinghy sailor, although with no prior big boat experience - would help sail it to its new home. On the voyage, sequentially, the rigging, engine and electrics all fail - and they are left two nights being swept up and down on the tide somewhere south of Portland Bill, before eventual rescue. It is a true mariner's tale, which deserves to be more adequately chronicled. Perhaps I'm making rather a big deal of this Land's End rounding.

Day 22 - 28th June

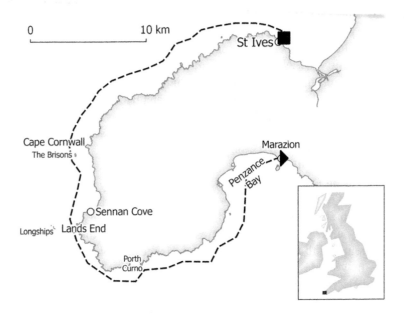

Wind and rain beat at the window as I fitfully sleep through the early hours. By dawn it doesn't sound so bad, but it is a grimy day outside. Coffee wakes me up and I force down some porridge.

I leave the house before James and Karen rise, and walk down to the dinghy compound with my gear. Visibility is poor. The other side of Penzance Bay is lost in the mist. I am not keen to sail, but no alternative options come to mind. The rational mind overrules emotionally led objections: I don't need blue skies to sail around Land's End. As Ian advised - I need puff. There is puff.

I rig sombrely and carefully, and suit up in the public conveniences, where at least it is dry. There is no colour to the day. I carry the board over sodden low tide beach, to the water's edge. By the time I have returned with sail and barrel, the water has receded another 50m. Wet sand sticks to everything. I lug the gear the final metres to the water, negotiate the rocks, and am sailing in clear water.

The mist hangs low as I zigzag my way upwind out of Penzance Bay. The zigs take me away from land, which with distance dissolves into the murk. The zags take me closer, eventually revealing an outline and clues to where I am.

Next come a series of headlands. The outline of each is revealed on final approach to the preceding jut of cliff. There is an obvious sea building the further I progress. Some distance on a sliver of sand shows through a nook in the cliffs: most likely Porth Curno. The beach looks steep and a foam border suggests that this wouldn't be a sensible place to put in.

I've been comfortable sailing until now. I realise that the sea state has gradually transitioned to become *lively*. The board is punching through the waves, and I am going faster, being carried by a current that wasn't there before. The veil of white mist has thinned and rocks are visible offshore. I realise that I am in *it*. This is Land's End.

The rocks - Longships - have a lighthouse. The sea around them is tripping over itself in all directions. Instinctively, I don't want to go there. The inshore route looks less hazardous. I pick my way carefully. The sea becomes steeper and waves ahead are crumbling. I am aware that - if I fall - getting going again in this confused sea will be difficult. And the waves could easily break mast or sail. I am not afraid, but my focus is intense. I catch myself muttering, with determination, "*You wanted this, mate!*"

As the coast bends, the angle I need to sail becomes more open. For the early waves I can point further into the wind and spear through them, but as the waves become bigger and the angle changes I modify my approach - controlling speed to avoid the steepest lumps, which might otherwise sweep the board away from under me. I narrowly avoid being sideswiped - slipping past a crumbling peak that snaps at the barrel laden tail of my board.

The wind becomes very light as I progress further round the headland. The little wind there is comes from behind me. All my effort and experience is required to stay on the board. I twist the harness lines away to prevent accidentally hooking in. There is no time for looking around, but I have a vague awareness that I have passed a lighthouse type building.

This area of horribly confused sea is where the currents from the English Channel and Bristol Channel meet. On my sail to Land's End there had been a typical south coast sea, generated by the overnight wind. On the west facing coast I can now appreciate that there is a big Atlantic swell. At Land's End itself, both the south coast sea and north coast swell have combined. The resulting maelstrom is made even more unpleasant by the meeting of currents.

Now onto the north Cornish coast the sea is smoother, but my problems are far from over. The sailing is very difficult. Once beyond the immediate danger of Land's End I stop to assess the situation.

With metronomic regularity, and eerie quiet, huge swells roll through. The separation between each bulge of ocean would accommodate a football pitch, perhaps two.

And the wind is light. Horribly light.

I had hoped that once onto the north coast I would be able to duck into Sennen harbour, but with no power I have zero confidence that I will be able to approach without being taken onto the outlying rocks and dashed to pieces. With practically no wind out here, I know the wind inshore will be non-existent. And making it to the beach in-between waves will be impossible too. With all my ungainly backpack and expedition gear on - drowning in the attempt would be a real risk.

At the moment the current is carrying me along the coast, in the right direction. But for how long? In this wind, will I still be able to make progress when the current switches? Or will I be pulled back to Land's End and the hideous sea I have just come through? For the first time on the expedition I am genuinely scared for my personal safety. There is no doubt about the situation. There are no landing options, I must reach St Ives, 30km distant, and I must avoid where the swells are turning into waves that are pounding the coastline.

Looking back at Land's End – the earlier chaotic sea replaced by eerie swells

I drain the water that has found its way into my drysuit, before recommencing the struggle of holding up my sail in the lifeless air.

The angle becomes broader - and sailing more difficult - the further I progress. The wind offers no assistance to stay upright as the board is pushed forwards then back by the ghostly swells.

It feels like I am going nowhere. Only the gradual approach of an island – rocks really, The Brisons - confirms that progress is being made. It is so difficult to sail that even getting my drinking tube to my mouth is a major operation.

The water surface does strange things. At times it is literally shaking, and the sea becomes a mogul field of dancing spikes. In other areas there is upwelling from the depths. The sea's surface is alive. It breathes to the pulse of the swells. It changes appearance as if by emotional response.

I head for midway between the island and the next headland, Cape Cornwall. On the approach I study the gap, occasionally seeing white water. Is there a safe way through? A big set of waves rolls in and turns white. I make a late decision to not find out. I thump the daggerboard down and harden up, pointing as high as I can - out to sea and away from the islands. But the current is still taking me north and the wind so light that I am struggling to clear the islands before being pulled past. I see and hear the waves unloading onto the island reefs whilst around me fishing buoys - small floats with three-metre long canes - are pulled deep underwater as the swells pass through. I make it out beyond where the waves are standing up and feathering, but keep pointing out to sea, watchful for any set waves that threaten to break further out.

I allow the current to take me past the island. Then it is back to sailing as low as possible, the most exhausting angle in these conditions.

The mist has lifted but it is still a drab and grey day. The weirdness of the water is spooky. The unrelenting white noise of waves on cliff is an unwelcome companion that talks at me continually - reminding of the threat inshore. Sometimes the sailing is so difficult I am forced to sail closer to the wind for more stability. Even then the shaking of the sea may be so severe that I am unable to hold the sail.

On one such fall I stop for a break. I call Gregg. There is nothing he can do other than confirm what I already know, but sharing my predicament is a help. I take a picture. Mist, sweat and seawater drip from my face. Fear shows through my haunted expression. The compact form of a puffin glides past. Its beak is the only colour I have seen all day.

Hour after hour I sail down the coast.

To check my GPS I first have to grab and hold it tight to prevent its violent swinging. The miles-to-go tick down. I notice that on the downhills of the swells my speed picks up and builds to around six knots - much better than I had thought, and on the uphills I am almost sliding backwards, making just two knots. The effort required to keep sailing is intense, but at least I know that I am making progress.

I am almost *at* St Ives before I realise that I will make it. A speedboat comes a short way up the coast and over to see me. The occupants take pictures and I am cheery, perhaps too cheery. My manner does not fit the ordeal I am emerging from. I talk with breezy confidence, as if today is just another day, much like previous days.

I sail into the harbour at St Ives. The sandy beach below the promenade is evenly spread with people. The sun is finally breaking through the clouds. For most people it *is* just another day.

For a while I sit on my board on the beach. A while later I strip off to my shorts and wade into the water. I lay face down, taking in the coolness, resting my closed eyes.

I sense that I need food so find a cafe, an empty one. I can barely speak as I order a cream tea. I find a corner table and wait, head in hands. Spent. When I lift my head there is a tray with scones and a teapot. I gather the strength to pour a cup. I don't take sugar, but put in two. I realise that I am shaking.

I am unable to drink at first. More willpower is needed to take that first sip than I have needed all day. We only need willpower to act when we have an alternative option. Drinking tea is a choice. There had been no alternative but to claw my way to St Ives.

The sweet liquid acts as a trigger. Tears start and don't stop. They run down my forearms onto the paper tablecloth, turning it translucent. I am now the only customer inside. Ordering more tea, I reassure the waitress that I am OK. By the end of the second pot - superficially at least - I am.

Day 23 - 29th June

My equipment stayed on the beach last night. I pulled myself together enough to send a message to Ed, who had signed up on the website some months ago. Apparently I'd taught him to windsurf way back in 1998. Fortunately, Ed's memory is better than mine.

I wasn't really sure I was up to being with people, but Ed, his radiantly pregnant wife, and the visiting friend - James - are so unassuming and easy to be around - that I am able to be there without feeling any pressure to entertain. They are busy and happy people. The normality of the domestic situation is a tonic. Dinner, a late take away curry.

St Ives is like an exotic country. The sun is out. People walk to or from the beach with surfboards, for there is still a decent swell running. Ed's enclosed garden is like an oasis. Plants you wouldn't expect, and an outdoor shower for waking up or washing away the salt after a dip. The vertically challenged swing door provides just enough modesty. It is all very well thought out.

I know early that I need a recovery day and broach this with Ed. No problem at all.

I'd told myself that I would visit the Tate Gallery, so I do. I am not altogether surprised to be wholly underwhelmed by the art, and more impressed by the building. A semi-circular entrance amplifies the sound of the waves and the glass panels reflect the beach scene. It is very immersive and I assume entirely deliberate. The roof-top café is very nice too. From it can be seen seals swimming along the waves that the surfers are riding.

By the end of the day I am feeling anxious. I can't really pinpoint the cause. Yesterday's trauma is the obvious candidate, but anxiety was a feature of my last relationship, and there has been contact on that front too, muddying the recently settled waters. Or

St Ives beach from the rooftop of the Tate Gallery

the angst may just be my regular self-inflicted worry about not sailing a sailable day. Still so far to go.

James is about to take the dogs out. I sense I could do with a stroll too and ask if I can come along.

We walk through a green lane. The dogs' poop is collected in little plastic bags. More normality - good. Then we reach the coastal path, with cliffs that stretch away into the distance. I am aware of the soft yet firm grass under my feet and feel safe. Feeling safe feels *great*. I am enjoying the walk and the scenery. Yesterday the cliffs were grey and threatening - they had none of the beauty that I see today.

If I had a life that was long enough to do all the things I wanted to do, one of those things would be to walk round Britain.

Pizza and a beer overlooking the surf beach rounds off the walk, and the day.

Day 24 - 30th June

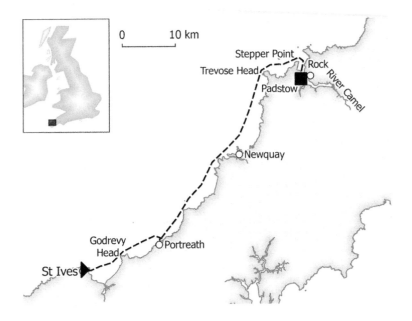

Ed drops me off at the beach at 7:30am. I am told that I can't leave my board here at night. That's not a problem.

It looks good for sailing. Sunny. The south-easterly wind is blowing offshore. Near St Ives there is a gentle summer breeze, although distant whitecaps suggest that further out the day will have a different feel.

I'm pleased to be on my way, but am soon on my limit for comfortable sailing. Rather than sail directly across St Ives Bay I stay inshore in search of less wind. This sets up a fast broad reach between Godrevy Head and the island lighthouse three-hundred metres offshore. Big seals wobble into the water as I pass.

Beyond the headland I am hit by more wind. I try to convince myself that it's fine, that it isn't really as windy as it feels and that I am just affected by previous days. But that is pretence. My sail is fully tensioned to dump power and I still have to take an extra wide grip on the boom to lever it under control. Sailing the required beam reach angle - ninety degrees to the wind - is very difficult. I try to sail tight then broad - a very open zig zag to avoid the beam reach angle. Tight I can manage, but broad is too out of control for comfort. Further inshore there is - on average - less wind, but the gusts are fierce and doubly tiring.

A hint of despair enters my mind. The seemingly continual battle against conditions is a strain that is getting to me. Where are the pleasant summer conditions I had imagined?

I give myself a talking to. It is silly to be pushing myself and equipment in these conditions. It is likely the wind will moderate later and I can make progress in the afternoon. Another fierce gust settles the matter. Directly upwind is a beach. A zig and a zag later and I am upon it.

Sheltered from the wind, it is a fiercely hot day at Portreath. The beach and village are packed with holiday makers. Amongst them is a Martian. It peels off a survival suit and protective layers, placing these on the grass next to its other worldly technology. Next it ingests an all-day breakfast at the beach café. Then it shields its delicate martian skin with a *travel-towel* radiation blocking device, and falls asleep in the sun.

By 2pm I feel sufficiently confident that the wind has moderated, and hurriedly prepare to depart, aware that miles are there for the taking. Target is Newquay, as a minimum. The launch is potentially complicated, as the waves have picked up with the tide, but a gust sees me safely out.

Thankfully, conditions are much improved: sufficiently offshore there is stable wind to blast along at nearly 20 knots. I'm also sailing directly where I need to go. No zigzagging. I reach and pass Newquay in little over an hour, where I at last see a dolphin. The sighting helps buoy my confidence. I am less perturbed and more accepting of the variability in the wind now. The valleys and hills channel or block the wind. *Local effects.*

Past Newquay sometimes I am planing at speed and at other times I am plodding along slowly. Maybe the wind is really this up and down, but more likely is that the wind is simply different at different places. With a different start and end point every day, my appreciation of local effects has become more acute. They can turn easy conditions into a struggle, and vice-versa. Conditions rarely stay the same as I progress along the coast.

I approach and pass Trevose Head. Once beyond the promontory, the familiar sensation of being a long way out to sea and in an area of wind acceleration. I harden up to bring myself closer to land. Then there is some protection from Stepper Point. And after this outcrop it is back into stronger wind funnelling out of the River Camel.

Traditional Cornish Shrimper boats are a welcoming sight as I sail into the estuary. The red sails leaning over in the breeze as significant swells raise and settle the craft. I'm impressed by the gameness of the crews. I carefully sail through the fleet so as not to impede. The Shrimpers take their racing seriously: not even a flicker of a hello.

I'm not sure where to stop. Further up the river the calm waters makes for pleasant sailing. Once again, I enjoy the arrival.

First I land at Rock. A wander around and a few phone calls convince me that I should be on the other side of the river, in Padstow. It is a struggle to beat the tide and by the time I get there I see that the water has all but disappeared from the river. Ten minutes later and I would have had to walk across.

Emily - a friendly face who I'd met out in Minorca the previous year, and who had messaged me the day before - shows up as I am de-rigging, and we work out a plan on the hoof. My board ends up snugly stowed at the Rowing Club - nice people, thank you! - and we end up at The Old Custom House to start the serious business of re-hydration.

Day 25 - 1st July

I chat tactics with Gregg this morning. With so few safe stopping options this north Cornwall coast really is a tricky place to navigate. Again the problem is swell. With 6-9 foot forecast for Bude - 40km up the coast - today is another tricky day. Gregg checks Reeds and Google Earth and confirms that I'll need to make it 75km up the coast before finding somewhere where I can be confident of landing safely. The wind is also *very* light. I'm particularly un-keen on sailing in a big swell and no wind, and need very little convincing to take a day off.

This turns out to be one of my better decisions. Despite it being recorded as the hottest day of the year - breaking temperature records at Wimbledon - here there is a mist that hangs over the coastal margins.

With no vibrancy and muted sounds, it is a medicated day that slips by without every getting going.

Guilt free - for I could not have sailed today - I enjoy a walk out to Stepper point. And later I am intercepted by Moira and family members, who are holidaying nearby.

Day 26 - 2nd July

It is another windless morning. John is my tactics man today. He is of the opinion that I should sample the famous Rick Stein fish and chips.

I go one step further and become a real tourist, visiting the lobster hatchery beforehand. It is an interesting project. Eggs from locally trapped female lobsters are hatched in tanks and the larvae nurtured to a point where they stand a more sporting chance of survival. The same boats that fished the mothers then return the baby lobsters to the seas where they were caught. It all sounds nicely sustainable.

The fish and chips are tasty enough, but - having not sailed for a couple of days - I don't really need them. By the end of my box I feel slightly overindulged, and conclude that the lobster hatchery entry fee was money better spent.

Emily and housemates are working long days as surf lifeguards, so I see little of them.

By late afternoon I've had enough of the bustle of Padstow. The sea beckons. With only a small swell forecast for tomorrow my anxiety about stopping options ahead is much reduced. I meet Tamzine and Moira on the waterfront for a farewell beer. We sit on the smooth stones of the harbour wall, which have been warming all day in the sun, legs dangling over the water. The gentle movement of the moored boats undoes the stress of the milling crowds.

Day 27 - 3rd July

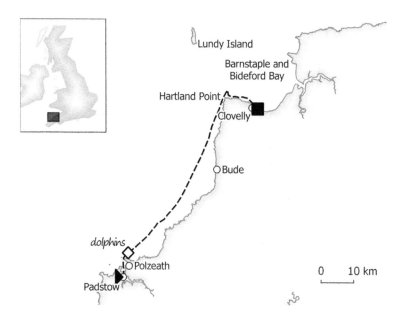

The Padstow streets are deserted when I walk down to the rowing club at 5am. Different timetable -different world. The early morning high tide has conveniently obligated the dawn start.

Sailing out, I observe that Polzeath beach is reassuringly devoid of swell. The smooth water of the river becomes a slight chop in the estuary. Further out there is a perfect sailing breeze and the ocean water becomes deep blue.

I spot bottlenose dolphins. Big animals, working as a team, schooling fish. They are obviously far too busy to be curious about me, and never come close, but this extended sighting is mentally logged as my first 'proper' dolphin sighting. To part-see part-imagine their hunting is a special way to start today's voyage.

Then twenty minutes later, from nowhere, I am joined by a pod of common dolphins. These most definitely have come to find me. Four maybe five individuals swim within touching distance, flanking the board, periodically breaking the surface for breath. I

Dolphins off Padstow

lean out over the ocean. The dolphins take it in turn to swim directly underneath me, rolled on to their sides. Eye to eye, we study each other.

Then, as suddenly as they arrived, they are gone.

I allow myself to pile significance onto the dolphins' visit: onto the message they delivered. Cornwall has been hard on me, but on my last day in her waters she has come to make her peace. I understand that I have been granted passage. Or that at least is my interpretation. For the next two months I will see dolphins almost every day - and each time I see them they will raise my spirits - but today is unique for having such close interaction.

I draw strength from the experience and cope well with the mental challenge of the rest of the day. I am becalmed somewhere off some cliffs. Where? I am not sure. An hour later wind returns from the southeast. The next 40km I take on as a headland hop, sailing far enough offshore so that all detail of the coast is lost. At times it gets quite windy: I crank on extra downhaul to depower the rig.

Lundy looms into view. Today it looks like an easy sail. But I have no intention of sailing to Lundy today. My strategy for crossing the Bristol Channel will be decided when I have consolidated today's leg.

Beyond Bude, a direct line takes me in nearer the coast. Inshore and nearer cliffs the wind is gentle. Cornwall becomes Devon as I make my way up towards Hartland Point, which is bathed in sunshine.

Hartland Point is potentially a difficult headland, so I deliberately slow up on the final approach, to let the worst of the tide finish its ebb. Ahead, a yacht - a rarity of late - goes past the promontory. The craft is leant over by the unobstructed wind and swept west by the strong current spilling out of Barnstaple and Bideford Bay. A useful indicator. I keep close in, making use of the back-eddy on the down-tide side of the headland.

I have noticed that a curiosity of the major headlands is that current tends to run out to sea along both sides, regardless of whether the tide is ebbing or flooding. A stronger current is on the upstream side; and a weaker back-eddy, or counter-current, flows out on the downstream side. The practical significance of this is that it is easy to be swept out to sea at headlands. The counter-current also offers assistance to approach them against the tide.

I approach Hartland Point in a gentle counter-current and enjoy the rounding. The lighthouse is the prettiest I have seen. Beyond it, I am in a fierce current that charges westward. After two long zigzags I have won only a handful of metres. I change tactics. Coming very close inshore and tacking regularly enables me to gradually claw my way up the coastline. The current loses intensity further from the headland. And thankfully there is *good puff* that allows me to power upwind. I identify potential places to stop in case of a problem and - with bolt holes identified - consider the rounding consolidated.

A few miles up the coast is Clovelly, where I land. This tiny and picturesque harbour is the first decent shelter north of Padstow.

Hartland Point lighthouse

With swell there are no other good options. It does feel good to have put Cornwall behind me.

I call Ian and Bella. A short time later we are back at their house, where Gregg and family also turn up.

And there is a package, from Gul: a drysuit of the correct size.

* * *

I've been chunking my journey.

If Clacton to Gregg's house was stage one, and Gregg's house to Ian's house stage two, then stage three is the rest of Britain. This thought is a sobering one. More sobering still is that I have to start this stage by crossing the Bristol Channel.

I basically have two options for reaching Wales. From here via Lundy Island in two hops, or further up the Bristol Channel in one.

My preference is via Lundy, mostly because it will save several days sailing, but also - perhaps - because of vanity. I'd rather not bottle out of the ambitious crossing.

The weather forecast complicates the situation: gales are due within a few days. Doubts fill my head. Do I have time to cross before the gales? Will the wind angle make the crossing longer than anticipated? Will I be able to cope with the sea state and wind strength? Will the tide races be problematic? Underlining all the questions is fear, stoked by my imagination.

There is the fear of extreme weather out of sight of land. I imagine Frank Dye and Tim Brockhurst in their Wayfarer dinghy during their *Summer Cruise*, of 1964. They sailed Scotland to Norway via the Faroes. Huge seas rolled their boat and they were lucky to survive. The video of their expedition is available on Youtube. It both inspires and chills.

My approach is different: not a long voyage for me. Rather a quick dash in a favourable weather window, and back to safety before serious weather sets in. Akin to how speed-mountaineers bag mountains. But the mountaineers are sometimes caught out, and perhaps I will be too.

There is also the fear of failure. I desperately want to avoid becoming a rescue statistic.

The weather forecast updates every few hours with subtle variations. I would be best advised to quit worrying, check the forecast tomorrow, and make a plan then. Instead, I remain serious and troubled, ruminating on the possibilities.

Day 28 - 4th July

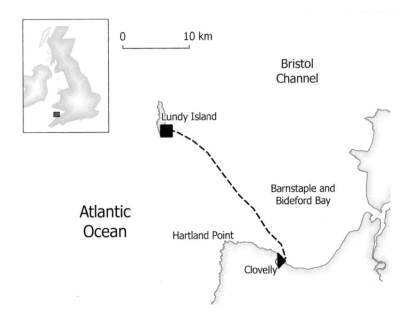

The forecasts have changed little. I've still no idea what my plan is for today.

Instead, an aching indecision has lodged itself in my mind. Lundy now, Lundy later, or push on east?

As the morning drags on my anguish intensifies. More forecast checking. Half decisions that are not binding, so are undone as quickly as they are made.

The inner turmoil is insistent, inescapable, exhausting. I crave relief, on a knife edge from breaking down. I plead with my own thoughts: *Please. Leave. Me.*

All present, except little Rafa, can sense my suffering. Their concern is obvious. The gestures of kindness trigger tears that roll silently.

There are some welcome distractions. I try on the new drysuit. The fit is good and the seals grip my ankles. That adds confidence.

At least if I do end up a rescue case in the Bristol Channel I won't be filling up with water.

Some proper wetsuit boots too. It was a mistake to set off from Clacton with low ankle shoes. Proper boots will overlap the drysuit seals. An extra barrier against water ingress.

I borrow a spare set of harness lines from Ian, and slip them on my boom. Ready to use straight away in case an existing line breaks.

Covering all the bases.

The midday forecast arrives and it is time to make a decision. Nothing much has changed. In theory I should be OK. Head to Lundy now and go early tomorrow morning for Wales. Safely ashore for when the gales arrive.

With indecision no longer an option, I resign myself to the choice that - deep down - I had already made. This is confirmation of the known. Given a tolerable forecast, I was always going to go.

My mind settles and becomes focussed. The worry has not gone, but the relief from indecision is tangible. Few words are needed as Gregg and I quickly load the car.

There is an offshore wind at Clovelly. The water is flat apart from a small wave that is wrapping round Hartland Point. Calm and peaceful looking here. I am well aware that a few miles north there will be a sea running.

A special hug to my niece, two kisses to María, a wave to cameraman Gregg, and I am away.

Beyond Hartland Point it becomes an exhilarating sail in sunshine and vibrant colours. Head high and closely packed waves roll in from the west. The current, flowing in the same direction, helps prevent the lumpy sea becoming rough. The board planes on a fast beam reach. I search for a smooth line, but occasional rogue lumps can't be avoided. The board spears through them. Drenches me in refreshing spray. Concentration is required and my mind is at last free from the worries of this morning.

I half-consider skipping Lundy and continuing to Wales. *Too late in the day for that, Jono.* I counsel myself to stay responsible.

The line sailed has taken me just east of Lundy. For the final few miles I change to upwind mode. The board climbs up and over each wave. It feels good to be dominating these conditions. And having been to Lundy before I know where I am going. Confidence has returned. I feel in total control.

Past the southern tip of the Island the water flattens and becomes more turquoise. The sheltered landing beach is just as picturesque as I had remembered. There are some swirly gusts to put up with on the final approach, and then I am on the beach.

Stage one of the crossing, 25km, completed. 55km to go.

I unzip and peel off my drysuit. Not a drop of saltwater has found its way in. A minor detail perhaps, but a real boost to my sense of preparedness for open sea sailing.

* * *

Emily and Mike, who work on Lundy, are expecting me. They had looked after Ian and I when we windsurfed to the island in the springtime, too. At that time we were given heroes' welcomes. We felt like heroes too - the first windsurfers to make the trip unsupported.

Lundy is only a stepping stone on this occasion, but the lush green island remains a special place. I enjoy a wander around the south end. There is a real calm about being stuck out on this rock on the edge of an ocean that surges past it twice daily in each direction. Despite its isolation it feels incredibly solid.

Later I link up with Emily and Mike in the *Marisco Tavern*. I've become distant again. Concerns about tomorrow are now back with me and I am subdued company. Emily and Mike's help is most heartfelt - I know they will be willing me across. I check the forecast and phone John to confirm tactics. A hearty meal, then back to my tent lodgings before dark, ready for an early start tomorrow.

Day 29 - 5th July

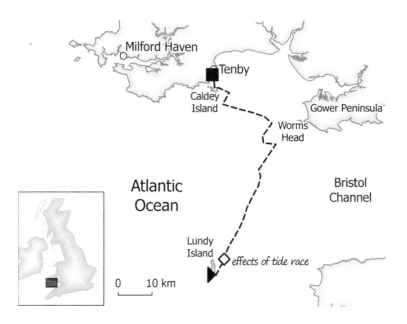

A 4:15am alarm confirms morning is here. I brew coffee and allow the aroma and texture of the warm dark liquid to soothe me to wakefulness. Less palatable but more nutritionally important is the Cuppa-porridge that completes breakfast.

It is wonderful being up at this hour. The flag above the church wafts gently in the wind. It is time for me to slip away. I descend the track that leads to the east facing landing beach. The sun lifts over the horizon and paints the sea orange.

I set off. The sea and the wind are coming from a southerly direction today. Both are pushing me towards Wales. But the wind angle means that my downwind sailing angles are roughly north-west and north-east. It is not *impossible* to windsurf directly downwind, but it is difficult and slow. In any significant amount of wind it is not a course that would be sailed. I will be downwind zigzagging today. Very long zigzags. Not many corners.

Sunrise start from Lundy Island

I surf the sloppy waves up to the North of Lundy. There is insufficient breeze to use the harness which makes it tiring for the first few miles. Then I sail into more organised waves. The lumps are *unusually* regular. I'm more than 3km from the tip of the Island but without doubt this is the North Lundy tide race. Closer to the island the standing waves might be problematic, but here the race is muted - fun rather than threatening. Beyond this diversion the sea is a field of smooth water, and at last there is wind to plane. Board speed doubles, comfort level quadruples, and Lundy recedes into the distance.

The post tide-race flats last only a short time. It is replaced by a sea that has grown more quickly than it has become organised.

I test angles on both port and starboard tack. Both get me further round Britain. I settle on starboard - which will get me back in sight of land more quickly. Wind strength is ideal for planing full speed down the adolescent swells. I push to sail broader at every opportunity. Sometimes I push too far, and spear through the backs of waves rather than over them. I try to avoid this - not stress the gear - but when I do take a nosedive the sensation of solidity transmitted through my feet is reassuring. The barrel feels rock solid. My express train powers on.

The constant need to scan the waves means that there is no time to look back, so I am unaware how far I sail before Lundy fades from view. The sea all around now is empty.

I stop for nothing, but occasionally harden up to the wind for a less hectic ride, which allows a break of sorts. With a hand freed up I can eat, drink, check progress on the GPS, and pee.

On water fuel of choice is the Snickers bar. My pockets are well stocked for regular - roughly hourly - snacking. Supplies are also easily replenished. For a particularly significant sail such as today's my in-pocket supplies are also augmented by the more satisfyingly meal-like Cliff Bar.

About two and a half hours and 30km after leaving Lundy I spot land. I immediately recognise Worms Head, on the Gower peninsula. I am well acquainted with the coastline here from my student days. It is still 20km distant, but a familiar landmark is a welcome rarity. Having a point of reference makes navigational checks much easier.

My line is taking me west of Worm's Head, so a landing on the Gower would be a forced rather than an elected choice. Land nearby reduces exposure though, so I continue until the headland is only about 10 kilometres away, which today seems close enough.

I gybe and sail on port for a while. The angle I can sail is too west and insufficiently north. No land in this direction. I stay on port long enough to allow my starboard tack muscle groups some recovery time. Then I gybe again – target South Wales.

When lower lying and more distant coasts start to populate the horizon I give port tack another try. This time my navigation checks suggest that I'm heading the right way for Milford Haven. I would have guaranteed easy stopping if I make it there, and it is a long way west. I feel good about the sailing and another 50km seems achievable. I set the natural harbour entrance as my new target waypoint.

Throughout the morning the wind has been gradually increasing, roughly keeping pace with my confidence level at managing it. But by the time I am level with Tenby I am having to sail tighter to the wind to reduce the crashing. It is becoming a very wet ride. And to the west the sky is darkening. A sharp increase in the wind strength prompts a snap decision to change plan. Time to consolidate.

Caldey Island is only 5km downwind of me now. I gybe back on to starboard, hoik on full downhaul to depower the sail, and crash through the waves to close the coast. Behind me the dark sky approaches. Spots of rain. As soon as the angle looks good for Caldey I gybe again, ready to take on the sky for a race to the island. The blackness spreads wide but my advantage holds. I charge inshore to where the island blocks the swells, and then the wind, at which point I know I have truly made it.

Within minutes of landing, waves of rain are falling, heavier with each passing gust. Thunder rumbles overhead. The Welsh mainland - only 2 kilometres away - is temporarily lost. I close my eyes and look up into the downpour, savouring the moment. Fresh water rinses away the salt and the stress of the last few days.

* * *

After the thunderstorm I have a wander around Caldey, which has lush vegetation and a monastery. A noticeboard informs visitors that the monks are of the silent Cistercian Order. Perhaps the monks are at prayer, or just don't like the weather. I don't see any. For all I know they could also be nocturnal, or arboreal.

I phone an ex-uni mate of mine who lives in Swansea. Matt immediately decides to drop everything to come and pick me up. We arrange to meet in Tenby.

There is a strong tide to beat on the sail to Tenby East Beach. The reward for the 3km sail is an easy landing. Having reached the mainland, the Bristol Channel crossing is officially complete.

Tenby sailing club is a hive of activity. I enjoy seeing the young sailors on the water, starting their sailing careers the way I did over 30 years ago. I wait for a quiet moment to arrange temporary storage for my gear, probably for a day or so, until the forecast gales have blown through.

Day 30 - 6th July

Matt and Clare look after me well, and their monsters Ffion and Owen are fun to be around.

I keep an eye on my reference tree - visible from the kitchen window. It sways about quite a bit. Definitely more wind than I want to be sailing in. No question. No guilt or indecision. I borrow Matt's bike and go shopping. Hallelujah. Normality.

My purchases are made with the utmost care. A fleece hat, merino wool thermal leggings and top, an additional thin fleece top, waterproof map case, waterproof stuff sack as a backup liner for my waterproof backpack, a refill of gas, a basic field compass to replace the one on my board which I smashed somehow, plus the regulation Cuppa-porridge and Snickers bar multipacks.

The clothing I should have bought before, anticipating that most of Britain is colder than Essex. I am very satisfied with my purchases. Retail therapy at its finest.

A new set of harness lines arrives, courtesy of Neil Pryde – a windsurfing brand. I post Ian's lines back to Devon and bin my old worn out set.

Day 31 - 7th July

Windier and wetter today. Definitely another good one to be sitting out.

My mind turns to the days ahead. I keep looking to Friday 10th. The forecasts suggest a moderate southerly or south-easterly wind. An Ireland crossing looks possible. The longer range forecast is for westerly winds, meaning that Friday is my one-day window of opportunity. I need to get in to position by then.

Planning this far ahead is new ground. I work out distances for each day to confirm feasibility, set waypoints in my GPS, and generally become quite military. I talk the plan over with Matt in person and Ian by phone. They both agree that if possible then it makes sense to cross. I experience a familiar narrowing of the eyes that comes from having a clear and consuming objective in mind.

With Gregg and family I am less candid. With them I emphasize the unlikelihood of a crossing happening, and talk about the potential alternatives. There is no point worrying my Mum or Dad yet about something that might not happen. Gregg probably doesn't need telling anyway, and is able to work out my intentions himself.

At some point the wind will moderate tomorrow. Matt will drop me in Tenby in the morning, and when it looks safe to sail, I'll push west.

Day 32 - 8th July

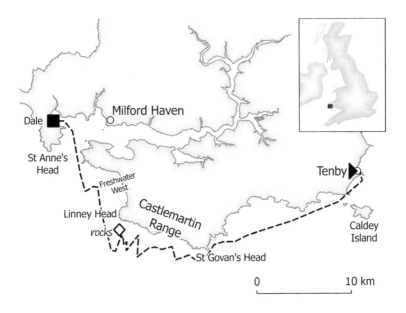

It is a blustery, cold and damp South Wales morning. Out to sea it looks rough, windy and generally unpleasant. Conditions are set to improve later, so I am happy to delay sailing.

Ahead is Castlemartin Range, another MOD obstacle. Yesterday, when I looked online to check firing times, I saw that there is activity programmed today. Part of me didn't want to know the exact times - so I hadn't phoned to find out - preferring to maintain the option of sailing through and claiming ignorance. But I feel nervous about the conditions and am looking for reasons to delay, so call the range now. "Clear to pass as of 4pm." I calculate that I should be OK if I set off 2 hours before.

I have a second breakfast from *Greggs* bakery. Then - to keep warm – hike to the out of town library, which unfortunately is closed on Wednesdays.

When I return to the town centre, the sun is breaking through. It brings welcome warmth to the bench I adopt in the church grounds.

I have a third breakfast - which at these hours we could call lunch - and then head to the sailing club, keen now to get on my way.

It is upwind zigzag sailing; flat until Caldey, but west of here the board thumps into a respectable sea. Initially I feel quite exposed, but the conditions continue to moderate and the coastline softens, allowing me to relax into enjoying the conditions.

From St Goven's Head the coastline is more exposed to the west. I tuck in to sheltered water before rounding the headland for a one-minute break. With the late start I can't afford to slow up.

Past the headland the water is sloppier. Board speed through the water seems good - up on the rail and sailing fast - but speed over ground is unimpressive. There is a strong tide running against me. The 10km upwind towards Linney Head is taking a long time. I come in close to the cliffs hoping for weaker tide and better progress, but am forced to stay further offshore when the coastline becomes more rock-strewn.

As afternoon becomes early evening the wind starts to die away. Progress against the tide is now very slow. Eventually I draw level with Linney Head but the tide is too strong and three or four complete zigzags later I am no nearer rounding than I was an hour ago. I can't cheat the tide inshore because of the rocks. I come in as close as I dare but with limited power to get out of trouble, and a big swell around, any closer would be foolhardy.

It isn't a good situation: unable to progress, no good stopping for a long way back, swell, night time approaching. Time to change tactic. I head way offshore in an attempt to escape the influence of the headland on the current. Three miles out and with the sun very low in the sky I tack again. GPS suggests that this time I am making progress and forty minutes later I am indeed past the headland.

Downwind now is Freshwater West - a fine surfing beach that has undoubtedly seen some good waves today. Not a landing option. Not without the required power to negotiate the final few hundred metres to shore. I must push on to Milford Haven. My objective is to make the harbour entrance by nightfall. Once inside the water will be flat enough to sail the final miles in darkness.

The swells rolling underneath me have turned glassy in the failing breeze. Vast numbers of seabirds settle onto the sea surface, where they will rest until morning. Black silhouettes on an ocean reflecting silver.

I am fortunate. The flow of Atlantic air continues to gently carry east, enabling me to work the angles west. Forty minutes later the glow of the lower horizon is extinguished, but I have reached Milford Haven.

The mouth of the natural harbour has better breeze and flatter water. I stay alert for shipping as I cross the channel, but the sea is empty. I am alone - as I am most days I sail.

Inside the harbour the water is reservoir flat, and there is land on all sides. The tension of exposure releases. There is a delicious tranquillity, as I glide through the gloaming, towards Dale, where I will overnight.

The *Griffin Inn* is open, customer-less, and I am too late for food. But it is warm, dry, and has comfortable seating. Sitting down feels *good*. Two pints of Guinness and the remains of a Tenby sandwich constitute dinner.

The barman closes up around me. When he is nearly done, I head to the snugness of my sleeping bag, and fall asleep within minutes.

Day 33 - 9th July

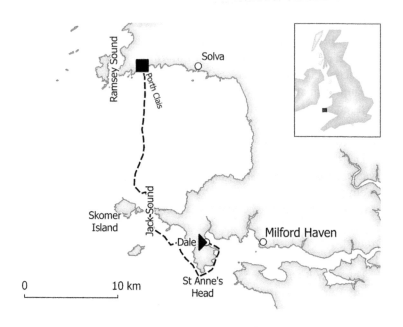

I'm up fairly early as there is activity in Dale and my roadside bed is a little public. Breakfast is the usual coffee and porridge. I wander along to the pub for their Wi-Fi. Very light winds are forecast: near calm. And mercifully no swell, which makes me feel more relaxed about heading out and not knowing where I'll get too.

Ahead are two tide races that John has alerted me to: Jack Sound and Ramsey Sound. I can expect strong currents and would prefer to reach them around slack water, on a current that then heads north. There are two fishermen nearby preparing their boat, who I figure can advise.

"One o'clock," by their reckoning.

I thank the fishermen, but am uneasy with their advice, which doesn't match my own calculations. Wandering back to my board the missing parts of the jigsaw fall into place. The fishermen recommended slack tide at high, fine if you've got engines or plenty of power, but no good for me on a day like today. I need the current switching and then carrying me north, rather than switching and heading south. I need slack at low, which is - fuck it! – now.

I rush through my preparation routine and am sailing by 8:15am. The breeze is pathetic. It will take me hours to reach Jack by which time the tide will be in full flow.

After 90 minutes' upwind slog of pumping the sail, I reach the limits of Milford Harbour. St Ann's Head is pretty without being impressive. Beyond this headland I am at last into the north-going tide. I can take a break from pumping and let the tidal conveyor belt deliver me towards Jack.

Approaching the Sound I am alert but not overly concerned. Friendly looking puffins are in abundance. The narrow divide between Skomer Island and the mainland has visible white water, but the scale is small. Overfalls? Rocks? No idea, I'll just try to avoid the worst of them. In the near absence of wind, my approach will determine my line. No different to the game of Poohsticks. I try to set up for an unobstructed journey through.

The current accelerates, and proximity of land blocks the breeze entirely. Small closely packed waves develop. Further ahead these tumble continually. I overbalance and fall onto the sail, but am quickly on my feet to lift it from the churning flow. I maintain the sail lifted half-clear of the water - a stable position.

And this is how I pass through Jack sound. A passenger on my 3.8 metre poohstick. Enjoying the scenery, the ride through more pleasant than scary.

Half a kilometre further on the current all but fizzles out.

I am now in St. Brides Bay, becalmed. Ramsey Sound, at the north of the bay, is 15km away. The beaches inside the bay are a similar distance to the East. For now, I'd just like to be able to get to land.

I go nowhere or in circles for a while, before a random puff of wind sees me sailing in the direction of Skomer. I try to approach the island but against the tide the attempt is futile.

A rest later and the ficklest of breezes arrives. There are two tankers moored in the Bay. I set about sailing towards the first of them.

Closure is glacial.

A while later a RIB (Rigid Inflatable Boat) approaches, from the direction of Skomer. The boat draws alongside and we talk. I had been spotted sailing or floating - flailing? - through Jack Sound and the boat occupants have come to check I'm OK. They see the *windsurfroundbritain.co.uk* stickers on my sail and are all *wows* and *well done's* and questions about the expedition. What nice people. I am struck by their friendly, non-judgemental, interest. They notice and engage, making life better.

I should be more like that!

The boat occupants share my opinion that I won't make it to Ramsey Sound before the tide turns, so won't get through today. As an alternative that isn't too far off route they suggest Porth Clais, just to the East of the Sound.

I pass in front of the first of the anchored tankers. Cheap parking out here.

Later on a gunmetal grey Fishery Patrol ship appears. It cautiously edges to within earshot. This time I can say where I'm headed to, but not really knowing where that *is* I ask which part of the coastline to head for. They've never heard of Porth Clais, but can eventually confirm it exists in the general direction of over there. It is reassuring that people know I am out here, and I enjoy their visit too.

The second tanker I leave well to starboard.

Progress is costly in terms of effort and time. Porth Clais could be anywhere along the strip of coastline that I am slowly closing on. I phone Gregg and together we cobble out a way of calculating the bearing I need. It isn't a slick system, but on this occasion it convinces me to keep heading towards what looks like an uninhabited lump of cliff.

The uninhabited lump of cliff slowly becomes bigger. Cliff-like attributes become better defined. But an hour after calling Gregg, and having closed to within a hundred metres of one of several candidate indents, my target still resembles a *lump of uninhabited cliff*.

I stop and ponder. Should I sail east or west in search of my porth? After six and a half hours on the water I am weary.

And then, out of what appears to be cliff, pops a bright yellow canoe.

The tiny entrance - cliff one side and wall the other - is all but invisible. I bump my way in along the wall and land on the slipway behind, as more canoeists launch around me.

* * *

I figure I need food and waste no time in demolishing some packet raviolis. Despite having contacts in the area I'm not expecting to receive any support here. I have - after all - gone significantly off track.

I am lost in my thoughts. At that moment I don't think an Ireland crossing can be on. I haven't got through Ramsey Sound. I haven't landed anywhere near a shop or source of food. I don't even have a mobile signal.

After two gruelling days I've come up short.

* * *

Two men wade through the shallow water between the beach and cliff-side slipway.

I pay little attention until they approach. Dave introduces himself. The other man is Andy, his dad. The latter wears a mischievous grin. Dave is registered on the website as a contact and has followed the tracker to locate me here. If I haven't got other plans, I'm welcome to stay with Andy and his wife Margaret at Lower Solva. They'll fix me up with whatever I need for the Ireland Crossing tomorrow.

"To make sure you don't drown!" adds Andy.

I am taken aback by their arrival and proactive kindness. And I don't yet realise the significance of the support they will provide.

* * *

Behind the wall is the River Solva. The garden is a green oasis and suntrap. My mind adjusts to the news that Porth Clais to Ireland is a possibility. A beer and comfortable chair aid the process.

The weather forecast is holding for tomorrow. South south-east force four, maybe five at times. The angle is a bit broad, but certainly good enough. Perfect forecasts don't happen.

Andy is an Irishman in Wales. It is obvious that he holds his homeland dear and would like to see me cross the sea tomorrow. He has also made the voyage himself, by yacht. He talks about it without mystique. Just another sail.

Nautical charts are laid out on the lawn. Hazards studied. The *West Coast of England Pilot* - Sixth Edition, 1910 - is consulted. By the time we eat, I have a firm plan in place for tomorrow.

Andy continues with his gentle teasing. Jokes about helicopter rescues and the like. But always reassuring in the end, tailing off into a soft Irish *You'll be alright*, directed at no-one in particular.

I have butterflies in my stomach about tomorrow, but do not experience the inescapable unease and gnawing indecision of prior to the Bristol Channel crossing. I feel prepared and capable. The adrenaline of anticipation builds within.

Before sleep, I carefully repack barrel, backpack and drysuit pockets. Safety critical gear most accessible. Strict adherence to practiced routine.

Day 34 - 10th July

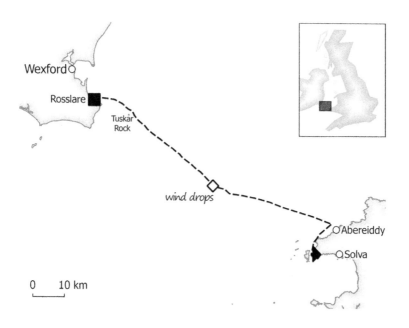

I stoop to see up and out from the low cottage windows. Clouds are scudding across the sky. Moderate south-easterly winds are still forecast. A delicious cooked breakfast fills the tanks and it is time to go.

We stop for additional Snickers bars before arriving - drysuit pockets now full - at Porth Clais.

Out to sea looks quite windy. Heading out through the gulley looks awkward. During final preparations Dave slips me some Euros, "for some food when you get there".

The handing over of the baton. I couldn't have asked for a better relay team.

I fend off the side of the harbour wall to reach the sea. Two quick tacks to navigable water, before starting an upwind zigzag to Ramsey Sound.

The Sound is supposed to be tricky, but with good breeze I easily overcome the south flowing current. The Bitches rocks are left to port. After these I use the full width of the channel, and find good wind for planing. Conditions are fantastic. I blast through the Sound in two broad reaches. Now in open water, my plan is to head up the Welsh coast until the angle is good to make Ireland in one broad reach. Gybe off too early and my line would be south of land.

The wind is brisk, but an offshore angle keeps the water relatively flat. Chop rather than a sea, and no swell. I charge along parallel to the coast in bright sunshine. Once level with Abereiddy, and about 2km offshore, I stop for final checks in these relatively sheltered coastal waters.

Further out conditions will be more intimidating. If the wind ratchets up another force I'll likely start to struggle, particularly with more sea state to contend with.

Drink. Snickers bar. Pee. Set GPS to Rosslare, Ireland. Check barrel is secure. A selfie to document the moment.

I set off on port tack at full tilt. My angle sailed is just south of Rosslare - missing the corner of Ireland. If the forecast is right I will be headed later in the day which will compensate and put me on track to hit land. I prefer this strategy to sailing further up the Welsh coast now, which would add distance unnecessarily if the wind does veer as predicted.

The board clatters over the wave-tops. Further from land the gusts become less severe. My fears about being unable to cope with the conditions fade. Feeling comfortable, I push as deep downwind as possible, urging the board closer to a course with land ahead.

I seek the speed and deep downwind angle that will deliver me towards Ireland. After nearly an hour Wales is losing its grip on the eastern horizon. High ground becomes isolated islands of land. Finally, these too disappear. Empty sea on all sides, save for the white horses that tumble in to and out of existence.

I work the waves to push deeper downwind. I run through the sums in my head. *An hour gone and one-third distance covered. 3 hours for the crossing.* My mind wanders. It seems too easy.

Final checks and a refuel before heading across the Irish Sea

This will make for a boring write up on the website. I register a flicker of disappointment.

And then, in a matter of minutes, the complexion of the day changes. The wind softens, and to maintain speed my angle sailed moves south. It softens further and I am no longer able to maintain the board planing. I shift my weight forward, changing mode to adjust to the new conditions. Mast-track forward. I am now supporting a limp and lifeless sail. The board sits like a cork in the water, and is bumped on all sides by the chop that has not yet been told the party is over.

In non-planing mode the going is slow and wobbly, but with effort I can sail any downwind angle. I am grateful for any wind that there is. Whilst there is still forward progress, I must keep sailing. The GPS indicates I am still making a few knots.

The ordered white horses that had accompanied me earlier become a distant memory. The sloppy sea here moves with the elegance and decision of a drunk. Sky and horizon are devoid of features. The air around my ears is quiet. Awkwardness of sailing provides a rough indicator of heading, but it is easy to find myself thirty or forty degrees off course. I must continually monitor GPS to stay on track.

I recalculate time remaining based on current conditions. No major concern, but this time with provisos. If the wind dies any more, or swings round to on the nose, then the situation could complicate substantially. I am alert to the smallest of variations in the fickle breeze.

I twist the harness lines away to prevent accidentally hooking in. Gently pumping the sail provides stability and a little extra speed. I think back to the swathe of green-orange on this morning's internet weather maps. I'd been concerned about too much wind, there was no hint that I might be becalmed. I reflect too on the comic irony of my premature thoughts about an easy crossing.

In the middle of the Irish Sea are two trawlers working their nets. I don't want to become catch, so pass at a distance. Do they see me, wonder what I am doing out here?

Past the fishing boats, in a dip in the breeze, I stop for a break. My usual routine. The Snickers bar and short rest restore energy levels. Progress comes a little easier when sailing is resumed.

On the horizon is what I decide looks like a sail, which I am closing on. A yacht? I decide it too must be heading to Rosslare, as its angle does not change. Maintaining a course is easier with a target to follow.

I enter and cross the shipping lanes. The only ship I see is very distant, and already departing.

The yacht sail doesn't look quite right. I realise that I am heading toward a lighthouse. I am pleased, since I assume this means land nearby.

Pleasure turns to unease when I realise the lighthouse is in open water. I later learn that this is Tuskar Rock lighthouse. Yesterday's navigational planning had focussed on beginning and end, and I hadn't registered this en route obstacle. For a few moments I consider that I may be horribly off course.

Near the lighthouse I see lumpy water extending well to the north: a strong tide running over shallows. I question my decision to head towards a lighthouse, on the basis that these generally warn of hazards. *What fool would aim for a lighthouse?* I adjust course to the north.

The day is overcast now. *Why can't I see land yet?* The horizon remains distant but empty. My unease is amplified by approaching weather. A fat cloud hangs its dark belly low over the sea and moves in from downwind. Storm cloud behaviour. Growls of thunder emanate from its dark interior. Thick raindrops pierce the sea and the wind drops to nothing.

The tide helps pull me north, away from the oppressive shadow, and I am doubly thankful for the feeble but consistent breeze that returns on the cloud's passing. I cross the lumpy water by the lighthouse.

It is early evening by the time I spot land. South East Ireland is low lying. Only visible at five or six miles from my sea level vantage point. Drawing closer takes time. I notice an improvement in the sea state near the coast. Easier sailing is welcome after eight hours afloat.

The final mile I allow myself to savour. A pleasant breeze carries me towards Rosslare port. A ferry from Wales appears from behind, rapidly closing the distance between us, although it too is throttling back on final approach. At the harbour entrance I cross in front of the ship, to make for a smaller anchorage to the north. I glide through the opening on mirror flat water. Small boats line the shore and there is not a soul to be seen. The fin grounds gently in soft mud.

* * *

I walk a mile inland to the main Rosslare road. At the crossroads there is a lively pub. Dinner tastes fantastic and is washed down with two pints of celebratory Guinness.

The realisation of how far I have come slowly descends upon me. Less than two weeks ago I was on the South coast of England. It didn't seem like I had achieved much. Now I find myself in my third country, with landmark crossings behind me.

I savour the release of accumulated stress. The Land's End trauma and the crossings to Wales and to Ireland are something

Heading into port just ahead of the Fishguard-Rosslare ferry: light winds from halfway across made mine a slow crossing

that I can now look back upon and - in time - process, rather than fear.

Pleasant chemicals bathe my brain.

The beginnings of a much deeper inner tranquillity, hitherto absent, settles somewhere between my ears.

Day 35 - 11th July

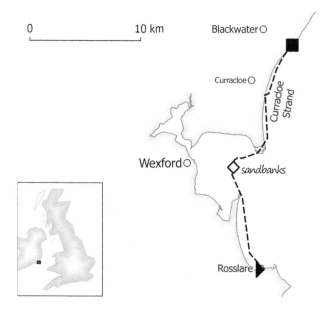

The forecast is for solid breeze from the south-southwest. On the west coasts it would be a day made complicated by swell, but here on the east coast land blocks its path, and it is flat. Reward for crossing the Irish Sea.

I am ready for an early start on my journey north. About to launch I receive a call from my ex. Maybe she hasn't heard that time and tide wait for no man. Maybe I'm just not very good at communicating that this isn't the best moment. It is a long phone call. By the end of the one-sided conversation the wind has clearly picked up to beyond comfortable strength.

Slightly irritated, I head out. The strong cross-offshore wind and mercifully flat water means the sailing is very fast. In twenty minutes I've zigzagged my way downwind to a spit of sand on the south side of Wexford Harbour. The estuary mouth is 5km across, and a maze of sandbanks complicates the route to the other side. In less fierce conditions I would simply head seaward of the obstacles, but I'm already desperately overpowered and sailing further out would put me in a very exposed position. I decide to stay inside the banks.

I navigate the channels between sand ridges, very aware of the shallow water around me. Grounding at speed could result in a bruising catapult fall.

As well as sandbanks, the estuary mouth appears to have veins of low lying rocks. It looks like there may be seals resting on them. The deep water channels I follow take me closer. It is nuclear windy, but the sandbanks that surround me provide a sense of security. I am curious to get closer to the seals. When I am near I let the sail down and decide to let myself be blown past by the wind.

I realise that the seals *are* the rocks. Hundreds - perhaps thousands - of the curious creatures are bunched together on the sandbank just a few tens of metres away. Many slip into the water and investigate from close up. Big dark eyes on whiskered faces surround me on all sides. The seals that approach from behind, out of my sight, come especially close. When I turn to face them they disappear in snaps of spray, and dozens more emerge from where I had been looking previously.

I am a full twenty minutes being blown past the sandbank. Land – the type that stays dry, or above the water at least - is miles away, and the wind is howling past my ears at a full force six; but the experience is so captivating that the awkward navigational circumstances are of no concern. I feel blessed to have been gifted this experience.

The crowd eventually thins out and I return to the job in hand. Crossing the estuary. The main channel winds out to sea. I attempt a short cut but end up on another bank in shin deep water, fin caught in the sand. I abort an attempt to walk my kit across the bank. Taking a breather on my return hike, I see a small yacht sail into the channel. I am pleased to see it well leant over with just a small amount of jib showing, confirmation that it really is windy, and it isn't just a case of me having lost my nerve.

I follow the channel, and then my intuition, until I reach the tree-lined north bank of the estuary. White sand scuds along the beach, airborne. Spray is ripped off the back of small breaking waves.

Close in to the shore gives some protection from the wind, but the gusts are still fairly savage. I'm uncomfortable in these conditions - teetering on the edge of a heavy fall.

I look for somewhere where I can sit out a few hours. Perhaps the wind will moderate this afternoon. A few miles on there is a beach with people, where I stop.

This is Curracloe Strand. Most famous – according to Wikipedia - for being where the Normandy landings were filmed in the film *Saving Private Ryan*. The coastline here certainly is long, straight, and sandy. By the beach there is a café - which I patronise, but little else. I head inland to the main town. Here I find a few supplies for lunch, but no cash machine, which is what I was really after, now that I am down to my last Euros.

I don't feel inclined to overnight here.

Back at the beach I screw up my face at the wind. It hasn't really moderated. I decide to head up the coast anyway. Whilst there is beach to land on, that doesn't seem too risky.

On the water I am massively overpowered. I sail short legs, to keep in the shelter of the land. There is no way I can sail broad enough to make significant downwind progress. It isn't sensible to be sailing in this. Three miles up the coast I stop again, this time for the day.

There isn't much here either. Not even a place name on Google. I quite like it though. Fresh water pours from a stream and there is a semi fallen cliff that will do as a camping spot. I select the least lumpy patch of available ground. Then I find a stick with which to prop up my sail shelter against the howling wind.

It is windy, cold and uncomfortable. Then it starts raining. Quite hard. A little bit miserable. I decide to find a pub. I put my drysuit back on over my set of normal clothes and splash 2 miles through the puddles to Blackwater. Great news! There is a little supermarket - open - and with cash machine, and two pubs. The second of which will even serve me food.

Warm, well fed, and feeling altogether more positive, I walk back through lighter rain to my dry two square metres of grass. Now pretty whacked, sleep comes easily.

Day 36 - 12th July

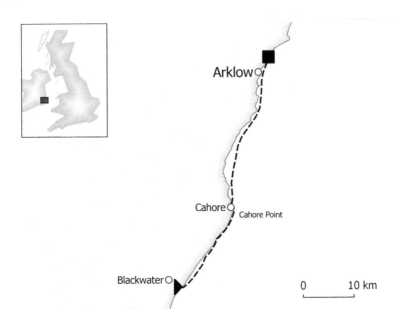

Arklow

Cahore
Cahore Point

Blackwater

0   10 km

Flat water, clear blue skies, and a gentle following breeze. To sail and not feel exposed - vulnerable - is welcome relief. Nothing psychologically difficult. Thank you, weather Gods.

With the tide against me, progress is slow. But that's OK. The board splashes through the water at a seemingly decent rate, although real progress - measured relative to landmarks on the shore - is slow. The sailing is so un-taxing that I am able to phone Clyde to wish him a happy birthday.

The beach here just goes on and on. It takes me all morning to finally reach a feature in the coastline. There is a small town behind Cahore Point, where I stop for lunch.

Cahore is a pleasant place. There is plenty of activity on and around the water: kayakers fishing, a few sailing boats, swimmers, people crabbing from the harbour wall, speedboats that look designed for lakes rather the sea. An ice-cream van pulls up. The driver and Mr Whippy operator is authentically grumpy.

He returns not a glimmer of a smile as cash flows into the van. That's odd. Is that a brain wired wrong or is life really that miserable?

I chat with a couple who have a small boat. They offer me a place to stay. I'm tempted, but after the tide turns the days should have plenty more miles in, so I politely decline the offer. They bring me a cup of tea instead, which is most welcome.

The day does have more miles. Sailing with the tide I add another twenty to the day's tally. The coastline becomes more varied, small headlands and bays, with hills inland. I pass the semi-major town of Arklow, eventually stopping a few miles north of here, where the camping looks good.

Previous revellers have left the beach in a bit of a mess, which is a shame. That aside, it is a very picturesque spot.

I find a path up the cliff to a road, wondering if there might be a pub somewhere near. I don't find one, or feel inclined to explore far, so instead retire early to my sleeping bag. Home cooked macaroni cheese from a tin is tea. It tastes pretty good, and also means that my barrel will be lighter tomorrow. I do like a light barrel. Not having to walk home from the pub is another bonus.

The ground is lumpy and covered in spiky vegetation, but I'm tired enough not to care. The sound of lapping waves lulls me to sleep.

Day 37 - 13th July

DUBLIN   Howth Peninsula

Dún Loaghaire ■
⸱Dalkey Island

Greystones ○

Wicklow ○
Wicklow Head

Ballinacarrig ○

Arklow ○   0   10 km

It has rained during the night. The wind looks good and some pre-sail nerves are with me again. Back to normality.

Porridge and coffee. Pack up routine. Launch.

I plane off the beach in the reaching straps. It feels like I am going fast, but the current is against me again. Course sailed is a compressed zigzag. But I still make reasonable progress, and the sailing is enjoyable. When the wind drops a little I change to non-planing mode, and keep very close inshore to cheat to tide.

With supplies running low, I could do with some water. I round a small headland - Ballinacarrig - and see sailing dinghies on the water. Behind the beach is a clubhouse or sailing centre. A likely resupply option.

The young sailing instructors are occupied with their groups. This is a world I recognise. I am directed to the building. The office team are warm, chatty and enthusiastic. It's nice that they seem excited about my journey so far. We drink tea and they apologise for the lack of biscuits, providing an apple instead. I check maps of the area and get an updated forecast.

Apparently, I'm on a private beach, or at least *access* is private, unless approaching by sea. The privilege of travel by windsurfer. Bono has a house somewhere over where a finger is waved. I guess everyone here knows that.

I could quite easily hang around and gossip some more, but that won't get me round Britain.

The long straight beaches are now behind me, and the coast becomes cliff lined. Wicklow Head is my first significant Irish headland. Its imposing lighthouse stands guard over the overfalls that extend out to sea. Sailing past the headland is exhilarating. I stay in close to benefit from the down-tide back eddy, and to stay in flatter water. And then emerge from cover of the lighthouse and am fully planing over the standing waves in the wind acceleration zone off the tip of the headland. It feels great.

Wicklow itself I don't stop at. The wind angle is wrong. Instead I sail a more open and faster line, reconnecting with land 8km further up the coast. There is a good wind rolling down from the Wicklow Mountains.

I continue to make good progress, and am ahead of myself in navigational terms. I need to check the map, and also eat something. I land where I see a dog walker. "There isn't much here", I am told "but a few miles further along is Greystones, which is a fairly major place".

Pulling myself and laden board up the steep shingle beach at Greystones just about finishes me off. I set off in search of food, and am drawn to a café by the quay. Maybe any fish and chips would have tasted this good, but the Harbour Café fish and chips go down in my expedition log as truly exceptional. I make an attempt to communicate my satisfaction to the cafe owner, adding that I eat fish and chips most days, from all manner of establishments, so am speaking with some authority. I sense that the proprietor doubts my sanity, but he accepts the comments graciously nonetheless.

Arriving at Dublin it felt like a landmark day

I could do with a siesta after that feed, but conditions are too good to sit around.

The wind blows over the cliffs and high ground behind. In search of more consistent breeze I stay further out. Progress remains consistent and I realise that I will make Dublin today - beyond where the information in my navigational working memory has prepared me for. I sail close-hauled and well powered up past Dalkey lighthouse. 10km ahead is Howth Peninsula. I consider the outcrop, and am reminded of Portland Bill. It would be a gamble to head out there late in the day, ignorant of what I might find. I decide to bank progress by stopping in Dublin.

With some telephone help from Gregg, I manage to reach my contacts, and make arrangements, whilst still sailing. I have the luxury of two options here. I'm certainly not fussy where I end up, but fate links me up with Des, who directs me to the local windsurfer launch site by Dún Loaghaire harbour.

Sailing into a city is exciting. Big infrastructure, impressive buildings, shipping. The scale is different to anything I have seen for quite some time. I feel the size of a flea. A vast Irish flag flies from a protective arm that embraces the harbour. The white and vibrant orange and green contrast with the city colours behind. I am grateful to Dublin for accepting me. It feels very correct that I am stopping here.

Des picks me up and we head back to his house. He's super busy with young family and a hundred other things going on, but he and Anne make me incredibly welcome. I have my first shower since arriving in Ireland, a great curry, and a warm and comfortable bed to sleep in. My foul smelling clothes even get a laundering.

I don't know how to thank my hosts enough, helping me out - a total stranger - just because. I also have a real admiration for them, indeed anyone bringing up young kids. Now that is a tough job. Windsurfing round Britain? That's not tough. That's a holiday by comparison.

Day 38 - 14th July

Des drops me off at Dún Loaghaire on his way to work. There's no significant wind, and Howth Head looks an awfully long way away, straight into the little wind that there is. The thought of floating around without the ability to manoeuvre away from the shipping is unappetizing.

The light wind is fortunate, because my ex, or is she ex-ex now - we've not agreed any change of status and I am confused to say the least, has arranged to visit. She's flying to Dublin - en route to London - and is due at midday. It's not particularly surprising that eventual arrival time is nearer three o'clock.

Familiar emotions rise and we slip back into old roles. Attraction is still there, but I don't feel at ease. That's more likely to do with me than her. It might not be coincidence that I am the one windsurfing round Britain.

* * *

I have a very good friend - Helen - living a few miles north of Dublin. I've made plans for us to head over to her place tonight. With my gear kindly being looked after by the Irish National Sailing School, we catch tram and train to make our way over to Skerries.

Helen screeches up to the station car park. She's the same as ever - welcoming, positive and full of energy. At home, we meet up with Helen's kids and significant other - Henry.

Henry's car has Newstalk Radio emblazoned on the side. Twenty minutes later I'm being interviewed on the beach as the sun sets behind Skerries.

It's a lively household. Helen and Henry are both fairly bonkers and very easy to like. They are also social-media hand grenades. I show Henry a picture on my camera of the Wexford seals.

Newstalk radio with Henry Mckean

Within minutes the picture is online and Tweets are rolling in with arguments for and against the oh-so-cute fish dustbins, all referencing the wsroundbritain hashtag.

I'm grateful for the lesson. More social media awareness likely means more donations and support along the route. Part of me thinks I should be more active in this area myself. But another part of me just doesn't gel with communicating in the quick and regular sound bite format. I think too hard about it. The real lesson is to not take social media, or life, too seriously.

Helen cooks a great meal and everyone gets on.

There's not any clarification on the off-plot relationship stuff.

The wind is forecast very light for tomorrow, so a day around Skerries is likely.

Day 39 - 15th July

Zero breeze is exactly what happens. The timing of this lull in wind is really quite convenient. Something of a Godsend. I've been having a few spiritual thoughts of late.

Having a full clear day is helpful to continue avoiding the issue. Neither of us makes any attempt to discuss relationship questions. In the circumstances - amongst friends - perhaps that is understandable. More likely - in my case at least - is that I am just avoiding. I'm unclear in my own mind. Plus I'm conflict averse. Fearful in the stuff of real life.

Instead we explore Skerries, a very agreeable little place.

Helen and Henry have work later, so we have a few hours to ourselves in the afternoon.

We go our separate ways for an hour and meet up in a café later. She's there having a chat with a travelling cyclist - animated and relaxed, both of them. He's a nice guy and I soon feel at ease too. He talks about how he enjoys the *meeting people* of heading off - somewhere, anywhere, wherever. I can understand that. Could I have said that a month ago?

It is likely, I imagine, that we are both more relaxed chatting with the cyclist than we are conversing with each other.

By the end of the day my mind is back on logistics. How to get back to Dún Loaghaire, via the airport, leaving myself enough time to windsurf round the Howth Peninsula. I'm looking forward to getting back to being on my own. My simple, single objective life. I can do that.

I can't remember now what dinner was, but Helen cooked it, so it was good. I just remember it was good.

Day 40 - 16ᵗʰ July

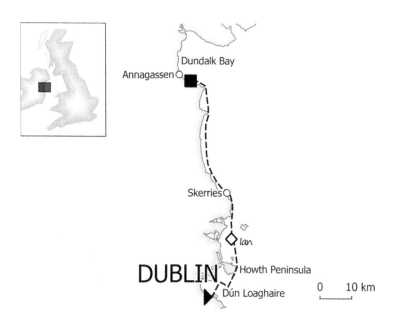

Helen drops both of us at Dublin airport whilst the clock in her car is still showing five-something. We thank her and head to departures. The London flight is already boarding, so there isn't time for awkward prolonged goodbyes.

That all went remarkably smoothly.

I take the train to Dún Loaghaire. There is a breeze on the water. I retrieve my equipment and am sailing by shortly after nine.

It is a long sail across Dublin Bay, against the wind. Towards Howth are the shipping lanes. It's not easy to know whether to pass in front of or behind the steel giants. I use the channel buoys as shelter - the ships are unlikely to hit those. I am between buoys when a pilot boat alters course to intercept me.

A crewmember comes on deck, his manner is tense. "Where're you headed?"

"Around there." I point to Howth. The crewmember follows my finger. Then he looks right, to an enormous cargo vessel, moving as surely as a tectonic plate. The steel island pushes a smooth bulge of stern wave.

"There's a ship there."

There is no disputing the observation. I agree. Patiently waiting for elaboration.

"You'd best pass astern."

I let the ship pass. The pilot stays in my vicinity. I'm instructed to cross the bows of the next vessel. The clear advice is welcome - comforting. When the crew realise I'm capable enough to not be a problem, they relax too. A mobile phone pointed down at me records the last moments of our encounter.

The wind around Howth is particularly light. Seabirds rest on a sloppy sea that bounces off the cliffs. I stay close in to the rocks, where the foul tide is less strong, but it is still a real struggle to get past the peninsula.

Once back into some breeze, I have more success punching the tide. Offshore of Malahide, I'm feeling a bit guilty that I haven't detoured closer inshore. I've a contact there who has been offering all sorts of help. Then I see a sail in the distance - unmistakeably a windsurf sail - it can only be my contact.

What an effort! Ian has sailed three miles out to intercept me. We stop for a chat and shake of hands. Two minutes later Ian ups sail to commence his wobble shoreward. The briefest of meetings, but one that brings a smile when recalled.

The rain comes down and I sail the remaining distance to Skerries with drysuit hood up. It keeps me warm and dry, but is disorientating. The sailing feels safe now that I am close to the shore.

I land at Skerries, finally having genuinely *arrived* here. Helen is waiting for me with packed lunch - an absolute star. We shelter from the rain, and drink hot tea. A reporter turns up for some sound bites and photographs. Conditions - current and forecast - are miserable, but I know I should get on.

I'm pleased when I do. There is more wind heading north of Skerries. It feels as if proper adventure has resumed. I semi-plane, parallel to the coast. Now with the tide progress is good.

Visibility continues to deteriorate, but there is no reason to stop. From the maps on my phone, I can just about work out where I am.

I reach Dundalk Bay, repeatedly grounding out in shallow water before making it past the point that marks its southern limit. The bay is eight miles wide, and set into the land by a similar distance. Cutting straight across makes navigational sense, but late in the day - and with such poor visibility - I'm not keen.

Instead I try to follow the coast. Shallow water forces me offshore. I am out of sight of land due to the disorientating misty rain, and dark is approaching. Still the fin grounds. I am sailing myself into a trap. The whole bay is emptying and will soon be dry. If I continue I'll be left miles from the shore, at night, on sand that will flood again in a few hours' time.

Having sensed the danger, I'd registered a last safe stopping place. There is nothing for it but to about turn and head back. The gradient nearer the point is less shallow, and I can get close enough to the shore to make hauling my gear over the drying sands a feasible option.

That is how I end up on an uninhabited stretch of Dundalk Bay sea wall.

It is a terrible camp location. I spend half an hour hacking back vegetation to make room for my sail shelter, aware of the strong winds forecast that will do their best to tear away my bothy overnight.

But it will do. Once suitably dug in, I set off on a hike, drysuited up in the pouring rain. Objective: a pub.

The village of Annagassen is only 2 miles away. What's more, there is a pub, serving food. All things considered, I've got lucky.

The rain continues to fall as I crawl into my bivvy bag later that evening.

Day 41 - 17th July

It is windy at night. The sail wants to gybe itself. There isn't enough space to set the sail at an angle that keeps it well pinned down by the wind. The sea comes right up to the vegetation bank upon which I am perched.

By morning the wind has swung offshore. The sail is buffeted, and the sea is awash with white horses. Far too windy to sail means an opportunity for a guilt free lie in. The wind direction is now better suited to the angle of my dug in sail.

I head in to Annagassen late morning. Buy bread and beans for dinner tonight. Then install myself in the pub.

I eat well and have my regulation one Guinness for the day. By late afternoon I'm fed up with the pub and head back to my sail, via the direct but wet route over the sands.

I have an early night.

The sands of Dundalk Bay

Day 42 - 18th July

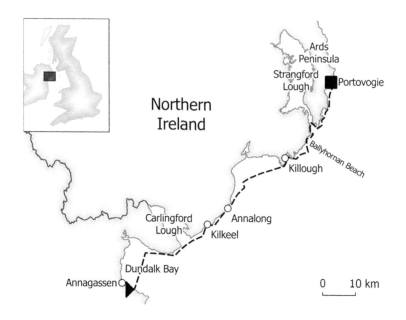

Morning. And I'm very keen to be away from here.

It is a long walk to carry first my board, then sail and barrel to the water's edge. A stiff offshore wind is blowing towards the mountains 10km away on the other side of Dundalk Bay. I'm expecting it might be quite a tough sail.

A planing broad reach starts on flat water that becomes choppy, then somewhat wavey. By the time I am nearing the mountains I am also nearing my wind limit. Too windy, too broad, too many gut wrenching decelerations. Sufficient spray to warrant a snorkel.

A small point marks the end of the bay. A beach tucked in its lee is sheltered enough to allow a stop. I get my breath back and eat a much needed Snickers bar.

I blast on past the entrance to Carlingford Lough where the wind briefly moderates. Beyond here it comes thumping in again. I feel battered and demoralised by the tough going. I search for somewhere to sit out a few hours. The town of Annalong looks promising. I haul my gear up the shingle beach and head off in search of a bacon sandwich.

The sheltered harbour is picturesque but mostly deserted, aside from the striking black guillemots.

I ask for directions and am directed towards the main town. The woman's harsh accent surprises me, puts me slightly on edge. This is Northern Ireland. Up the road union flags are flying, which further pique my alertness.

I have no idea where I crossed the border. Sea is no respecter of national boundaries.

Curb stones are painted alternate red white and blue. Some of the walls are painted with murals.

In town I find a café. Decor is spartan but it is spotlessly clean. The waitresses beckon me in despite the seawater that drips from my suit. They are disarmingly welcoming. Bacon roll and tea are fantastic.

I learn that the flags are left over from 12th July parade. The waitresses don't seem to consider the parade or the flags as a big deal. I follow their lead.

Walking back to the shore, I ponder how predisposed I'd been to be wary of these people. The Northern Irish accents around me now sound friendly rather than harsh.

The wind has also mellowed. I take the opportunity to knock off Dundrum bay as a point to point 20km straight liner. A quick stop for an excellent broccoli and stilton soup at Killough, then back to making miles.

A band of rain is passing through. I head to Ballyhornan beach. An island here provides shelter from the lumpy sea, making it an easy landing spot.

From the beach I can see white water to the north. It is distant. That I can see it white means that it is big. I phone Gregg for a navigational update, but he is out walking the dog.

I manage to bring a map up on my phone, and work out that ahead, around the next headland, is the entrance to Strangford Lough. I really don't like the look of all the white water, but decide to continue with caution regardless.

Level with the headland the sight before me is frightening. The tide is on full ebb, and water is pouring out of Strangford at a rate I wouldn't have thought possible. This torrent of water is charging into the oncoming sea waves. The result is overfalls several metres high extending out as far as the eye can see. I have absolutely no intention of sailing through this.

I edge closer. Where the sea is like a river, with land on both sides, the water is flat. If I can beat the current and sail upstream to where the mouth is narrower, I will be able to cross. What I mustn't do is become trapped in the fast moving stream and be pulled out into the overfalls. That would be disastrous.

The shoreline is rocky. I stay as shallow as possible, my fin occasionally snagging on the rocks. The current races past an outcrop. I don't know if I'll make it past, but judge it safe to try. If I get pulled back, retreat is still an option.

Even with decent wind, the current is an even match for board speed. I slowly gain on my reference points - rocks, static contours on the water surface as it rushes over underwater obstacles. I claw level with the outcrop. Water races past. Every metre has to be won. With the jut of rocks clear astern I subtly change course, creeping back towards the weakest currents in the shallowest water. I start to pull forward more confidently. Made it.

With distance between myself and the overfalls out to sea, I grow more confident. The technical sailing is fun and the scenery is beautiful. I head a long way upstream to where the mouth of the lough narrows. When the gap to the north shore is less than 1000m, I feel confident that I have the sea room to cross safely. With no rain around the wind has been more reliable. I don't want it to desert me now.

I set the board to cross at forty-five degrees - sailing into the stream at an angle. The current is astonishing. It pulls me back into the wind, transforming a force 2-3 into a solid 4. One-third across and I'm fully planing, yet still moving backwards relative to reference points on land. I continue crabbing my way across. In the final third I am once again able to hold station relative to

Flags at Annalong leave no doubt that this is Northern Ireland

land. Back in the rocky shoreline fringe the flow is less strong and the detour nearly complete.

I ride the current back out to sea. In places, the water has a visible slope. At first opportunity I sail off from the outgoing conveyer belt, hugging the coast on my journey north.

I liaise with Diane, my contact from Bangor, and we arrange to meet at Portovogie, which is a fair trek for both of us.

The coastline of the Ards peninsula is remote, rugged and spectacular. Something is different, I realise I am north. A slight vertigo sets in when I consider how much further north I have yet to go.

Portavogie is a fishing town. Islands and rocks protect its harbour. I land on a wet low tide beach. Our threadbare rendezvous plan falls into place. Diane has linked up with a local fisherman - Robin - who offers his garden for board storage. Three strangers collaborate. A little bit of warmth flows between us. Trusting to fate has allowed things to work out.

Day 43 - 19th July

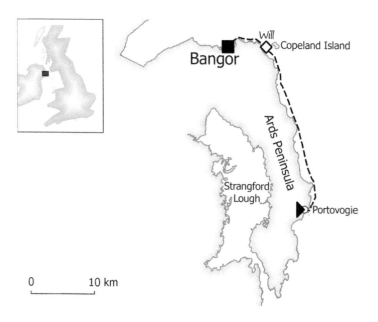

The morning is calm. Diane gives me a tour of Bangor, including a stop for a full English breakfast. I'm developing a taste for these.

I trust that a breeze will fill in. We head back to Portovogie early afternoon, ready to catch the north-going tide.

Robin's ducks are guarding the board. The beach is right behind his back gate.

The sail to Bangor takes four and a half hours, and the sun shines from start to finish. The lightest of following breeze ripples the water. Scotland is visible in the far offshore distance.

I pick my way through rocky reefs that sit offshore of golden-sand beaches. Seaweed stretches to the surface of the clear water. I peer down at the life below me. This is raceboard cruising at its most relaxing.

About to depart from Portovogie on a blissfully pleasant day. Photo: Diane Burgess

I'd been told to be aware of currents at Copeland Island, but they just don't happen. Instead a paddleboarder called William comes over to say a quick hello, then paddles off again.

There is a bit of current to contend with on the final miles to Bangor, but nothing troubling. I have a newfound confidence to deal with conditions after my experience yesterday.

I land at Ballyholme Yacht Club, linking up again with Diane.

Some more windsurfers catch up with me to say hello, some yacht sailors advise on the crossing to Scotland. A smooth Guinness goes down particularly well.

We get Indian takeout for dinner. Diane's friends come round. I listen intently as Maia points out all the places I can stop as I head up the coast.

Day 44 - 20th July

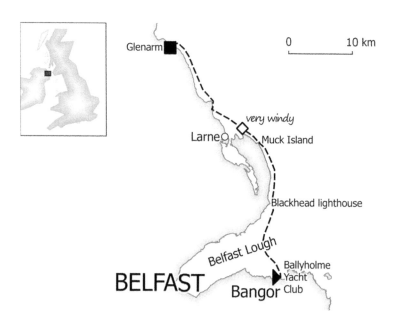

I've noticed that the strip of flexible rubber that seals around the daggerboard has started to peel off. Potentially this is a major problem. Even a small opening here seriously compromises performance. And once the flusher starts to peel, a small hole rapidly opens up into a larger one...

I'm in an ideal place for repairs. I buy some epoxy glue, and a couple of other glue types as backup alternatives. It is raining outside, but the yacht club have a marquee up, which I can use as workshop. I meticulously prepare the operation and stick the flusher, then use weighty rocks to hold everything in place whilst the epoxy goes hard.

It's a slightly unnerving day. Lost in the mist is the other side of Belfast Lough. The coast heading north is cliff lined for 20km. One of the forecasts I habitually check is forecasting winds of force 6-7, but there's not much wind at the moment, and other forecasts don't concur.

I lunch porridge and stuff extra food in the barrel, unsure where I'll next have the opportunity for a decent refuel. Oban?

The kids and instructors at Ballyholme Yacht Club wave me off and are then swallowed up in the mist. I follow GPS to the shipping lane. Buoy hopping seems the safest strategy. An outgoing ship disregards the lane entirely.

Blackhead Lighthouse marks the beginning of open sea. Waves rebound off the cliffs to create a messy, unpleasant, tiring, sea state. I'd been told these cliffs have a spectacular walkway, restored from Victorian times, but I can barely make it out in the poor visibility. I stop among a concentration of shearwaters, temporary diversion from the downwind discomfort.

I'm learning to be less affected by these difficult times. Am developing a philosophical acceptance that they always end. Sure enough there is eventually a change of conditions. I pass inside of Muck Island. The water in its shelter is blissfully flat.

Beyond, the coast bends round into the port of Larne, which leaves me a few miles offshore. A breeze from the land blows the mist away. Above the hills spectacular clouds have ballooned upwards. On the water - I can see the wind long before it hits.

I harden up on to a true beat, land ahead at forty-five degrees, ready to do battle with the advancing army of white horses. In the closing stages before impact I fully tension both outhaul and downhaul.

The wind thumps in. In a way I'm lucky. This overpowered, anything other than upwind sailing would be unthinkable. I don't need to tack and ahead is land where I can stop. I have about 5km to sail. An extra wide grip on the boom and pushing like buggery on my front arm prevents the sail dumping in to windward. Wide stance on legs and minimal daggerboard prevent the board capsizing itself.

Muscles burn. The distance to land halves, then halves again, and eventually I make it to shore. More luck is that nothing broke.

I don't sail again for a few hours, wary of more punishment. When I do head out the wind has moderated substantially. I don't sail far enough offshore for constant wind. On-off planing is preferable to another struggle back to shore.

I make it to Glenarm by early evening. A few tacks take me into a small marina. A yacht sails most of the way in too - just taking a tow for the final part. Engine failure. None of the gathered parties appear to notice me sail in. I gently settle my board on the concrete slipway.

It turns out I was noticed.

I'm looking for a camping spot. A man wanders over. Weather beaten. My dad's age or thereabouts.

He squints a hello, then turns to observe the cluster of people by the stricken yacht, and her saviour. "These your friends?" The yacht crews' voices are excited; they are on a high having successfully dealt with the engine crisis. I explain our coincidental arrival.

Curiosity shifted, he turns to consider my sail, board, barrel. "And where'll you be staying?"

I indicate to the patch of green above the slipway. "Here, probably."

He looks up, clear blue eyes scan seaward. A pause before addressing no-one in particular, "Aye, we'll see about that." The words float away on the breeze. Then another question. "And what'll you be eating?"

"Rice meal, probably. Pub, maybe." I don't know the options yet. More words are released onto the breeze. "Aye, we'll see about that too."

Twenty minutes later I am in a warm and dry cabin. A plate of beef and potatoes steams in front of me. I've been taken in by David and Maureen, who are travelling in convoy with their daughter's family in the yacht moored alongside. They are lovely people. I couldn't have got luckier.

* * *

I'm one hop from Scotland. My original plan had been to head to Rathlin Island first, but I can't make the tides work for that. I talk it over with David and Maureen - who are also headed to Scotland - and phone John too. Second and third opinions are comforting. I'll start early and head up to Cushenden, against the tide. That will leave time for a quick stop and refuel, before catching the first of the ebb for re-crossing the Irish Sea, destined for somewhere on the Kintyre Peninsula.

Onboard welcome from David and Maureen

Day 45 - 21ˢᵗ July

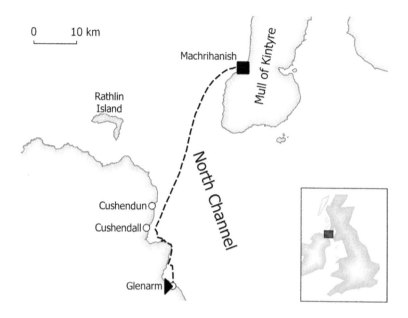

A cooked breakfast starts the day well, but a frustratingly light headwind leaves me further and further behind schedule. Passing outcrops and headlands against the tide is a real battle. Sometimes I just can't make any progress, or a zigzag sends me backwards. The wind drops to nothing for a while - an opportunity to stop and eat something. Five hours after leaving Glenarm I'm still miles short of Cushenden. I scale back my objective. Mentally accept that I won't be crossing to Scotland today.

Now heading to a revised destination of Cushendall suddenly a breeze fills in. The tide has also turned. Speed over ground is healthy. I'd been hoping to cross to Scotland around slack, to avoid strong current in the channel - and am late for that - but the improvement in conditions has me in two minds.

I still don't think I should go, until far out to sea I notice a brace of yachts heading north, with wind. I immediately recognise the tall elegant lead rig - and smaller craft behind - as my friends from

Glenarm. The sighting prompts an immediate decision. *Fuck it! If they're going, I am too.*

For half an hour conditions are ideal. Tide assisted, I sail past Cushenden, speed over land around 10 knots. I make up some lost ground on the yacht sails, which are further over towards the Mull of Kintyre - pitching into the chop like pecking hens. I sail far enough to be fully committed, where the wind drops off to a less than reassuring force 2. Possibly the earlier breeze was a land effect. Provided it doesn't drop further, I'll be OK.

A fairly uneventful crossing unfolds. The yachts outpoint and outpace me - presumably under engine power – until they become specks in the distance. Level with the Mull of Kintyre, for about a kilometre, the water is upwelling and turbulent - disturbed enough to know that on the wrong day it would be quite unpleasant. Progress is steady and consistent. Further north the current is less strong and no longer sweeping me away from land.

There is quite a shocking contrast of scale between the pleasant hills and valleys of County Antrim, and the monumentally large lump of rock that is the Mull.

The last hour or so I no longer need to hold my upwind advantage, and progressively free off, towards Machrihanish - the most southerly village on the Mull. I pump the sail to put myself further inshore, anticipating a windless evening.

I take a break, before cruising the final few kilometres in reflective mood. Ahead is the fifth country of my journey. I experience a sense of homecoming, or at least that is what I nostalgically recognise it as. But it is not a sense of homecoming - I struggle with the concept of home, not really feeling that I belong anywhere. Rather it is a sense of peace at returning to a land of wilderness and open spaces. A refuge of distant horizons that offers escape from having to be social. Not unlike the sea - in fact. But without the fear.

I am proud too - at having arrived here by my Route One. And relieved - to have completed the last of the major crossings. With me, for today at least, is a calmness and serenity that I've been missing for years, or perhaps had never previously achieved.

Day 46 - 22nd July

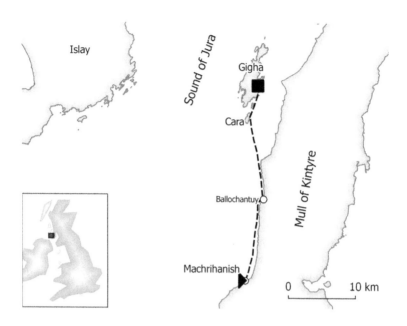

I have an offer of breakfast this morning. A family with a holiday cottage in the village invited me. In the pub yesterday there had been a pub quiz and we'd been persuaded to form a team.

The cottage has big windows that the Scottish rain has left spotlessly clean. Outside are views up the Sound of Jura, which today is bathed in sunshine. A gentle south-westerly breeze ripples the water.

A full English, fresh fruit, and coffee set me up for the day. Gordon and clan take a few photos as I sail off, that later make it into the Campbeltown Courier.

It is mostly slow sailing, but progress up the Sound puts me amongst the Scottish Islands, which will provide protection from Atlantic Swell up until the North Minch.

There has been a shift in my attitude to sailing. I'm no longer in such a hurry. Route One has left me on track for getting round the top of Scotland before I run out of summer. I can afford to play it a bit safer. I also want to *enjoy* the west coast of Scotland.

I cruise north, stopping for lunch at the quite smart Argyll Hotel, in Ballochantuy. I leaf through the newspapers.

The Scotsman has a piece about the worst summer storm for forty years. I guess that was when I was camped on the edge of Dundalk Bay. It has been a summer of low pressures, and looks set to continue that way. Low pressures bring wet weather - but also wind - so I can't say the weather pattern is unfavourable. I generally manage to just accept the weather for what it is.

Further north I approach what I assume is Gigha island. A pair of perfect white sand beaches curl out to meet each other on seaweed covered rocks. Lush ferns and other vegetation provide a gentle backdrop. The sea below me is a forest of life. If I sail past this beach I will regret it forever. I drift into the shore slowly and silently.

The beauty of the spot opens an emotional tap. Perhaps the build up to the crossings had generated a tension within me, and with the three major ones now behind me, that tension is finally released. I'm absolutely alone apart from the birds and the fish and the astounding, mind blowing, extraordinary beauty that surrounds me. I realise the privilege. And I realise that moments like this are few in life.

It turns out that I was on uninhabited Cara Island.

5km further on is Gigha.

I round the rocks that guard the safe anchorage - I recognise two of the yachts. Before I've sailed over to say hello David and Maureen are beckoning me on board. I'm welcomed like a good friend who had been expected to show up.

A plate of food is set down in front of me. I had been expected. I've been tracked all day.

I also learn that I hadn't been alone crossing the Irish Sea. The good shepherds on their pecking yachts had their eyes on me from start to finish.

Day 47 - 23ʳᵈ July

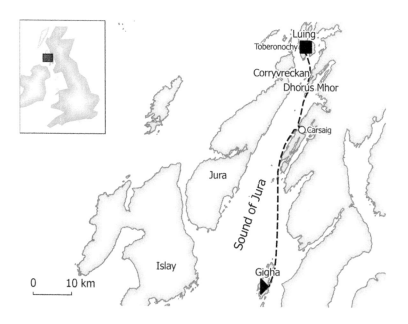

A wet and windy morning is forecast to gradually improve throughout the day, freeing up the morning to explore. I leave board and belongings on the shore, so am independent.

I'm keen to scope the sea on the island's windward side - to properly assess conditions in the Sound - so head west along green and pleasant tracks, dodging rain showers. At, literally, the end of the road, I realise that my phone is no longer in my pocket.

This is a problem. I comb the entire route, twice. But no phone appears.

At the beach is a pretty cottage with immaculately kept garden. The cottage owner - Marian - calls the device. I consider the phone most likely to be nearby, although concede that it may be turned off as a battery saving measure. We search for an hour.

It is time to concede defeat. I thank Marion, who has helped me beat bare the nearby vegetation in fruitless search, and bid my farewell. Hope all but extinguished, I ask for the final favour of another call fifteen minutes from now.

At the allotted time I am behind a hedge where I'd earlier taken a pee. Breeze rustles the vegetation but there are no other sounds. At T+5 I jump the puddle back to the track, and start walking to my board. Defeat truly conceded, my thoughts turn to how to source a replacement.

The phone is abandoned - by rights destined to a decay in the Scottish elements - when I hear it. I race back to the source of the sound. The black and grey device is nestled amongst long grass, safe and well.

I phone Marion, and walk back too, to personally thank her. I can't quite believe it. The timing was too exquisite. How could I even hear the phone at that distance? *Carried by the breeze*, I tell myself. A Goldilocks breeze. *Just right* to carry the sound without drowning it out.

How is it that things are working out, I ask myself? Every day problems resolve themselves, good fortune comes my way, things just fall into place.

I consider the divine, but settle on the psychological. When you're in a good place, life rains gifts on you.

The subjective experience of all this 'luck' I take to be what a more spiritual person might call *grace*.

* * *

By the afternoon I am back on the water, having lunched and finally sent some postcards off to folks and support team.

The sailing is fantastic. Broad reaching, clattering over the waves, heading straight up the narrowing Sound of Jura, as if threading a needle. Even cynical old hand windsurfers like myself can still find a simple joy sailing conditions like these. I stop for a break on the lee side of some rocks, just because I can really. The ten-year-old explorer in me. I pull in to Carsaig, wondering if I might be able to buy some lunch. I can't, but have reserve bread and cheese to fall back on.

The Sound of Jura has narrowed from 23km wide at Gigha to just 4km here. The currents run fast as a result. The colander of islands makes it difficult to predict speed and direction of the draining water. On the other side of the sound I can see a line of breaking water. The intersection of currents running in opposite directions.

Good breeze gives me confidence. This is a time for being bold, as John had advised. I set a waypoint for the Sound of Shona.

The route is unclear: islands or headlands block my path. I sail it as I see it. Intuition guides my navigational choices.

I stay east, away from fiercer looking currents, until ahead shows signs of becoming a dead-end loch. There is a gap, between an island and - I presume - a headland. Last exit. Water charges through the constriction. Post expedition I learn that this is the *Dhorus Mhor*.

In upwind mode I cross the line into the current that floods into the channel. Water thumps against the daggerboard with violent force and I am swept downstream. *This is frightening*, I say out loud.

I track across the divide towards weaker current on the north shore, where I will be able to calculate my next move.

Ahead the sun is low. It shines straight through the Gulf of Corryvreckan. An infamous stretch of water with whirlpools that can swallow small boats. From my angle here the Gulf looks impossibly narrow. Towering mountains rise vertically on each side. For me in these moments they resemble the gates of Hell, to be avoided at all cost.

Dhorus Mhor negotiated, the next current flows south-west. I hug the cliff-line but the water is deep, and - unimpeded - flows strong. Where available I use rocks and outcrops to effect my advance. Then attack with full power those sections that require confrontation. I have increased confidence in the *sail it as you see it* approach now.

There is a long, final exposed section, during the crossing of which I gamble on constant wind, before making it to the more benign waters of the Sound of Shona. The currents become trivially weak. Corryvreckan, and imagined fear, fade into the distance.

Another privilege, to have sailed that stretch of water. The purity of the experience is powerfully emotional.

The exhilaration subsides. Post battle serenity settles within me. These private experiences are intoxicating. Since Carsaig I have sailed without human witness.

Toberonochy view from a bivvy bag before dawn

Day 48 - 24th July

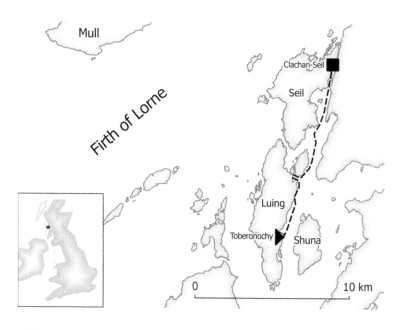

The gentle patter of rain soothes me through the night. Comfortable and dry under my sail, I occasionally open my eyes. The broken clouds reflect off the calm waters of the sound. It never really gets dark.

I've an appointment at 9am. The offer of a cup of tea turns into a full English breakfast. I'd met John yesterday, he had been cursing the swallows nesting in his boat. Swallow crap in exchange for midge control seems reasonable to me. Repeat offenders – no doubt. Before I depart from Toberonochy I receive from John's son a *Bing Blazer* t-shirt to add to my wardrobe, and fishing spares. Grumpy John wishes me well and seems to mean it.

I keep finding nice people. I know that my sampling is selective: I am unlikely to develop a rapport with people who tend towards unhelpfulness. But, notwithstanding this, I firmly believe that all of us would – at a fundamental level – prefer to be friendly and co-operative. The apparent exceptions are for the most part easily explained, and the remainder at least *have* explanation.

The breeze is almost non-existent. I reach a point where mobile signal returns and stop for some admin.

The fittings on my board, already well used before the expedition, are feeling their age. Mast track is worn and not working properly. Footstraps are decayed. The fin is also old and tired - and I have concerns it may fail at an inopportune moment. I talk with Gregg and with Tushingham. Together they work out a plan to get me some spare parts ready for pick up in Mallaig. I'm left no doubt that Tushingham's support is genuine and beyond the strictly commercial. I feel happy to be part of this team.

It takes me 4 hours on the water to cover the next 4 miles. For most of the time there isn't a breath of wind. I resort to attempting to paddle at times – surfer style, whilst attempting to balance the sail on the back of the board using my legs - and do at least progress a few hundred metres this way.

It is hard work for little gain, but I have a clear target in mind. Alice and John were early sign-ups to the website. I'm keen to take them up on their offer of help; and frankly, I could do with a shower and re-introduction to soap.

I head up a narrow channel between Seil Island and the mainland. Just before Clachan Bridge is the village of Clachan-Seil. Alice and John's garden backs down to the water's edge. They are on the lawn when I arrive. I haul my gear on to the lush grass and we exchange hellos. It takes me a little while to place them at first, but then I remember teaching Alice windsurfing, and chatting to John on occasion on the beach in Menorca. Calm and gentle people.

I am very well looked after. Later on we take a very agreeable stroll down beyond the bridge, following the narrow channel until reaching the sea. On the return journey we stop at the pub. Behind the door is a small room, lots of people, noise, chatter from all directions, roof too low. The evidence before me suggests that this should be an agreeable environment, but I feel a familiar discomfort. Fortunately there is a quieter adjoining room. I retreat there, pretend to inspect the old photographs that hang from the walls, and properly savour the wonderful taste of ale.

Paddling, or at least attempting to

Day 49 - 25th July

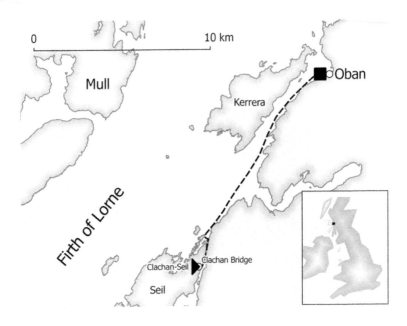

Alice and John wave me off as the morning tide turns to flood. A gentle wind blows north to south through Clachan Sound, but the current will at least assist my progress.

I sail under the single stone arch of Clachan Bridge. The kilometre long channel that leads to open waters is shallow and weed clogged. I sweat my way through the vegetation, to freedom. The cheeky shortcut is pleasing, and cuts miles off my day.

I wait for wind and admire the views for a while. Across the Firth of Lorne are the mountains of Mull. A dolphin lazily makes its way seaward. The scene is majestic.

A variable combination of breeze and current then carries me towards Oban. Land is close and conditions are benign. It is an unusual day because personal safety is not a pressing concern. It is also warm, and really feels like summer.

Heading up inside Kerrera Island, a yacht rounds on me in an unexpected and slightly violent manoeuvre. Not piracy, just a friendly hello from another lone traveller, who wishes me well on my journey. Another new friend. Yet more evidence that life is better being someone who notices.

My Mum and step-dad Peter have travelled to Oban by train. Elbows on railings, they are looking out to sea, soaking up the sunshine, as I coast in towards a landing spot at the sailing club.

Mum is relieved that I appear to be essentially the same me who left from Clacton 49 days ago. I think she had imagined a shipwreck survivor with barely the strength to drag himself to dry land. There are days I feel tired, for sure, but physically I feel fine. Mentally I am feeling good too. The top of Scotland holds more fears, but I am in a far better place that I was after going round Land's End. That trauma I feel is now behind me.

Of course, in some ways I am a changed me. It couldn't be any other way. But I'm not chasing personal growth or looking to ring any changes, yet. The processing of experience takes time.

* * *

Oban has a town centre, tourist shops, tourists, opportunistic seagulls, ferries, pubs and cafés. It is a pleasant place to spend a sunny afternoon. We eat and stroll. I borrow Jen and Peter's hotel room for a shower and a nap. Before more eating, I manage a blog post for the website.

I turn down the offer of a hotel room. There doesn't seem much point when I'm just as happy under the sail. Also - by recent standards - this is a major conurbation, so it's probably not a good idea to leave kit unattended.

Day 50 - 26th July

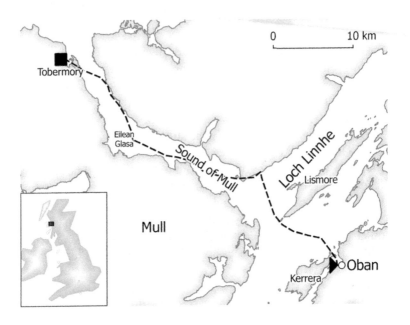

I have a hearty breakfast with Jen and Peter. I hear that the adventurer's Mum had been up at dawn to check on her son. Cocooned in my sleeping bag and bivvy bag I was oblivious to her visit.

We chat with a fisherman during pre-launch procedure. He reassures me about the days ahead - says I've done the trickier bits already.

It is unusual to hear knowledgeable and non-alarmist advice. More often locals seem to take pride in having a treacherous coastline, and are keen to describe theirs as being particularly fearsome. Gentle enquiry usually teases out that their advice is based on reputation or notoriety, rather than first-hand experience. I've become quite discerning about the advice I heed.

I'm pleased my Mum hears the fisherman's calm analysis.

It has been a perfect rendezvous. I sail out of Oban dodging the *Calmac* ferries and am back on my journey.

It is a significant crossing of 14km to the north side of Loch Linnhe. Here a mountain drops down to the sea and under its steep side is a bay that reminds me of childhood adventure. I stop for a while, just because I can. I clamber the rocks and then sit quiet and still, observing nature.

The tide is against me heading up the Sound of Mull. It is a long haul, but technically easy - with an exposure level as low as it gets. I enjoy the scenery and wildlife along the shores.

Seals are taking their siesta - noses pointed up to the sky. Most notice me early and silently slide into the depths. Some notice late and perform a powerful combined turn and dive. One doesn't wake at all, as I glide past close enough to count the whiskers on her face.

I stop for a break on an island in the middle of the Sound, a mile from each shore. The island is little more than a rock but is home to seabirds and - to my surprise - an otter.

The weather turns grottier in the afternoon. A stiffer breeze, and drizzle, coincide their arrival with my own, at Tobermory, on the island of Mull.

The town's anchorage and marina is full of yachts, and space on land is limited too. Via intercom, with whoever is inside the locked marina building, I negotiate permission for a one night stay on the patch of land behind their office. It's certainly not luxury but is at least slightly private. I am quite pleased with my effort and reward.

Dinner is fish and chips. Only five out of ten.

The weather, and perhaps idealised memories from childhood holidays, likely has something to do with it, but I find myself a little bit disappointed with Tobermory. I recognise the signs of overly intensive and highly seasonal tourism. Tired and jaded workforce. No real resolution of the paradox that there is a slight resentment of the tourists, but that these are the ones paying the bills, supporting the pubs cafés and shops. I saw it where I lived in Spain, and I see it here too.

Day 51 - 27th July

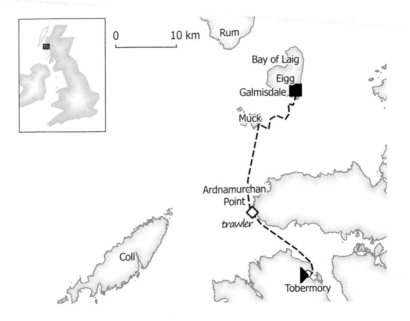

By breakfast time, the rain is a gentle and pleasant pitter-patter on my sail shelter. A visitor, who has presumably seen me from the harbour master building's window, pokes his waterproof clad head into my space "What are you doing here?" Even I do better greetings that that. I explain that I have permission.

The hooded figure grunts and turns, I presume to verify my story. I amuse myself with the thought of round Britain windsurfing vagrants becoming a serious nuisance. Let one sleep here and they'll all want to...

A pair of harbour officials come over to chat. They are friendly and helpful. I imagine they've checked the website and seen my route so far, and have reached a *fair do's to him* conclusion. I think I've been accepted as a fellow mariner. I'm sure I could stay a week if I wanted to. I don't. But my fondness for Tobermory is mostly restored.

A few yachts soon head off into the Sound. I follow them out, grateful for some company on the sail toward Ardnamurchan Point. It's a cracking downwind blast to the headland. The easterly wind funnels directly out of the Sound of Mull. The landmass of Ardnamurchan then blocks the wind. It becomes so light that I struggle to avoid a trawler, and end up uncomfortably close to its nets, that are being paid out into the depths. Anything that becomes entwined in those is going straight down with them, I observe, with a chill. The crew are friendly, and take a picture.

Finally, clear of the headland, I'm back into wind. I have a choice to make. Either follow the mainland coast east, then sail north tomorrow. Or sail more north today - to the Isle of Eigg - then sail more east tomorrow. The wind direction is unfavourable whichever route I choose, but heading to Eigg will likely mean I'll have fewer miles to sail. There is also reputedly a pub on the island.

I head out into open water. The east in the wind means that I am quite exposed. With no land to leeward, any problem would be significant. Eigg is about 17km away. Slightly nearer and a few kilometres downwind is the Isle of Muck, which is roughly the angle I can make. It's another good sail, thumping upwind into the waves at 8+ knots. I reel in and then leave behind one of the yachts that had departed Tobermory before me.

I take a close look at Muck but decide against landing. Facilities there look non-existent. I press on to Eigg. Short zigzags keep Muck downwind of me: a safety net in case of a problem.

Eigg is impressive. If I were going to design an island I'd look at this one for inspiration. It has a fine natural harbour with white sands. Behind this, graceful green contours rise to a craggy peak that reminds me of what I imagine the Eiger to look like. I land at a fantastic camping spot. A short while after that Dean comes over to say hello.

The tall thin man reminds me a bit of me. He explains how he kayaked over here 12 years ago and never left. I consider 12 years on the island, and imagine myself 12 years later at this very spot. *The faint ring of alarm bells.*

Isle of Rum from Isle of Eigg

At the time, and now, I'm pretty sure that twelve years on Eigg wouldn't be for me. But on reflection, perhaps it *could* have been, had I not developed a connection with a different island instead.

Dean heads off to do some house building. Apparently he has built several on the island, but hasn't got round to building himself one yet. I inspect the Galmisdale Bay Cafe, which doubles as the pub most evenings except Mondays. Poor timing on my part. A bacon roll is quickly sustaining before I set off for an explore.

I really enjoy my walk across the island. A sign from Eigg Electric informs that the island is self-sufficient in renewable energy. I pass a number of dwellings and the smallest, most picturesque school I've ever seen. I take a picture for Alba. The camera comes out again at a point overlooking Laig Bay, with stunning views towards the Isle of Rum.

I'd come back to Eigg - to explore some more - with more time.

As it is I head back to my camping spot. Rehydrated-something is dinner. A t-shirt and sun visor combination keeps the midges away from my face, but complicates eating. I settle down to sleep in the peaceful twilight.

Day 52 - 28th July

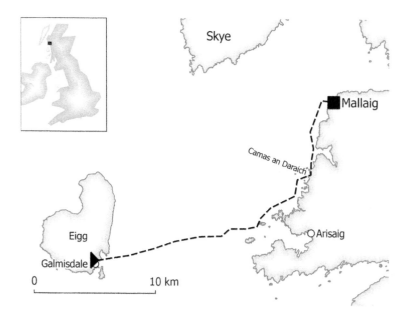

There is a very light and cold wind this morning, coming out of the north. If I head out and the wind doesn't fill in it will take all day to reconnect with the mainland - so instead I make a return visit to the Galmisdale Bay Cafe.

Late morning I witness the arrival of three kayakers. I greet them much as Dean greeted me, minus the shipwreck story my imagination has saddled him with. I've already got the best camping spot but cede rights to a nearby patch.

The kayakers are a guide and two clients. They started out from Arisaig early morning. Conditions were perfect calm for their crossing, and they saw a minke whale. I'd like to see whales too, and people I meet are convinced that I will. Perhaps even killer whales - there is a pod in these waters, and another on the north coast of Scotland, apparently.

At one o'clock a breeze fills in at last, allowing me to set sail.

Upwind sailing in light airs is not very energetic. After an hour and a half on the same tack my hands are ready to drop off with cold. No whales either.

I put in regular tacks up the indented mainland shoreline to encourage circulation. A beach stop - to stretch out and readjust my multiple thermal layers - and at last I am at an agreeable operating temperature.

And I *love* my fleecy hat. Similar to how, as a kid, I loved my dungarees.

The wind fills in some more and I enjoy the upwind sailing the rest of the way to Mallaig.

Approaching from the sea, the concrete harbour wall and steep crags behind Mallaig remind me of a fortress town. I like the non-compliance with twee. I cruise in at slow speed, on the lookout for a camp location. Thin pickings.

A floating pontoon has a few yachts moored up. I'm being waved at - beckoned closer - by the crew of the end boat, a traditional sailing vessel from before the era of plastic. On board are two men with identical big hair - surely brothers. A young blonde girl - a daughter? And of similar age a good looking lad who I immediately recognise as Johnny Depp's Captain Jack Sparrow, from the film *Pirates of the Caribbean*.

They had seen me rounding Ardnamurchan Point two days ago, themselves rounding further offshore. I remember seeing them too. Their boat doesn't have a spare cabin, but I am welcome to sleep under the boom tent if I would like. I do like. I long ago resolved not to be picky about offers of help.

The crew of *Lassie of Chester* head off in search of food. I delay, sorting out my gear. I don't really need the time to do anything in particular, but it allows me to transition away from my world at sea and back to a world with people.

Refreshed, I re-join my shipmates. The pub's fish chowder is excellent.

The two older men are indeed brothers. One is Adrian, *Lassie's* skipper

Rosie, the blonde girl, is Adrian's daughter.

Sparrow is hired help. The most experienced sailor amongst them, he has the prettiness, elegance, and - to my ear - occasional fantasy of Depp's cinematic character.

Lassie started her summer voyage from North Wales. Sparrow came on board at the Isle of Arran. They've put in to Mallaig for engine repairs.

Having my own repairs to do here, I fit right in.

The proud crew of *Lassie*

Day 53 - 29ᵗʰ July

First job today is find Mallaig Boat Yard. The spare parts sent by Tushingham haven't arrived yet - but are apparently on their way. I keep fingers crossed for an afternoon delivery.

There is a Fishermen's Mission behind the harbour, with adjoining café, which I am pleased to patronise. The mental image of those plunging nets off Arnamurchan Point returns to me. Also the rusted machinery grinding away on board, and the contrasting soft flesh of the operator in such close proximity. Dangerous enough work in benign weather. A form of Russian Roulette the rest of the time.

I like Mallaig. It seems to me an honest place, and to have a sense of purpose.

In the afternoon my spares turn up. Wary of dropping the fiddly parts in the sea, I move ashore to a convenient "No Parking" area to fit them. I don't get moved on, but do have an agreeable conversation with an enthusiastic Dutchman.

Having completed the work, the mast track slides freely as it should; some of the footstraps - the ones I also use to lift the loaded board and which therefore take more abuse than normal - have been replaced; and the fin and fin bolts - which are also particularly stressed on my modified craft - have been changed.

The work gives an opportunity for a thorough inspection of the board. The previously smooth underwater finish has developed a rough texture, which I sand out. Borrowed silicon spray is used to lubricate all moving parts. The full service is good for confidence. My only slight concern is the new and significantly larger fin. I hope it won't lead to control problems in stronger winds or put too much additional stress on the board's fin box.

My adoptive family here have been working on *Lassie*. She is a Morecambe Bay Prawner, of wood build. A classic. They have struck up a friendship with an interesting local builder and sailor - Toby - who shares a passion for things wooden. Toby is an acknowledged expert in classic boats and looks after *Lizzie May*, a new-build traditional Pilot Cutter, moored just a few metres away. We've been offered a sail this evening. I understand this is quite a privilege, and so decide to abandon my guilt at lack of progress today and look forward to a new experience instead.

Before we head out, our neighbour - Peter Prawn - appears from below the decks of his boat with about 20 kilos of freshly cooked langoustines to share round. Peter is another friendly link from the Bangor area of Northern Ireland. He has some sort of family connection here, hence the free bagfuls of 'prawns' from the trawlermen. We all gorge until full, before heading over to the *Lizzie May*. I'm glad I decided to stay put today.

It is a memorable sail. *Lizzie May* sails beautifully. Conditions in the Sound of Sleat are mind-blowingly fantastic. A stiff northerly leans our gunwales into the water. The tumbled clouds and towering mountains are painted multitude shades of grey. This rates as one of the most breath-taking arenas in which I have sailed.

We tack upwind to Doune, in Knoydart, where Toby grew up. The ancient settlement was re-colonised by Toby's parents. It has access by sea, or by a 30-mile mountain walk from the nearest road.

There is a lot of wild man in Toby. At one point he climbs the mast and scans the majestic surroundings, as a wolf would scan its territory.

Toby drives the *Lizzie May* hard. There is a little bit of showman in him too. But I believe not for show is the importance he places on seamanship. We sail off our mooring and sail back to our mooring. Having an engine is not reason to use it. I'm of that opinion too.

We stay aboard until late. And although the wolf in me would rather be roaming now, than below decks amongst whalers' songs and whisky, that barely matters. Because *Lizzie May* and the Sound of Sleat have provided something close to perfection this evening. When I think back to today and my eyes glaze over, it is out there on the water that I will be.

Lizzie May powers across the Sound of Sleat

Day 54 - 30th July

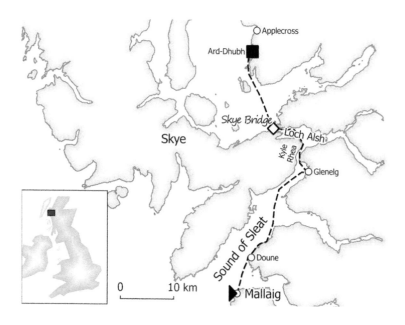

A gentle southerly breeze propels me out of Mallaig. Conditions are once again perfect for easy and non-threatening progress. I sail a few hours, across loch mouths and following the contours of the coastline in between. I am in awe of the landscape around me. It is like being in the spectacular opening sequences of a film, and the camera never stops rolling.

More wind comes in around Sandaig - where the Sound of Sleat narrows. The board picks up on to a plane with particular ease and feels more balanced with the new bigger fin. The kit feels solid.

Further ahead is Kyle Rhea - a narrow channel between The Isle of Skye and the mainland. Apparently there are strong currents here I should beware of. I have a few hours to wait before the tide goes slack, so put in to the shore at Glenelg for a break, and to bide my time.

The village guards the entrance - or exit - to the Sound of Sleat. It has a nice feel. Although there are jutting peaks on three sides, and water on the fourth, there is level ground and a sense of space. The houses I see suggest a small resident population and some second homes. Services include the Bike Shed - I meet Jake the proprietor - and small primary school with adjacent village hall-cum-café. I meet Lisa, who works in both.

The slim brunette is pleasing on my eyes and has a cheery manner. I could do with a weather update and she has Wi-Fi at home. It's a good connection. Sat on the front step of her house, we chat in the afternoon sun.

I could stay longer, but the proverb about time and tide rings in my ears. Lisa says she will cycle down to wave me off, which makes me happy.

I suit up next to my board and delay departure hoping Lisa will appear. She doesn't. Oh well. Slightly deflated, I haul up the sail and glide away.

Kyle Rhea separates the Sound of Sleat from Loch Alsh. A strong current flows but the water is flat and the experience barely raises my pulse. I sail past the Glenelg ferry, which was originally operated by Lisa's grandfather, apparently.

The wind in Loch Alsh is abysmal. The high mountains on all sides suggest this would be par for the course.

The route out is under the Skye road bridge. Against the tide, progress is a real battle. I stay very shallow where possible, passing inches over rocks upon which is perched a lighthouse.

Back in open water, wind returns. That's good - I'd like to get somewhere and am short on daylight. The day has turned overcast again. The arrival of the next weather system is imminent.

In my mind I would like to make it to Applecross. There is a pub there, my research suggests. A pub is good when there is bad weather about. The foul current delays progress. None of the land I pass has signs of settlement.

It is nearly dark before I reach a habited shore. There is an inlet with a few dwellings at each of three locations. A misty rain leaves everything dripping. I ghost over to each of the first two locations, but these appear to be poor camping options. The third option looks less promising still. I head back towards the first location - marginally my favourite. No pub or signs of life anywhere.

Then out of the misty gloom come voices. Two men are frantically - chaotically - rowing. The sound of crabbed strokes and bounced oars is unmistakable. I look round for an explanation to their efforts, but in the closed-down visibility there is only mist and wet hills. I am perplexed. But they do seem headed to me, so I glide closer which saves their splashing.

The men are out of breath. They explain - panting - in fragments: I must come and stay with them. They've got a spare room. Well, not a room, a campervan, and it's not theirs. But I can stay there. It's broken down. That's OK. And they've just got back. Late. Sailing late. In their Wayfarer. That's why they're in trouble. But not now! Because look how late I am! They really would be in trouble if they were that late. Thanks to me. They're off the hook! Come and stay. I must be knackered! Who are they? Oh. They are Matt, and Matt's son - Chris.

And that is how I meet the Oglethorpe family. They are absolutely the sort of people who notice. The rain in the evening is torrential. Once again I've got incredibly - inexplicably? - lucky.

* * *

Inside, the shoreline cottage is cosy. An open fire keeps the cold out. I meet Matt's wife - Lucy, and their daughter Emma. Lucy sends Matt to visit the hen house and ten minutes later serves up egg on toast. The runny yolks couldn't taste better.

The cottage is home to Lucy's Auntie and partner, who work on the local Applecross Estate. I've actually come up short - Applecross village is a few miles north. This is Ard-Dhubh, a regular escape for Matt and family.

The spare room for the cottage is a broken down but well-appointed campervan. I squelch over the sodden ground to my lodgings and a very comfortable night's sleep.

Day 55 - 31st July

It hasn't stopped raining. I make tea from under the covers. Views through the windscreen are out over the Inner Sound to the Island of Raasay. It is windy too. I'm not keen to sail.

Matt and family are instantly understanding that conditions are unsuitable for sailing. They know of a MOD submarine sounding station just up the coast at Sand. We call them to check on passage rights and wind readings. There are no subs to worry about today, but with winds gusting 30 knots they recommend I stay put.

With that settled it becomes a guilt free and mind calming day off.

We compare notes on sea safety. Though of limited experience, Matt and Chris are intrepid explorers with their Wayfarer dinghy. The opportunities for wilderness adventure around here are exciting to consider.

I enjoy talking with Matt. Like many of the family men I meet on my journey, he clearly finds aspects of life a bit tame. He's done some interesting bike expeditions in the past and misses the freedom he had as a younger man. At the same time he fully appreciates and adores his family and understands that life is a compromise. I admire the groundedness of men like Matt. And it's no surprise at all that Chris and Emma are such nice young adults.

We go for a drive up the coast. Past Sands Bay and then on barren moorland until the coast bends round into Loch Torridon. Waves of rain roll up the Inner Sound. Cleansing, nourishing fresh water beats down on the windscreen.

We stop at a strategic point to survey my route for tomorrow. The vibrant green landscape contrasts with panoramic folds of advancing grey cloud. In the blustery wind I close my eyes and

Looking south down the Inner Sound during a break in the rain

look up, open mouthed. The taste and touch of salt free water is delicious.

For parts of the day I am lost in thought. I realise just how far I've come. Physical distance, and personal journey. I am finding more peace in myself.

I also reflect on yesterday's chance meeting in Glenelg, and on the Ireland meet up with my ex. Talking with Lisa was easy and there was attraction. That was unexpected. Between my ex and I there has been some contact, but - to my ear at least – it has been increasingly distant of late. With nostalgia but positivity I know that it is best to leave behind what perhaps could have been, but that wasn't meant to be.

That evening I receive a good luck message from Lisa. She'd cycled round to see me sail through Kyle Rhea. I'm pleased, and can imagine or remember seeing a figure on the rocks there.

Day 56 - 1st August

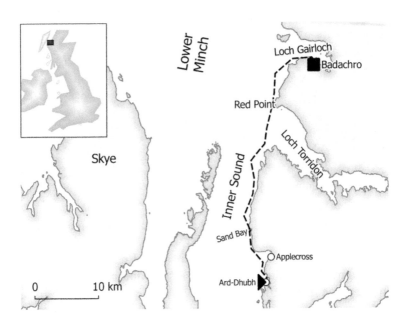

Squally now, rather than non-stop rain. Windy enough for me to not be overly keen, but I don't want to overstay my welcome, and the forecast is for conditions to improve.

I am waved off by the small community. Waterproof-hooded figures line the shore. I sail a few runs in the shelter of the cove to test conditions - which I judge as borderline OK - before heading out, broad reaching downwind.

I don't get far before the next big squall catches and is upon me. I'm thankful for yesterday's familiarisation with the coastline as I know I have Sand Bay as a bolthole. Overpowered and in heavy rain I make it in. Matt and family show up too, they've been driving along the coast road taking pictures at various vantage points.

There is a bothy to shelter in here. Matt explains that Monty Halls lived here 6 months as a crofter for the BBC programme

En route to Sand Bay before yet another downpour. Photo: Emma
Ogglethorpe

Great Escape. Inside is empty, but the rebuilt roof keeps out the
now torrential rain.

After the downpour it really is goodbye to my new friends Matt
and family.

I leave land behind once again. Heading north the Inner Sound
opens up into the Minch. The Isles of Lewis are 50km offshore.
Although there is useful protection from Atlantic swells in the
Lower Minch, the sensation is of being on exposed coast.

I cross the 6km wide mouth of Loch Torridon. To the east rise
steep mountains dressed in rags of cloud.

Fine beaches either side of Red Point, and others further north,
go admired but unexplored. Still early in the day I reach the
calmer waters of Gairloch.

I have contacts here, at Badachro. When Meredith and Rob
signed up it was a real boost. The flag they put on the map is right
in the middle of the most remote stretch of coastline I will face.
Their help turns one huge stretch of unknown into two large but
significantly less daunting sections.

I sense a slight rise in anxiety about not making more progress today. The terrible weather these days has me worried that summer has gone, and with it my chances of getting round the north coast of Scotland. I think it through and consider the situation more rationally: on a coastline this deserted I need help wherever it is offered. I also want to meet these kind strangers.

A winding channel takes me up to Badachro. A current flows out: seawater topped up by fresh that drains from the hills. There are a few moored boats, and a scattering of houses.

Meredith and Rob and their polite boys offer every comfort a windsurfing adventurer could wish for. They settle me in and then get back to their day. Like most people in remote parts they survive off a mixture of work. Rob fixes boats and skippers them for people – recent customers are the BBC who were filming orcas. Meredith has a craft shop (*Latitude 57*) and an obvious flair for making and selling things: arts that she is training her boys in. They come and go, as do a mixture of friends. It is a fun and lively household and doesn't feel at all like a lost outpost.

I head out for a stroll and get rained on.

Later I attend a birthday gathering where I meet Rob's Mum and other family members. They are welcoming and unassuming. To my surprise they know some other contacts of mine on this coast. They also know and have helped other adventurers. I become aware that although northwest Scotland is geographically big, in terms of community it is a more connected world than I had imagined.

Day 57 - 2ⁿᵈ August

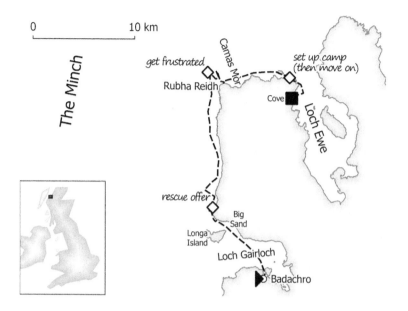

I leave early, supplies augmented by a square foot of Meredith's calorie packed Rocky Road crunch bar.

The lightest of airs take me across Loch Gairloch, then between Longa Island and Big Sand. Beyond here the wind dies completely. With the sea like a mirror I lay the sail in the water and rest on the board. A couple of hours later a gentle northerly breeze fills in. Enough to resume progress tacking upwind.

I haven't got far when a small fishing boat motors over. A serious expression asks me if I am the windsurfer in difficulty. This requires some thinking. I cast my mind back to the people I'd seen on the beach at Big Sand bay. I remember being told that a few years ago 4 people lost their lives there in a canoeing accident, an event that traumatised the community. I begin to see how my resting whilst drifting on the tide could have been misinterpreted as being in distress.

I concede that - although I am not in difficulty - in the absence of there being any other windsurfer in difficulty, then it is likely that I am the windsurfer who Stornaway coastguard are looking for.

The crew of the boat use their VHF radio to bring up Stornaway coastguard, who seem content to have the situation resolved. I receive a minor telling off for not having my own handheld VHF turned on. Fair point, particularly when it isn't obvious that I am OK.

I generally keep my electronic gear turned off to save battery. I don't want to appear argumentative though, so don't explain this. I also do get into the habit of using the VHF more – the shipping and inshore waters forecasts make me feel less alone.

I am alone now on the long upwind slog to Rubha Reidh: the next - and a significant - headland. It doesn't look bad on the approach, so I ride the back eddy to the tip hoping that guile or board speed will see me past.

I try for an hour without success. All strategies result in zero or negative progress. Offshore I am swept away down tide. Inshore there is no wind next to the steep cliffs. The sea state is uncomfortable. After a while I just want to be on land. I get pissed off and lose my rag, venting my frustrations at this fucking headland.

It is a rare and brief outburst. I am tired and had become inward focussed on the discomfort of the current situation. This is a puzzle to be solved, not cried over. I investigate around the rocks in an area of dead current by the lighthouse. With difficulty I could get ashore here, but everything tells me it's a terrible place to stop.

I remind myself to play the long game. Tidal cycles are only 6 and a bit hours. Something will change.

It does. Wind? Tide? Both maybe. Anyway, I slip past the headland.

Camas Mòr - a spectacular beach I know from a long-ago but memorable holiday walk - that I had been excited to be returning to, but now just want behind me, surrenders too.

Next is the entrance to Loch Ewe. A few miles in there is a settlement with a pub.

The ebb is now flowing out of the mouth of the Loch. When the wind drops again to practically nothing I can barely beat the current so give in and look for a camp spot. Truly I have had enough today. Anywhere will do.

An awkward landing later I attempt setting up camp. Water wells around my every step on the waterlogged grass. Sheep dung and undoubtedly ticks abound. There's not even a stick to prop the sail with. I set off inland in search of road but find none.

Without doubt this is my worst campsite yet. When I see a puff of breeze on the water I undo it all and head back out to fight the current into Loch Ewe.

With pub coordinates in GPS I make it halfway before the wind dies once again. At this rate of progress it will be dark before I make the watering hole. But the distance I've made has given me an alternative option. Directly downwind is a small settlement of a few houses.

I land at the tiny harbour and contentedly survey surroundings.

A quad bike thrashes down the hill, at each bend using only half its compliment of wheels. Good brakes stop the machine a few metres from the unexpected obstruction that is my board and sail. The young driver - orange hair and orange chest height waders - wears an expression of having confronted alien life.

We strike up a question and answer. Where have I come from? Where am I staying? What do I eat? I reply with my by now well practiced answers, and am in fact very happy with my options now. *Staying over there. Under my sail. Eating rehydrated rice.* I can see that the lad wants to help out but is not yet independent himself and can't quite work out how.

Then he has a light bulb moment. With eyes wide open and nodding head urging an affirmative reply, "do you want a lobster?"

I am genuinely moved by the offer, but decline on grounds of practicality. The mental image of lobster in my tiny cooking pot is humorous. I chat some more with Jamie before he goes off to a stack of creels and I, contented, to a grassy knoll that looks perfect for camping. I like Cove.

I'm setting up camp when Hamish ambles over. He and partner Nicky have a cottage here and I am offered an upgrade to solid roof accommodation.

I don't jump to accept. Part of me feels that I should be roughing it more. I am also tired and really just want to rest. But another part knows that *where I need support* I should accept it with the good grace with which it is offered. To do otherwise would be churlish. And from a more selfish perspective it leaves me in better shape to start each day, increasing my chances of expedition success.

I pack up my things for a second time and head to the cottage. Nicky - unassuming and calm - transforms my boring rice into something really quite delicious. Hamish is of Northern Irish descent and characteristically warm and sharing. They are sailors and divers. We talk of the tides, and I hear a scary personal tale of their being swept from a dive boat near Rubha Reidh.

Good fortune landed me at Cove

Day 58 - 3rd August

The forecast is for a lot of wind. Somewhat irritatingly though it is a nice day. Were it not for Hamish repeatedly pulling up wind forecasts maps on his tablet, gleefully pointing at the red bits and telling me I'd be mad to go, I would feel an obligation to sail. Hamish and Nicky say I am welcome until the bad weather passes through.

I decide that the least I can do is make myself slightly useful. My offer of help is accepted and the lawn round the cottage receives a decent trim.

With low tide approaching we head down to the harbour. There is a community project underway to extend the slipway. Another Hamish is orchestrating the effort. Machinery is rolling about and swinging round. A pair of wellies, and the occasional shout of "mind your back!" have health and safety covered. The need for manual labour is limited, but I like to think that my contribution is at least not detrimental.

Unfortunately, the last load of cement is contaminated with what looks like animal dung. Project manager Hamish takes this quite personally.

A second misfortune is when volunteer Geoff slices his hand on a tractor bonnet. The lumpy slipway section seems less important after this. It will soon be covered with seaweed anyway.

In the evening I go fishing with Jamie and a few other Cove locals. A glorious sunset in a disturbed sky tells of weather to come. Safe - a fish I had been unfamiliar with - are the major catch. We land a few mackerel too. Jamie is catching to bait his creels, the rest of us for our dinner. I take some mackerel home. They taste almost as good as if I'd caught them myself.

Day 59 - 4th August

The Loch is covered white with cresting wavelets this morning. Beautiful windsurfing conditions for a small board and sail, but unsailable for me. I am glad. Decision to stay put vindicated.

Hamish is keen to drum me up more support in the area and has arranged for a live interview on Two Lochs radio, in Gairloch. Sitting in comfortable car seats currently rates high up my list of pleasurable things to do, so being chauffeured there and back is fine by me.

Two Lochs is a one woman show. Since it is live, when you are off, you really are off: pointed towards the door, literally. The good news is that after you are off you can head to the pub.

Hamish picks up some supplies on our day trip, then we head back to Cove.

Later on there are drinks with friends of Hamish and Nicky. I have surely met almost everyone in this tiny hamlet now. Cove attracts those who seek remoteness. Our host, like a number of the folk in these parts, has a forces background. I enjoy our conversation. Unlike the majority of people to whom I explain my journey, he doesn't ask *why* I am windsurfing round Britain. I imagine that like me he just considers it a pretty reasonable thing to do.

Later still we call in to see Geoff. His hand is stitched and thankfully there has been no nerve damage. The whiskys flow and I join my companions in a dram or two.

Day 60 - 5th August

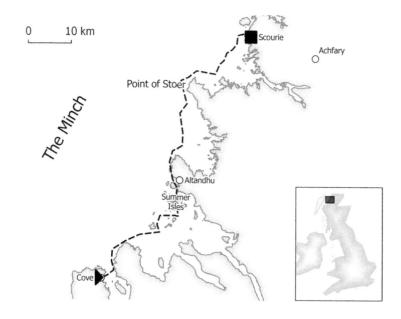

It is with some trepidation that I set out this morning. Away from the shelter of the land a solid force 5 puts me distinctly on the limit for downwind sailing. Misty rain compromises visibility as I head across Loch Ewe and then out into the open waters of The Minch. My immediate target is the refuge of the Summer Isles, 25km distant.

The isolation adds to the exhilaration. It is truly just me. I tuck up small to show as little of the sail to the wind as possible, and navigate myself into a position upwind of land, in case of breakage. The second half of the passage is rock strewn. The larger rocks are steep sided: islands really. Chop hits into their windward faces and splashes in all directions. The smaller rocks lurk around or just below sea level and reveal themselves only at the last moment.

The more densely packed Summer Isles have a calming effect on the wind and waves. I stop briefly on one to examine the offering of flowers on its lush thatch of vegetation. Fittingly, the sun threatens to break through.

Back in touch with the mainland I pass Altandhu. The place name sounds fantastical. I take advantage of sheltered water behind an off-lying island for an early lunch stop. Seals lazily investigate the transparent waters, their dark bodies contrasting with white sand.

Pushing north again. In more exposed waters conditions are now ideal. Planing, picking a line through the swells, fleece hat pulled over my ears to calm the constant whistle of wind. Objective: north.

I stay offshore and sail in bold broad reaches towards Point of Stoer, cutting off another huge swathe of deserted northwest coast. I feel immensely privileged. Many times on this trip I have been called an explorer but today I feel like one. I think of the other round Britain windsurfers - pioneer Batstone and record chasers Cooper and Russel. They weren't alone, and I can't help but think they missed out. I think of the now deceased solo windsurfer Arnaud de Rosnay.[4] I know that this experience is unique, and doubt there will be other moments in my life that match it.

Approaching the headland a strengthening wind requires tighter reaches to minimise the likelihood of nose-diving the board into swells. All the time I am analysing risk, but my mind is free and without fear. Another 25km is ticked off.

I have grown in confidence, enough to stop in the choppy waters off Point of Stoer. I want to take in the panorama of natural beauty around me. The sea is dark and empty, being chased northwards by the weather approaching from behind. Beyond the lighthouse a rock stack climbs out of the sea. Around my head a Great Skua adjusts on the stiff breeze. An attack seems imminent. I dissuade its approaches with a waving arm.

I finish passing the headland and this time follow the coastline inshore. Less wind. Less sea. Less exposure. A fishing boat: first of the day. Tiredness begins to catch up with me.

---

[4] French windsurfer adventurer who completed many solo crossings. He died in 1984 attempting to cross from China to Taiwan.

GPS points me to the small town of Scourie. From Google Earth I know it has good landing options. The coastline downwind is rocky, barren and steep. Without my waypoint I would never find the inlet.

A small open boat bobs around just outside the entrance. The two occupants are pulling mackerel out of the sea almost continually. Around a hook of rock I find the bay. An easy landing and dry land are welcome. There is a campsite too. That most likely means there will be somewhere to buy food nearby.

My instinct to push further north needs to be tempered by an analysis of where I am, and of the forecast for lighter winds towards the evening. I coach myself to be ambitious but not greedy, and settle for reaching here today.

I am not expecting support, but it arrives. Richard - a friend of *Viking Renewables* Richard – lives and works on the Reay Forest Estate, half an hour away into the hills. Richard had mentioned that his pal might help out, but I hadn't really considered this as anything more than chat.

After a beer at Scourie campsite we drive through the hills to the hamlet. Achfary is tiny, and surely as remote as anywhere on the UK mainland. The nearest supermarket - Inverness - is a 120-mile round trip. Misty cloud hangs in the valleys. The midges are ferocious.

I'm curious about Richard. To live out here is quite an extreme lifestyle choice. We talk a bit over a few beers. Richard is a pretty good cook and knocks up a filling dinner. Maybe there are a few similarities between us. But I'm not quite sure.

Day 61 - 6th August

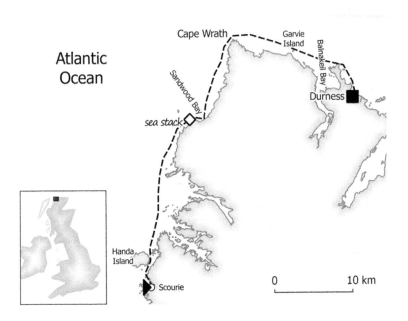

I am in a good place mentally as I prepare for heading round Cape Wrath. It hardly seems possible that I am within touching distance of the northwest corner. By focusing on a day at a time, and - some days - on hours at a time, great leaps of progress are unexpectedly realised.

We get going before the day does, driving through mist to Scourie. The rhythmic clunk of windscreen wipers fill gaps in conversation. I bid Richard farewell, then take shelter in a convenient bird hide that overlooks the beach.

Before Cape Wrath is the famously beautiful Sandwood Bay. I plan to stop there before pushing round the corner. On the north coast of the headland are the highest sea cliffs in Britain, rising to 281m. The high ground to an extent creates its own weather. Sometimes the MOD fire out to sea, but not today, thankfully.

The Inshore Waters Forecast is for wind from the south, with mentions of force 5 in the Cape Wrath area. Swell should be

Breakfast in Scourie bird hide

slight. I don't know quite what to expect from the headland but have a strong conviction that today is the day to find out.

The rain eases. I purchase mosquito net and fresh GPS batteries from Scourie's filling station store.

The sky clears and I head out. Handa Island flattens the water and is soon bathed in bright sunshine. Scotland has pulled its familiar trick of turning grimness into outstanding beauty. Cape Wrath no longer seems threatening and I enjoy the morning's push north.

A huge sea stack rises from the sea off the headland that forms the southern boundary of Sandwood Bay. I pass close by the base on the gently heaving sea, craning my head back, jaw agog. The Jenga-esque masterpiece is silhouetted against a bright blue sky.

Sandwood Bay is indeed beautiful. Periodic pulses of North Atlantic swell break upon the shoreline. I glide over clear turquoise waters - Mediterranean hues - but with a winter freshness and a cleanliness more southern waters do not know. I

Sandwood Bay sea stack

beach behind some rocks. Before lunch is unpacked the sky is again overcast.

I delay restart to time arrival at Cape Wrath with a slack tide. Sailing up to the headland is almost trivially easy. In the gullies that punctuate the cliff line I spot hundreds if not thousands of fishing buoys. Washed up there never to be collected.

I pass the lighthouse close enough so that all but the tip is obscured by cliff. It is slightly too easy, but grey and ominous.

Now on the north coast I proceed in an easterly direction.

Sea cliffs rise vertically out of the water. Wind rolls over them and plummets into the void below, creating an unsailable mix of gusts and lulls within a mile of land. I am forced offshore, where ferocious gusts test my arms' resolve and the integrity of my gear. It is a very exposed position. Any problem and I would quickly be pushed by tide and wind into remotest north Atlantic.

The next miles are a battle. I seem to be going fast – the board charges through the water - but I am slow relative to land. The current is far stronger than the tidal atlas had suggested. Time too passes quickly. Absolute concentration on the task at hand.

As the cliffs start to descend I adjust my line to come in closer to land. The tide tears past an isolated rock - subsequently identified as Garvie Island, and of note for being a target of live firing by NATO jets.

I cross Balnakeil Bay and round the next headland. The final upwind legs before making land are through a maze of rocks. I'm so tired and accustomed to the fierce gusts that I almost forget the wind is still unpleasantly offshore and the exposure level unrecommendable. I consider continuing, but instead come to my senses. The landing on Durness beach is gentle and easy. A number of tourists witness my arrival without obvious interest. I look round to the calm water off the beach. To a casual observer there is little of interest out there – no evident challenge.

I, however, am in no doubt about the significance of today. A major objective has been achieved. I am past Cape Wrath and in at a place of safety. Again, there is the sense of satisfaction at having knocked off a difficult bit. A satisfaction tinged with sobriety though - the sailing today *was tough*. I now want off this exposed north coast, before bad weather pins me here.

I haul my kit halfway up some cliff steps to a hollow in the grass. That will do for sleeping, and will provide a nice view in the morning. Dinner is a private affair at the Sango Sands Oasis: Guinness with fish and chips.

Day 62 - 7th August

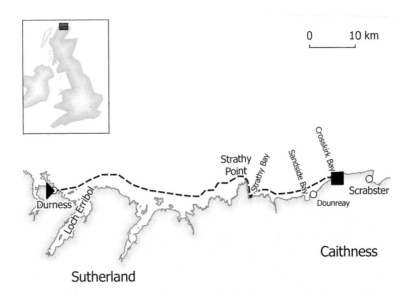

I start sailing mid-morning. Conditions are similar to yesterday. A south-westerly wind funnels out of Loch Erribol. I cut a scallop-shaped course across the mouth to reduce exposure. Then high sea cliffs rise vertically and I am forced far offshore in search of stable breeze.

It is a lonely sea out here. The sailing provides a drip feed of adrenaline to my system. I'm not searching for that, but do enjoy the way it focuses my mind.

There is not a leg of my journey where I have increased risk for the sake of excitement, yet I am reliably branded a daredevil, thrill-seeker or similar in the press reports that have followed me. The clichéd labelling does not fit with the image I have of myself. I consider myself risk averse. My decisions are guided by a desire to bring nearer completion of my goal in a way that minimises risk. The gambles I take are rationally calculated rather than daring.

But I do also derive great satisfaction from what might be termed a sail-it-as-you-see-it approach. How far offshore to sail? Where to gybe? Reading the water for rocks, currents, and wind. It is totally absorbing sailing in conditions like these, and I have confidence in my ability to read the risks I face.

No, I would not choose to put myself in a compromised position. But I am a willing participant in this physical and tactical battle with sea and weather. And I do relish - thrive on - the sensations it brings. There is a thrill from the risk, but I do not seek the risk in the first place. And here I am, solo windsurfing Britain with no backup - so neither can I really claim to be risk averse. Maybe risk tolerant fits better. Or boredom intolerant. Does that make me a thrill-seeker? I am not so sure now. The press labels may have some truth – but to paint me as borderline-kamikaze is clearly wrong too.

Maybe the problem is labels. At best they only capture half-truths.

Further east the land becomes more low-lying. The wind moderates and I am able to sail further inshore. Soon there is barely any breeze. A sloppy sea remains and makes balance difficult. I wobble downwind, discomfort having replaced menace as feature of the day.

Relief comes in the lee of Strathy Point. Flat water and a gentle wind acceleration over the headland allow me to coast into the stunning Strathy Bay. I realise that this is a beach I know from a road trip to the north coast with Clyde and Gregg, many years previous. We'd marvelled then at the beauty of this place and I am similarly in awe now.

The crispness of colour gets me most. A horizontal brushstroke of sand dissolves into a turquoise and then dark-denim sea. Above, there is a fade of greens, then dune grasses that shimmer silver in the breeze, and then more lush green that forms a sharp undulating horizon against an intensely blue sky.

I haul my equipment above the high tide line and then scramble up the dunes to a churchyard overlooking the bay. Amongst the grasses are hidden wildflowers of all colours. Nature *always* gets colours right.

I have ten minutes to myself before I am joined by my Dad –
Andy - and his partner Nadia, who have taken this opportunity to
make a pilgrimage north.

We hug, have lunch, and take pictures. I take delivery of an old
phone that will be of more use than my current model – a poorly
suited last minute choice that now has a broken screen. Good
riddance. Andy also hands over paper photocopies of the tidal
atlas pages from Reeds Nautical Almanac. A4 paper does not go
wrong or object to rough treatment. Sometimes, the old ways are
best.

I am happy that my journey has brought Andy and Nadia to this
special part of the world.

* * *

Out to sea I observe a pleasant sailing breeze and my imperative
to push on resurfaces. The north-east corner of Scotland is on my
mind: the Pentland Firth. The waters of the Pentland are the ones
that my imaginings most feared at the beginning of this adventure.
The tides here are exceptionally strong, 12 knots on springs and
in some weather conditions 16 knots have been recorded. Weather
conditions now are good and the tides are relatively small. This is
a good opportunity and I am anxious to be in position for a
rounding as soon as possible.

I feel a little bit conflicted. Andy and Nadia having made the
long journey north and almost immediately I am heading back out
on to the water. I rationalise the snub: realise that it is in my mind
only. They too realise that the north coast is an exposed place, and
would not want to hinder progress in any way.

My target is Scrabster. The last of the tide carries me east, out
of mountainous Sutherland and into the much flatter Caithness
region. I'm in a hurry, pumping the sail to catch free rides on the
waves. Sandside Bay is registered as a potential stopping option -
the wind is already failing. The large white dome of Dounreay
nuclear power station passes more slowly. I'd have no qualms
about stopping here, but the coastline is inhospitable to landing.

The tide sets against me. It will gather strength now until after
dark. The wind fades to nothing - that looks like it for the day. I

need a landing spot and want to avoid a retreat on the tide to Sandside Bay; these miles have been hard earned...

Two-hundred metres ahead there appears to be a north-south running inward fold between fields. The elongated dip suggests a stream and therefore possible landing site. The coastline itself reveals nothing at this distance. It rarely does. I push to within fifty metres. When the angle is just right I can see in. Stream water pours over seaweed covered boulders. It is still an awkward spot, but a precious find indeed. The gulley has a small wave on its point - too tiny to surf today but surely known by local surfers. I let a micro-swell carry me past the point, close enough to the breaking section to tell myself that I have surfed a Caithness reef.

I have landed at Crosskirk Bay. The land bordering the stream - technically a river and with abundant fresh water - is secluded, grassy, flat, and comes with enviable views. A stick sail prop is easy to find. It is my best camping spot of the expedition, evidence to me of the value of doing something different - of being curious.

I am tired. After phoning Andy and hearing that they are in a B&B some distance away we decide to meet up again tomorrow morning.

A rare treat of tinned macaroni cheese is dinner, and reduces my barrel weight by a full half kilo. I watch for the splashes as seals hunt salmon, and at some point fall asleep.

Day 63 - 8th August

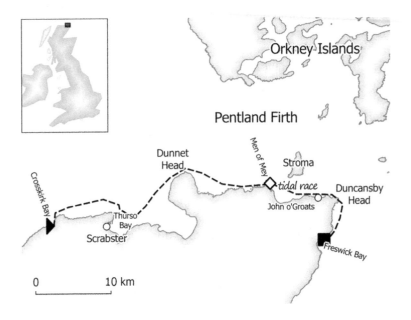

High tide today, for Scrabster, is around 4:30pm. My plan is to take the last of the east-going flood through the Pentland Firth, and round Duncansby head when the tide is slack. I don't want to arrive late - as once the current switches it may be too strong to sail against; but equally I don't want to catch the Pentland too early, when it will be in full flow, potentially with severe overfalls.

The schedule means that this morning can be enjoyed. I watch the occasionally leaping salmon some more over breakfast. Andy and Nadia arrive. They bring a local area Ordnance Survey map, which allows me to better study the section of coastline I will later sail.

I brew coffee and we take a short stroll to investigate the ruins of a nearby chapel. Nerves catch up with me. I doubt my calculation that there is time to spare, declaring that it is time I was gone. I run back to my board in mild panic.

On the water I make reassuringly good time to Thurso Bay. Now concerned I may be ahead of schedule, I double back towards a fishing boat. Here is an opportunity to run by my plan with people who should know what they are talking about.

The boat turns out to be a fishing *trip* boat with a dozen rod-dangling punters. The skipper emerges from the wheelhouse. He seems authentic, and considers my plan. I await his opinion whilst fishing rods play up and down.

To the collective relief of all present he thinks I should be OK. But he is concerned that I'm already late to make it through today.

The analysis buoys my confidence. And I know I am faster than he thinks. Suddenly I am up for it. Fuck this waiting for slack tide business. I just want to get through ASAP. Now on a mission, I sail north-west, my sights on Dunnet Head.

The headland is the most northerly point of mainland Britain. I pass close by impressively vertical cliffs, slightly revelling in my newfound daring. I am now in the Pentland Firth.

Beyond the lee of Dunnet the current makes itself felt. I harden up to get closer to land. The sail has a reassuringly solid pull. I stay close in and sail towards the gap between Stroma Island and the mainland.

There is a strong current now that is picking up pace all the time. The constriction - smooth from a distance - now churns with white water. My preferred tactic would be to stay close in, but the Men of Mey headland is strewn with outlying rocks, making that unviable - the current that rips past could pin me on the jagged reef.

I back off the power but barely slow down. White water now stretches across the entire channel. It is slightly surreal to be sailing at what looks like a line of barely submerged rocks. Six weeks ago I'd have been scared, but a lot has happened since then. I stick to my line and am ready to plough through.

With slightly alarming speed the water state becomes altogether more violent. Waves break in strange ways all around me. There is too much to take in so I focus on ahead. I am also bombarded by noise. The background din of rushing water on all sides. I barely hear my board as it thumps through the confusion of waves.

Then it is gone. I look back and already it seems small and insignificant. The water now is flat. I head upwind to get near shore again. GPS records an unlikely speed over ground of 15 knots - fifty percent or faster than I would expect for the conditions. I pass John o'Groats and am soon approaching Duncansby Head – Britain's north-east corner.

The approach of higher ground forces me further offshore until I am East of Duncansby. I am now in the North Sea. I delay my tack, wanting to easily clear rather than scrape past the headland. Current continues to smash the board through the waves with unusual aggression. When I do tack my angle takes me almost parallel to the coast. There is good puff. I pass Duncansby head for a second time. This time I take a hand off the boom to pump a clenched fist. I bare the whites of my teeth and let out a battle cry of approval.

Real victory lies 5km south of here. When I tuck into Freswick Bay to consolidate the day's sailing, I have really made it to the East Coast.

* * *

There is a tiny harbour on the north side of the bay, in the well-tended grounds of a commandingly positioned house. I am granted permission to leave my board here. The owner – Mrs Brown, a Christian name is not volunteered - explains that this is the old Pilot's House. The Pilot would have kept watch for ships coming from the south, and intercepted these to guide them through the Pentland Firth. This fortuitous – or maybe inevitable, for where else would I stop? - connection with journeying seafarers from the past sets my imagination on the run, and moves me to tears.

I return to the North coast as a tourist tonight. Andy and Nadia have booked me a hotel room. I enjoy a hot bath and then fall asleep watching Match of the Day.

Passing Duncansby Head and now into the North Sea heading south

Day 64 - 9th August

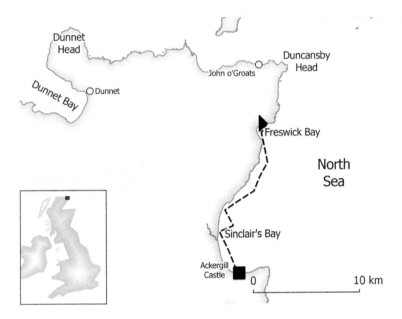

After breakfast Andy and I go to the village of Dunnet. There is a road sign there that Gregg and I once 'corrected' by the addition of a second T. Andy and I recreate the photograph from 1999. This time my finger forms the upright of the T but it is Andy's finger that forms the horizontal. It seems like an important thing to do.

Andy and Nadia are heading south later, or to an airport, I'm not really sure and neither are they. By lunchtime their travel plans are still refusing to resolve. They are stressed and the day is in danger of turning sour.

I surprise myself with my calmness and ability to steer the day round. I buy a few provisions for a picnic they haven't yet agreed to, and we drive to Dunnet Bay for a lunch they don't yet know they want. I brew coffee despite Andy's assertion that my camp stove won't work in this wind.

It is a fantastically sunny and brisk day, and we are connected with it now. Dunnet beach is flat and wide. We paddle barefoot in 3 inches of cold and clear water that the breeze whips up around our ankles.

Before I am dropped off at Freswick Bay we do the tourist trail.

John o'Groats has good ice-cream. It isn't quite as far north as Dunnet Head, but it is the farthest away habited place from Land's End on the British mainland. It spells itself "John 'o", which isn't the Essex spelling. Must be Gaelic or Norse or something.

Next stop is Duncansby Head. I could wander the grassy clifftops here for hours: admiring the stacks, observing the currents. Walking is so pleasurable and free of fear. I am happy to have had the opportunity to revisit where I sailed.

I wave Andy and Nadia off late afternoon. I decide to sail: conditions and coastline are easy and more distance from the Pentland will be a comfort.

I tack upwind for a couple of hours and make it as far as Sinclair's Bay. Now 20km from Duncansby Head I am confident that whatever happens I won't accidentally get swept back round.

The landing and the camping here are both very comfortable. The long twilight silhouettes Ackergill Castle against a spectacular sky.

Day 65 - 10th August

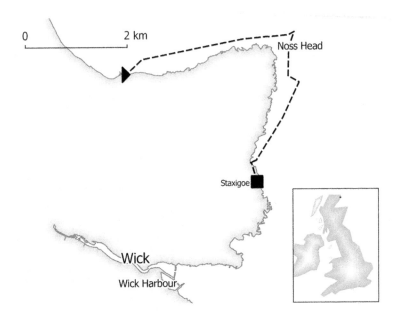

I nearly lose my fleecy hat today. Panic! It is like a talisman for me. A walk of the shoreline rescues the hat, and the beginning of my day.

The sailing day starts with light winds and a gentle drift out to Noss Head. At the lighthouse the current checks my progress, and I must pump to win distance. If I stop for a breather I go backwards. After two hours I am past the headland, but have had enough of this game. I put into the first nook between rocks that offers a landing option.

I am thinking *food*. The town of Wick is a walkable distance but first I must reach a road. I bushwhack my way up a steep bank that is thick with thistles, nettles and brambles.

On the road to Wick - with red and stinging legs - I see that I would have had a much better landing option just 300 metres further on.

It rains in Wick. In fact, it chucks it down. I head to an empty harbour, where I can keep an eye on the wind. I install myself in the Harbour Cafe for an All Day Breakfast.

Displayed in the cafe are fascinating photographs that show Wick when the herring trade was booming. Many hundreds of sail powered fishing vessels fill the port and there is activity everywhere. Barrels full of fish are stacked sometimes a dozen high. The pictures astonish me, and I am also surprised to find myself interested in something which is undeniably *history*.

I can't make my breakfast last all day. Instead I call Jan - a Local Contact here who is family of friends from way back. I could do with some company and a cup of tea would be nice.

The rain stops and I call by. Jan is very easy going. After a tea she drives me back to the nearest access to my board. There is wind on the water now and I feel I should use it.

I suit up but do not like nor trust the wind I see. Also, beyond Wick I have not established good stopping options. When I realise that I have left my sun visor in Jan's car, I take it as a sign that I should rein in my ambitions for progress today.

In strong winds I sail 300m up the coast to the better landing site at the hamlet of Staxigoe. By the time I am back at Jan's house there is not a breath of wind. I have the opportunity to check Google Earth for landing sites south of Wick, and see that there would have been none – really, nothing - for at least 20km.

There are further downpours and an impressive electrical storm that evening.

Day 66 - 11th August

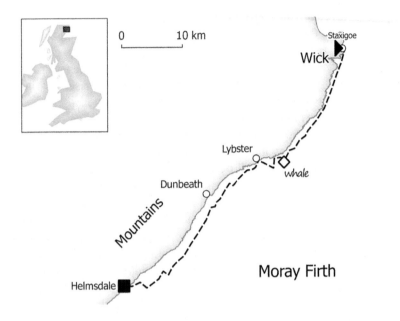

I set sail at 8:30am, attempting for a second time to get past Wick and off this long stretch of cliff-lined coast. There is an angled headwind but conditions are otherwise favourable. Pushing a bit further south feels good. I make good speed until the wind swings more squarely on the nose and then fades.

Past a small headland what I take to be a whale makes leisurely progress in the opposite direction. It is bigger, and breaks the surface - rotates forward - and slides out of view much more slowly than the dolphins I have seen. The movement is strikingly serene. A lifetime's practice of controlling the breath must help.

The low cliffs are continuous. They have few features, aside from the occasional stream where brown water tumbles into the sea. The air near the waterfalls has a curious taste of salt and peat.

After three hours I reach Lybster, a narrow inlet. I am lucky - on a rougher day it would be a difficult place to stop. The Heritage Centre meets my needs for caffeine and calories.

Curiosity is also satisfied: I read more about the herring trade that was once so important to this area; and possibly identify my whale as not a whale but rather a Risso's dolphin. But now - at the time of writing this and after extensive whale ID research, I am in fact sure it was a small minke. 50 percent sure.

It doesn't look windy out to sea. But there is the odd beach further on, so I head back out with the intention of reaching a less hostile coastline by end of day.

It is slow to Dunbeath, where there are stretches of sand. Beyond here mountains slope down into the sea. There is a bit of wind coming off the hills so I continue.

It is a good decision. Despite the poor forecast I benefit from a decent force four, and make good distance deeper into the Moray Firth. After another five hours of tacking upwind I reach the town of Helmsdale. The coastline here is more open, a welcoming boulder strewn shore rather than cliff. I am tired but very pleased with progress.

There is perfectly flat grass to camp on. A Local Contact in the area has also tipped me off about a good chippy. I locate the garishly decorated La Mirage restaurant. The *fish supper – large*, is excellent. Not a mushy pea is wasted.

Day 67 - 12th August

Close inshore is dead calm. Far out into the Moray Firth perhaps there is a fickle breeze at times, but the direction couldn't be worse, and I am not tempted out. From Helmsdale to the south side of the Firth is about 50km, a significant enough crossing to warrant waiting for good puff.

It is a glorious day and I allow myself to enjoy the return of summer.

With a lap or two of Helmsdale village under my belt I stroll to the harbour. I recognise a man who has just parked up and whose dogs are tying him in knots with their leads. Alan and I know each other quite but not very well, from occasionally crossing paths these last few years. He has tracked me here and come to offer practical support and words of encouragement. We take the dogs for a walk and have a brew-up back at my board. I appreciate Alan's visit.

After another lap of the town I rest in the sunshine on the old bridge over the river. I've barely got uncomfortable before my anonymity is blown once again.

"You must be the windsurfer!" says a voice extravagant with enthusiasm. I give it some thought, check for other candidates, then accept that this seems likely.

The lady on the bridge introduces herself as Jeanetta and offers me a place to stay and a meal, if I would like one. I initially decline. I haven't done anything today to earn hospitality, and neither do I require it here. But I'm realising that this is a narrow and isolationist point of view. I should welcome the opportunity to interact just because interacting is nice.

So I head back with Jeanetta to what she describes as a bothy, where I also meet Corrine. They are both so much more interesting than my bridge.

The bothy is a few miles up the glen, set back from the river Helmsdale. When I am near the sea the issue of progress nags at me. The river and the hills are a welcome change and an opportunity to properly relax.

The bothy is constructed of corrugated iron, but this is no cowshed. Masses of hard work and artistic talent have created something special. Outside it just fits. The painted panels sit with the surroundings as naturally as trees. Inside is antique but not stuffy. It doesn't hugely surprise me when leafing through the Bothy-refit Scrapbook to see it featured in pages pulled from House and Garden magazine.

We walk the dogs along the river before dinner. At risk of offending Mum and late grandmothers, this is probably the best roast chicken with trimmings I've ever tasted. Jeanetta has a rare talent for combining things, whatever the medium.

A short while later I enjoy a bath in my antique chic bathroom and then retire to bed. A tough life, that of the expedition windsurfer.

Day 68 - 13th August

Breakfast is so good I wonder how I'll cope when back on my standard Cuppa Porridge fare. I am then dropped off back in Helmsdale, neatly slotted into the run for the morning papers. I say goodbye to Jeanetta – mistakenly anticipating that today I will make progress.

The sea in the Firth is mill pond smooth. Force zero: calm; sea like a mirror; smoke rises vertically. The Beaufort scale describes it well.

Early mornings are often like this and sooner or later the sun's warmth usually injects some movement into the air. But today that doesn't happen. Instead there is a rare full day of *morning glass*.

I add two more laps of Helmsdale to my tally, inspect preparations for the weekend's Highland Games, hunt wildlife with my camera, and generally have quite a nice day. I decide to fend for myself this evening, so head to the village store to buy supplies.

Before turning to matters culinary it's time to catch up on voice notes. These are recordings I make for every day to help with subsequent recall of details of the expedition. Some people have suggested I write a book. I doubt I will - I'd not have much interesting to say - but I would like to remember the expedition for me. I sit on a rock that looks out to sea and tell myself about the last few days.

There are dog walkers around here. I am a couple of hundred metres away from my board. That's too far to save my dinner from the errant Labrador I now notice rooting through my things. The Labrador has the owner well trained and she stays well clear until the food is mostly gone. I tell the lady not to worry – her hound has had a balanced meal, and I quite fancy chips again anyway.

So I end up back at La Mirage. Polishing off the *Fish Supper - Large* is more challenging today. Either I'm not so hungry, or the locals here get bigger portions.

Calm in the Moray Firth

Day 69 - 14th August

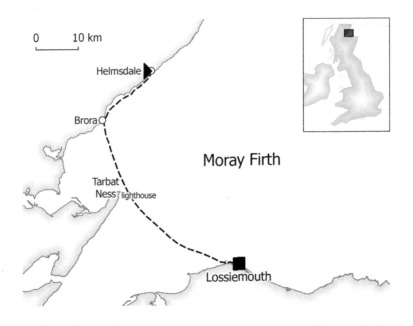

Back to it today.

My plan is to head deeper into the Moray Firth, where it is narrower. Here, and depending upon conditions, I will either cross to the other side, or I will cross as far as Tarbat Ness – a conveniently located tonsil of land deep in the throat of the Firth, or I will postpone for another day.

It takes minimal effort to reach the town of Brora. Conditions are good – a following breeze that seems reliable. Tarbat Ness lighthouse looks almost close and the angle is favourable.

I make a quick stop to double check forecasts and strategy. A hurried cheese sandwich completes crossing preparations and puts real food in my stomach before the drip feed of Snickers bars that will follow. Minutes later the last of the incoming tide carries me towards Tarbat Ness. If my timing is right, then once past the lighthouse and closing on the south side of the firth I will also benefit from an eastbound outgoing tide.

It goes remarkably to plan. I sail a broad reach towards the lighthouse reaching Tarbat Ness in about 90 minutes. That's about one-third crossing distance. Level with the peninsula I change angle to point at the nearest land on the south side on the Firth. The tighter heading means I can hook in. I make good speed and as land slowly comes nearer I tighten up further still, to make more distance east. I briefly ponder the lost social opportunities of doing this: I'm now jumping past Local Contact Scottish John - who I know, and Beverley from Findhorn - who I don't. Contacts Eilidh and Alan have already been skipped.

It's easy to underestimate the distance to land. Seeing it and getting there are very different things. I remind myself that I am still a long way out, a long way north, in a summer of most unsettled weather, and that I am still a long way from finishing.

I refocus. The current pushes me into the wind, which helps add more power to the sail, which in turn helps me keep the board up on its edge and cutting efficiently through the choppy sea.

I see lots of dolphins. There's something reassuring and pleasantly distracting about seeing dolphins. For a few minutes they help you forget about your aching neck and the seam of your fleece that is trapped by your harness and pressing hard into your side.

I get in touch of land and tack upwind a few miles before the breeze goes light. A long sandy beach precedes Lossiemouth. I stop on the wet sand to rest my backpack-sore shoulders. It is also an opportunity to consult with Gregg over where to head for. A sailing club just before the harbour sounds a good plan.

Another mile to go. Periodic and well-spaced bumps of swell are starting to arrive. They lift me up and settle me down as I glide over the reef and sand seabed. The water is beautifully clear.

Before I have pulled my gear out of the shallow water I know I've been tracked down. *Who is it on the beach waiting? Which Local Contact?* Embarrassing not to know. The man seems familiar in some way.

I need to hear his voice for the penny to drop, then break into a grin of recognition. I know Jim from Minorca Sailing and fun times windsurfing – we'll call it coaching – with him in Fornells Bay. I'm touched to hear he's been following progress. Before retirement Jim flew in the RAF from Lossiemouth. He and his wife Katie know the area well and are back holidaying. There is a spare bed that I am welcome to use.

Before that though there is tea and cake in the cafe. The friendly cafe owners make some calls and link me up with Steve - who has keys to the sailing club. Steve comes down and he too is strangely familiar but I can't quite place him either. It turns out Steve instructed in Minorca a decade or so back. Since then he's rowed the Atlantic, cycled through Indonesia and now operates an instructor training business.

Jim and Katie look after me well. Rain comes down that evening - pretty torrential – and I am glad to have a roof and warm bed.

Day 70 - 15ᵗʰ August

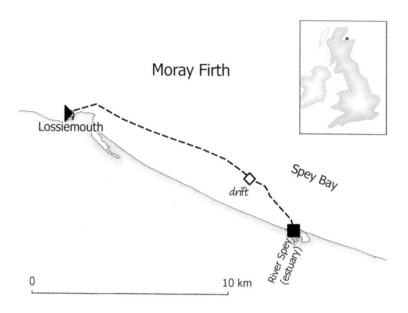

It rains less hard through breakfast and on the drive back to Lossie. Jim stops the car above the river mouth and we look out over the sea and along the coast. Good quality surfing waves break onto the sandy beach that stretches east. The lunging waves leave behind a trail of spray in the still air.

Jim and Katie are off to bag a Munroe. I take shelter in yesterday's cafe and the day gradually improves. A plate of chips – house compliments – arrives. Aperitif to coffee and carrot cake. A welcome breeze fills in. I am keen to be off.

Protected by the harbour, the high tide launch here is relatively uncomplicated. I sail past the protective wall at a prudent distance, observing the waves crashing into the barrier and over the rocks upon which it is built. An identified safe landing is 20km ahead.

238

Lossiemouth surf

The discomfort of sailing downwind in light airs and in swell is something I am accustomed to now. With some justification I might even claim it as a speciality.

Initially, progress is acceptable, but after only a few miles the wind switches off and in these conditions that means you can't sail. Even holding the sail up is a pointless exercise in rapid exhaustion. I sit on my board and observe progress by GPS. A fraction of a knot - the outgoing tide. Very soon I am feeling quite seasick.

I know I've just got to sit it out. The situation will change eventually.

I am here a while. Big fat raindrops come and go, as do curious seals. A steady stream of gannets adjust their flight paths to pass directly overhead.

The tide brings me nearer to a rivermouth. It seems likely that there may be the possibility of getting in through the waves here. Churning stomach and the arrival of a hint of breeze are encouragement to try.

The waves around the rivermouth are in fact small and fun. The swell has also dropped off and probably low tide has flattened the sea out too. A wave picks me up for a tame ride in to the shingle shore.

This is Spey Bay. This part of Britain's coastline is all new to me, but I like it here. Sailors rarely mention the east coast, and in the various round Britain accounts I have read it receives quite cursory treatment, but here at least it is stunning. The Moray Firth had always sounded a rather grim place to me – ugly like the eel that shares its name. How wrong I'd been.

The river that gives Speyside its name is small and picturesque. In its final curves before meeting the sea, ducks and waders go about their business, and sea eagles survey for pickings from above.

Rain is on the way again. I erect my sail on the pebbles to take shelter from the downpour. A rainbow forms. One end embeds itself into a spit at the rivermouth. Where the colours fall birds become busy, as if thrown to wing by a colossal force, or prospecting the riches to be had.

It is a typically Scottish day: mostly grey and shitty, redeemed by a few minutes of spirit-lifting spectacular.

Under the sail, mine are now the only dry pebbles on the beach. I'm comfortable and peaceful here so don't bother to search out a pub. A couscous meal does for dinner, and sleep comes before dark.

Day 71 - 16th August

Moray Firth

Conditions are tranquil when I set off this morning – flat water and a light but slowly filling breeze. A couple of hours upwind sailing gets me to just past Buckie, where I take advantage of a conveniently located beach café. Two bacon rolls, a cappuccino, and toilet visit later I sail off into the distance.

With their easy parking, food, and conveniences: beach cafés really are the motorway services of the long distance windsurfer.

I enjoy the next few miles on this surprisingly busy section of coastline. A few small cruising boats from local harbours sail towards Cullen Bay. Now round the corner we all have a gentle following breeze and sunshine. One sailing boat – no cabin, not much more than a dinghy – is sailed by a very elderly couple. I remember them because they look so happy. It's rare to see that sort of contentedness and I smile to think of them now.

The town of Cullen sits on the left of a sweeping bay and is backed by rolling hills that are spanned by an arched viaduct. It's very pretty and today the town has bunting up and is busy with people. The festival is their Harbour Day. 2015 will go down as a good year I think. From a distance I catch the end of the lifeboat display and the start of the rowing skiff race. I don't have a programme slot though, and don't want to gate-crash, so sail on - leaving the town to their day.

As I leave the bay some dolphins pass me on their way in. They are close by, occasionally breach, and are big. Bottlenose dolphins. Bucking the usual trend, I manage to get a picture.

The coastline is indented and interesting and I sail onto Portsoy in high spirits. Here I have a contact, but - despite it looking like an interesting place - it is still too early in the day to put my feet up. Instead I push on towards Banff. Now tacking upwind again in a wind that can't make up its mind.

I stay offshore and when the wind shifts am in a position to benefit, more or less heading seaward of the next headland. Banff passes at some distance to leeward. I am encouraged by good progress. The day is getting on and I am wondering how ambitious to be when I get a phone call. Unusually – for it is a day of unusuallys – I hear it *and* manage to answer.

It is Rob at the other end. I know Rob from Minorca. His wife – Lynne – worked at the sailing centre before my time and they then sailed around the world - having two children on the way - before settling in Scotland. I've windsurfed with them on a few occasions. Their technique is similar to that of other ocean-hardened windsurfers I know: accomplished, and based on an excess of power.

Rob is majorly enthusiastic and supportive of my expedition and very keen to help. I'm equally keen to link up. I mention that I might try to reach Pennan today and Rob takes it as a definite. Rob and son Danny are heading back from some camping in the highlands and we'll meet up later. Decision made to push on, I push on.

The late afternoon breeze falters on the approach to Troup head, and I am getting tired. It has been easy sailing today and as a result I have been sloppy with my eating – insufficient Snickers bars have been consumed for so many hours on the water. My limbs are OK, but my brain is slow.

The fin of my board has caught a bin liner. That's bad luck. Seaweed I can usually reverse out of but the bin liner has just become more entangled. I need to stop to clear it by hand.

I lay the sail down, kneel on the board, and am immediately side-tracked by the need to have a pee. I operate the drysuit's 'relief zipper'. The subsequent relief is considerable. Then I remember why I'd knelt down in the first place.

I shift my weight on the board – rearward, towards the fin. The black bag is nearly within range but when I stretch further my rucksack topples forward over my right ear, causing the tail of the board to sink too deep, and me to lose my balance. I fall in head first in a roly-poly type movement, which is stupid enough. More stupid though is doing this with the 'relief zipper' still wide open. Cold North Sea rushes in around my nether regions.

I'm quickly back on board and zipped up, the consequences are no worse than a bit of cold, but I take it as a lesson against complacency.

What feels like the day's last gasp of wind gets me to Troup Head, and a truly magnificent spectacle. Thousands of Gannets are on the cliffs. The white birds take every available space. Hundreds more birds are still on the wing and these circle or hang on the wind above my sail. They are graceful, silent and curious. I tilt my head back to gawp at birds as they glide in all directions at different airspace levels. The scene is a kind of avian Battle of Britain. A soundtrack of propeller powered engines would work well here.

The final 2km to Pennan is an upwind struggle against an adverse strengthening tide. The cliffs block the wind, which is only dispensed in meagre and occasional puffs. Finally, I escape the pull of the current.

I'd wanted to stop here since learning back on the west coast that Pennan is where a significant proportion of the movie Local Hero was filmed. I was probably primary school age when I first saw the film. Mark Knopflers instrumental soundtrack score "Wild Theme | Going Home" has been playing in my head for days.

It's quite emotional to actually make it here. The tiny village is a short row of houses, one of which has the word Hotel painted on the roof. The steep cliffs allow no back gardens so out front are washing lines for drying clothes. There is a red phone box. Above the roof line an impossibly steep single-track road curves around until out of view. It is exactly as in the film and every bit as pretty.

I see Rob and Danny on the also ridiculously pretty beach, and slowly glide in over clear water and fronds of kelp. We beam smiles as we shake hands, and Rob's warm words and enthusiasm spill out everywhere.

The Hotel is open, good news for all of us who are keen to eat. Rob heads off to check they'll keep the kitchen open, whilst Danny helps me stow board and sail out of reach of the tide. A few minutes later Rob returns.

"My treat and the menu looks great, and they've given you a room for the night."

We all knew they hadn't.

***

It's a nice hotel too, and the Thai Green curry is memorably good.

After dinner Rob and Danny drive south to reunite with the family at home, near Stonehaven. I am left in no doubt that I am very welcome to stop by when I reach there, and I know already that I will.

I tread the soft carpeted stairs to my room, humbled by my good fortune and by Rob's kindness – which today stands for the kindness of all those who have helped me on this journey.

Day 72 – 17th August

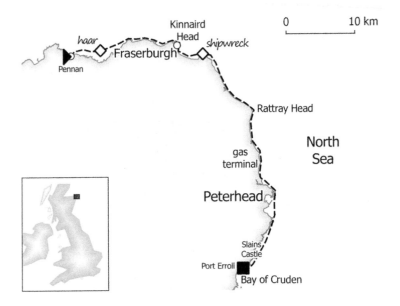

I've been sporting the Robinson Crusoe look for a while now, but maintaining that doesn't really seem honest given my regular access to comforts. The beard goes.

Fried breakfast for breakfast and then toast and coffee. I stock up on a few sachets of marmalade before thanking the proprietors and checking out. It's a beautifully sunny day. I wander around this bizarrely picturesque hamlet and don't want to set sail, because that will be this experience over. When I do sail away, it feels like closing a chapter.

I have a confidence sailing now. The cliffs are stunning and beautiful rather than intimidating. I'm pleased to like this coastline so much. It seems to me that – in writing, in the way people speak - the East Coast gets a raw deal compared to the West. That seems an injustice. Perhaps the East Coast is just shier. I try to take pictures of the sculpted crags, but with the sun behind nothing good comes out, supporting the conjecture.

I part from the cliffs, staying offshore for a direct route to the next outcrop instead of following the convex coastline. Ahead, the line between sky and sea is painted wrong – too close. It gets increasingly wrong until there can no longer be any doubt that a wall of fog is rolling in. Now closer it moves fast. It consumes the land where my board is headed. A shore based wind turbine I'd been navigating by is next to disappear.

This is haar – a sea fog that affects these north-east coasts. It forms when a sea breeze sets up that deposits warm air from the land over cold sea. The haar then travels in from the sea to complete the cycle.

I doublecheck that GPS is pointing me in a sensible direction, and check handheld compass for agreement, before entering the whiteout.

The fog is cold and visibility is minimal: metres, just a few waves ahead. I regularly check compass and GPS - wary of any undetected change in wind direction that could put me off course. And I listen intently. I want to get in close proximity to the coastline – get in closer than other craft will be. I think that will be safest. Better to take my chances with rocks than marine traffic. I'm lucky that there isn't any swell today.

A shadow emerges from the white. Land: a shoreline of jagged inlets. A left turn to continue the silent progress: listening, checking water depth. Right a bit when the shadow of land fades or is lost; left a bit when rocks complicate passage. I am lucky too that the water is so clear. All the time: scanning for shadows.

Navigation by depth takes me past a few harbours, identifiable as such by fog-shrouded protective walls that suddenly loom dark and high. I know that eventually I will find a bigger harbour – Fraserburgh – and that just beyond there will be beach.

Engine sounds arrives from an indistinct direction. A helicopter? Oil rig transport, maybe.

A kink in the coastline with a lighthouse and fog horn – Kinnaird Head, I can later confirm. And now a harbour wall. Shadows of an industrial scale fishing fleet extend above from the other side: this is Fraserburgh. I follow the wall to an opening. A huge trawler materialises out of the fog, inbound. I hang back

The haar rolls in: a few minutes later visibility was practically zero

until it has passed through and then hurriedly pump my way to the other side of the gap.

The next wall leads to calmer water, bends round and then is gone. Ahead of me now is a long expanse of sand, and a haar that is less thick. There is also a beach café.

Bacon sandwich in hand I consult the map. From Fraserburgh descends a line of yellow. Beaches - heading south - for miles. Good. Simple. Simple is good. I feel mentally tired, like having just finished an exam, and enjoy the release from effort.

* * *

Progress is made a few metres from the beach – or beaches. The boundaries between them are unclear or easily missed, but visibility is no longer problematic. Sand stretches away into the middle distance ahead and behind. Close in I escape the pull of the tide.

Fraserburgh wreck

A shape ahead turns into a shipwreck. Cormorants take flight from the decaying vessel as the tide whips me over the suddenly alarmingly shallow reef upon which it foundered.

A small swell rolls onto the beach. I position the board just beyond reach of the teetering wave crests. Playing with the waves is fun and keeps me alert. Aside from the tufts of marram grass that top the dunes, there is just sand. It is like sailing the edge of a desert.

Rattray Head is a rare feature. The lighthouse sits a few hundred metres offshore upon a round base that must itself sit upon a skerry. Some miles further on the tide rips past another reef. My passing scatters thousands of seabirds and dozens of seals.

Further south, appearing in the valleys between dunes, flames leap from the flare stacks of an oil refinery.

Eventually the beaches come to an end. I land on the last bit of sand for a progress review and cheese sarnie.

Ahead is Peterhead, the eastern-most point in mainland Scotland, and a difficult place to get past in the wrong weather by some accounts.[5] I have a contact here who has kindly offered advice and support. His sign-up message stuck in my mind – something about Rattray Head and that I *will* struggle in this area. The message was welcome and well meaning, but the definitive tone I took as a challenge. It made me want to prove my contact wrong.

So I sail at Peterhead with particular focus and just slightly narrowed eyes. Once engaged, I am engrossed in the challenge. There are strong currents but there is good wind too. Multiple headlands, islands and shipping must be negotiated. I sail it as I see it, creeping up behind rocks in weaker currents and back eddies, punching across the main flow between islands and the mainland. I hugely enjoy the sail and feel no tiredness despite the physical effort. A few hours pass in minutes.

The coastline is jagged cliff now. Peterhead retreats into the distance although the poor landing options mean it isn't quite beat. The board powers along – borderline planning and surfing down waves – but the current pulls relentlessly and checks progress. Eventually fatigue sets in. Beyond Slains Castle, backlit by a low sun, wind and tide start to run out of steam too. I reach and pull in to the smoother waters of the Bay of Cruden.

* * *

The sail provides shelter from the drizzle. I'm not expecting any help here, but am located by Rob, his daughter Megan and her friend Lauren. This is a different Rob to yesterday. He runs a kids' windsurfing club – the Sea Gorrilaz - in Newburgh, a few miles further down the coast. I choose to abandon my gear for the evening and accept the warm shower, cool beer, and hot chilli-con-carne that Rob and his wife Wendy have on offer. An easy decision.

I meet more Sea Gorrilaz, and am shown their sailing location in the muddy reaches of the River Ythan. Rob and the kids are enthusiastic about windsurfing and have been following my trip,

---

[5] My pre-expedition research revealed that Richard Cooper (windsurfer), Fran Gifford (Wayfarer) both had problems getting past Peterhead on their round Britain journeys.

Slains Castle

even planning their own expeditions. I am struck by the basic set up of the club and the sense of community around it. I imagine the kids having fun in their river, and perhaps sailing local beaches when they are bigger. I'm in no doubt that their experiences will help them develop into nice and well-rounded people. The few words I write here don't do justice to the value of what Rob makes happen.

Day 73 – 18th August

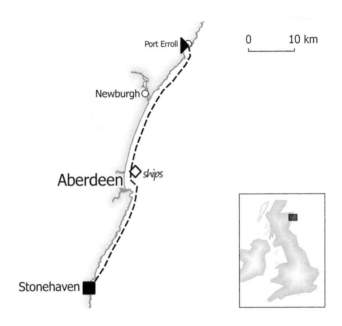

Fresh fruit on my porridge is a treat this morning. Rob drops me off at Port Errol on his way to work.

It's been raining all night and is still raining now. I suit-up in the public toilets. No point getting wet needlessly. Back at the harbour I glumly survey the scene. Swell rolling into the bay, further out the open sea is rough and intimidating. Grimy viz. Wind from the north-east, strong enough to concentrate the mind.

I tighten the barrel's straps just a little more than normal, add an extra securing knot, triple check everything. Pump chest. Exhale. *Let's do this!*

Swells roll underneath the board. At the corner of the bay rocks snare them and turn the sea white. Near the cliffs the sea state is ugly and confused and the proximity to danger is unnerving. I sail further out. The swells here are more clearly defined.

The sailing is complicated but rewarding. Memorable, in fact. I experiment with different techniques. Mast track back is sometimes good, but generally is too fast - too often I outrun the wind and lose power, or crash into the wave in front, or both. It uses too much energy.

I work out that it is best to stay in sync with the waves, to surf them for longer and link them together. I sail out of the harness. When I have a wave I dump the sail's power and just surf – five seconds, ten seconds - until I'm ready to jump to the next one. The linked up ride is continuous. I move my weight to gently carve left or right for the best line.

The nose does sometimes bury, but there isn't the brutal deceleration of a normal board, the extra weight from the barrel pushes it through like a torpedo, and more often than not we resurface dripping but intact.

The coastline soon changes to beach, a long beach that runs all the way to Aberdeen. The sea state is transformed. Beach allows waves that reach to shore to properly expire, to dissipate their energy rather than reflect it back out to sea. The wind also comes slightly from the land. Between the waves now it is flat. Cleaner.

Sailing normally now, I position myself further inshore to catch the fast moving swell lines, riding them each for hundreds of metres at a time.

I am getting tired and take a fall on the approaches to Aberdeen. A good time for a Snickers bar break and situation review. A beach landing looks nasty. Sailing into the major port at Aberdeen would be an option, but does not appeal. Out to sea dozens of ships that service the oil industry point their bows shoreward. Free parking for them out here, and for me too. The day is still misty. I'm not sure whether this is drizzle or rain, but the freshwater rinse is not unpleasant.

Beyond Aberdeen the coastline reverts to cliff, but conditions now are less testing. The next 25km to Stonehaven take just 90 minutes.

Lynne and Rob – that's Rob from Pennan – sail dinghies from Stonehaven and we've prearranged to meet at their club, inside the harbour. The bay and harbour entrance have a lively sea when

Parked-up ships off Aberdeen

I arrive. Lynne is there on the harbour wall. She offers directions and cautions about a rock that sometimes becomes exposed with the rise and fall of the sea. To be honest, this is child's play. Compared to this morning – a few rocks... a few waves... No bother.

But it is *great* to see Lynne. We stow my kit and head back to their house. I feel at home and at ease. It feels, like with the Bournemouth and North Devon pit-stops, as if I am with family.

* * *

Tomorrow's forecast is for big swell and no wind. I have no appetite to sail this coastline in those conditions and decide early on to extend my open ended invitation an extra day.

Rain beats down overnight.

Day 74 – 19th August

It is a productive day-and-a-half off. The mast track has another service to restore some ease of use, camp stove - bent during a fitful night's sleep – is repaired, pictures and voice notes are backed up, replacement gas is purchased, leaky dry-bags are repaired. Rob and Lynne donate supplies of Cuppa Porridge and Snickers.

Gul have sent ahead a replacement pair of wetsuit boots. My existing boots, that were new in North Devon, have worn through. They leave my feet unprotected, and the North Sea that continually circulates around my toes, even in August, is surprisingly cold. I ceremoniously dump the old pair.

Lynne assumes responsibility for my neglected PR duties, and arranges an appearance on Scottish TV. The piece is filmed as a combined feature with 'fellow adventurer' - kayaker Nick Ray.

I'd been vaguely aware of Nick's challenge to paddle to every RNLI station in Scotland. By unlikely coincidence we are *both* in Stonehaven on the day I finally google him.

Together we float around on the swells by the harbour wall, before landing and each saying a few words for the camera.

Job done, Nick suggests we go for a pint. I'd been thinking that too. *The Ship* has a good selection of draught beers. Predictably, we both go for *Wanderlust*. It's pretty good.

Talking with Nick is interesting. In the eyes of many people I am an adventurer. So what are adventurers like? I want to compare notes. I ask Nick if he is enjoying his adventure and he replies without hesitation that he has loved every day of it. That surprises me – I couldn't claim that - I know how much I struggled early on. There have been so many amazing moments but also the worry and fear of compromised situations. For me, at least early on, I can't even claim to have *enjoyed* the experience, the mental side has been too tough. I hint at my mental struggles and am relieved that Nick relates to these too. Perhaps Nick is a more experienced adventurer. It occurs to me that at the beginning of my trip I was not an adventurer - but that now I may well be, and am certainly a changed man. I am better equipped to deal with fear now – it takes less time to process a fearful day into an amazing day.

I conclude that our experiences are not so different.

There is none of the brash adventurer about Nick. He is self-effacing about his achievement so far and seems to consider it to be less significant than my own. It isn't, of course, and it saddens me to hear this. We each take on the challenges we think we can complete. Scale of achievement relates to personal difficulty to the individual rather than miles covered or any other arbitrary measure of impressiveness.

Back home, mutual friends and Minorca Sailing connections call by. We enjoy a relaxed beer and pose for a timed photograph. Left to right: Hamish, Katie, Danny, Lynne, Rob, Shona, John, and myself. Missing from the group photo is Shona and John's daughter - another Katie - who is out in Menorca, doing my old job.

We talk about adventurers. Shona contrasts me favourably with Richard Branson, which is nice.

* * *

I've enjoyed this time with Lynne and Rob. It can take a while to be sure that people you meet in a work setting, or friends of friends, are really your friends too. I'm there now. I was too guarded before, and sometimes missed seeing deeper.

I come to understand that we now share what might be called an *adventurers' bond*. There is a commonality of experience, an appreciation that we are *of the same clan*, with a shared familiarity of *exposure*: that excitement difficult to discern from fear. Rob and Lynne miss that – tell me they miss that, though I sense it first. They miss what I am experiencing: the thrill, the fear, the intensity.

I also learn that Lynne has a lasting bond with Menorca as I do. The pre- round Britain me never engaged enough to discover that.

Chatting with expedition kayaker Nick Ray, suited up for the BBC Scotland cameras. Photo: Rob Skinner

Day 75 – 20th August

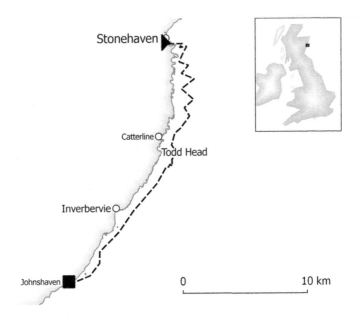

On the drive down to Stonehaven harbour I receive a call from a journalist. Nothing particularly unusual about that, but this one is uniquely hilarious and wacky. I give her a few soundbites about the expedition; she is generous with enthusiasm and offers a place to stay at her farm somewhere I've not heard of. It probably won't happen. I archive the bizarre conversation.

Lynne and I survey the sea state. The swell is much smaller and there is a superimposed choppiness that suggests a wind that is not really there. "Looks alright," we both say. I don't think that, and guess that Lynne is probably kidding herself too.

I head out and the wind is indeed *supremely* shite. It takes a long time to get past the headland of the bay. The sloppy sea stops the board dead, pitches it, knocks it off course. Progress is a painful one mile per hour.

After three hours I do have an option to end the misery - Catterline bay – but heading towards the cliffy inlet looks even more unpleasant than life out here. Even if I make it in how will I get back out? I procrastinate long enough to miss the turning.

A small beach by Todd Head is another non-viable option. I attempt to pass the headland, where – remarkably - conditions manage to deteriorate. Now there is not a breath of wind. The slop is more boisterous and random. Balance is near impossible - I can't string together more than a few exhausting seconds with the sail raised.

I sit down, hoping to be swept forward or back, anywhere other than here, but that doesn't happen. The waves and current have me pinned here off the headland. I try again to sail forward – hopeless. I try back towards Catterline – also hopeless.

There is a veil of harr that sits inland and has the day paralysed. I call Gregg to complain about the conditions. He checks online and tells me I have 12 knots of breeze! To that I avoid a *complete* sense of humour failure. Just.

I study the lighthouse that sits upon the headland. The owners are signed up as Local Contacts. I had been excited about the prospect of stopping here. Perhaps they can see me now.

It is uncomfortable out here, but that is not worrying. Worrying is the thought that I might be stuck until nightfall. And worrying is the thought that I might have to make a decision to accept or refuse rescue. Rescue would feel like failure. Refusing rescue - depending upon the circumstances - might be a very selfish choice. It is a decision I don't want to have to make.

But I'm not too worried. I know now that *the bad times pass.* They always do. Either conditions change, or we adapt to them. The brain isn't wired to do bad times indefinitely.

So its grim for a while but then the harr just goes, and behind it comes a wind: the 12 knots Gregg had told me about. From dead in the water to punching through the waves in a matter of minutes. I clear the headland and continue south.

Now I have wind I don't want to waste it, despite there being a risk the harr could return. I could, but don't, stop at Inverbervie – the now less hostile looking shoreline justification for this decision. But the good breeze doesn't last, and a few miles further on I am struggling once again.

My phone rings. I'm better at answering it now.

"Wow, you've made good progress!" Although, obviously, I haven't. "Are you stopping for a cup of tea at Johnshaven?" It is Turid, that wacky journalist from earlier.

From my point of view a landing doesn't look possible, but Turid says there is a harbour.

"I can get in?! Brilliant! Of course I'm stopping!"

"Great, see you in ten minutes!"

"Mmm. There's no wind, I'll be forty-five."

How kind that the wind switched off again right *here* - to deposit me right at the front door of Johnshaven. Fate shouldn't be argued with.

The entrance to the harbour is tiny, and rock strewn. Turid is on the harbour wall. I know it's Turid: the slightly crazy dress, actress pose… It all fits.

It doesn't take long to establish that we get on well. That I will be staying is assumed. We dump my gear in Turid's Mum's front garden, and head to the farm. Camilo and Pierre are lodgers helping out, so I meet them too, but soon we are off again. Spanish Camilo is Montrose Football Club's latest free transfer and is training that afternoon. It seems as good a place as any to be interviewed, so Turid grabs her notebook and we head to the stands.

Turid is a true professional. She softens me up with a few rounds of hangman and makes insightful comments about the talent on the pitch. We have each other in stitches. I haven't laughed so much since an unexpected carrot reference caught me off guard last year. We head back, detouring via the pub. My stomach-muscles are cramping.

The farm has an outdoor hot tub, actually the ex-Edinburgh zoo penguin pool. Pierre is charged with getting the wood-fuelled boiler going. Turid knocks up some vegetable-flavoured water. I compensate with a brace of emergency Snickers bars. We drink a reasonable quantity of red wine. That loosens up the stomach muscles.

Sometime after midnight we head to the hot tub, slip off our robes and slide in to the… freezing water. The moral of that tale: never trust a Frenchman with your hot tub.

Newshound Turid (second left) and team Johnshaven

Day 76 – 21st August

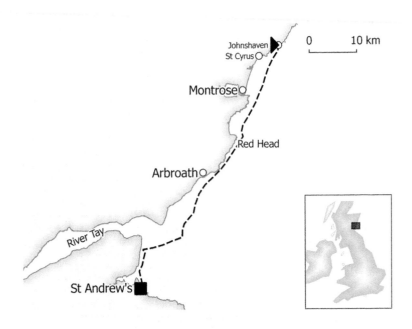

A small entourage sees me off from Johnshaven - Turid's Mum and a sailing couple originally from Essex swell the numbers. These are very warm people and I miss them even before I have set sail.

It is a choppy sea today. I sail out of the comically small opening to the harbour, and set the board up on the rail in upwind mode. In theory the wind is dead against me today, but I find myself able to sail parallel to the coast or better. I enjoy cheating the weather. Soon I am far off land again. I am happy to be back in my own company too.

A lifeboat passes me far out to sea. It has bunting flying. I recognise it as the Shannon Class boat for the Montrose station – Turid is due a ride later as she has to write a piece on it for the *Montrose Review*. I expect the prose will benefit from Turid's mastery of nautical terminology and double entendre. Montrose is slightly lacking in news according to Turid – the big scandal this year is that a topless sunbather was spotted on St Cyrus beach. Gasp!

I have to put a tack in to get past Red Head, but other than that make Arbroath in one.

The wind does shift now, and I need to sail zigzags to get past the Tay estuary. The Tay is a big river with strong currents, and sandbanks that stretch a good few miles out to sea. I stay offshore and pick my way through the outer banks, tacking to avoid the shallowest parts where waves are breaking.

Getting past the river takes longer than I anticipate and I am keen to get to land. Sloppy preparation means that I have run out of water, and I have a particularly dry throat. It may not be a coincidence that yesterday was one of the few days I've broken my unofficial three-unit alcohol limit.

When I do reach land it is a long sandy beach backed with pine forest. No fresh water nearby. Bread recharges batteries without dehydrating too much, and I head out for the final 9km to St Andrews. It's howling windy this bit. I keep my tacks short to minimise exposure in the now cross-offshore wind.

Pleased with progress, but tired, I call it a day at the home of golf.

I receive a call from the Dundee Courier, they ask a few standard questions and ask me to stay put for their photographer, who is on his way. Steve – when he arrives – sets me up on the beach under my sail, propped up by a stick, with the town of St Andrews in the background. Straight away we both know he's got a great shot. It is the shot on the cover of this book.

Lots of people have said I should write a book. I never thought I had a book in me, and never thought enough would happen to warrant a book in any case. But now I am coming round to the idea. I guess that I am allowing myself to think that I will finish the expedition, and that allows me to think of what happens next.

Day 77 – 22nd August

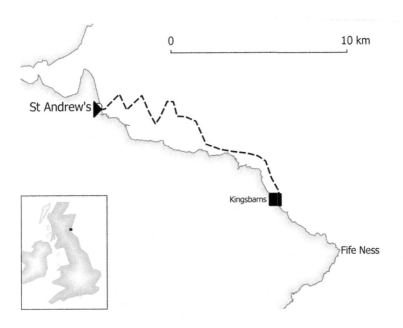

A slow day today. There is no wind early on and not much more later. Late morning there is sufficient to move, but with the direction unfavourable I make just 8km for four hours sailing. Vertical smoke from distant chimney stacks confirms that it is a fairly hopeless day for sailing.

A small beach a few miles short of Fife Ness offers a welcome landing opportunity. Families make the most of the nice weather: kids exploring the gullies, bigger kids on canoes. A picnicking dentist stops for a chat and then returns with a donation of *Rocky Road*. Very tasty and sugary. Definitely a Scottish dentist. An apple would be nice too.

The sea is now mirror flat again. I look ahead to tomorrow and the crossing of the Firth of Forth. This is a good setting off point, but the wind is forecast strong. I plan an unusually early start to hopefully blast my way across before the day gets too lively.

This is posh golf course country and there is a links behind the beach. In the absence of handy sticks I borrow a rake from a bunker to prop my sail.

Towards evening a group of campers show up. One mega-tent, supplies for a week, alcohol for two more. They are an agreeable bunch and invite me over for a beer around the camp fire. A torrential but short-lived thunderstorm temporarily relocates us to beneath their tent's awning. Better here than under my sail.

Later, with the camp fire resuscitated, some revellers stumble over. The pair are on a first date, we hear, a few times. A few times more than is necessary, from her. He appears to have lost most of his clothes. She isn't wearing much either, though possibly she started out that way. They are looking for some drugs or the sea. We point them in the direction of the latter. You meet all sorts on Kingsnorth Beach.

I retire when the inevitable whisky comes out. Early start tomorrow. I'm pleased to have a good excuse to get away. I would never say I *enjoy* parties, even beach parties. They are like visits to the dentist. I go because I know I should. There is sweet relief at being back under my sail. Ordeal over.

Day 78 – 23rd August

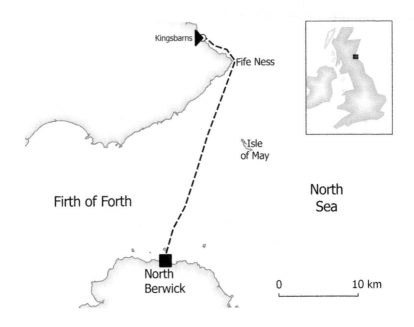

Kingsbarns

Fife Ness

Isle of May

Firth of Forth

North Sea

North Berwick

0   10 km

    I am breakfasted and sailing by 6:30am. It is a blustery morning. A day when I do well to remind myself of John's advice about being bold. When you go – go with decision.

    It is dead upwind to the headland at Fife Ness. This is the way to wake up! Facefuls of spray and biceps straining to keep the sail in trim. I shift harness lines and hands further back on the boom to match the pull of the fully tensioned sail, and find an equilibrium of sorts.

    Past the choppy headland waters I change to reaching mode. The angle is good for a fast sail across the Firth of Forth. Ahead starts as empty horizon. Behind, the headland recedes. The swells out here are cleaner and the wind a little less strong. Conditions couldn't be better.

    I'm not fussy where I will make landfall. The same as for every day, priority is just to make land somewhere. But I have Contacts in North Berwick, and the angle is good for there. Initially I sail to a bearing, but soon there are islands of land to aim at.

The 25km crossing takes just one hour. By 8.00am I am cruising into the sheltered and very picturesque North Berwick Bay. I'm pleased at how I sailed that. And although it seems slightly ridiculous to be hanging up my harness for the day before most people are out and about, I know that consolidating here makes sense. The wind will be in stronger later.

My Contact Fiona and toddler Duncan find me on the beach. I know her and partner Paul (aka Morph) from instructing days. They are members of the East Lothian Yacht Club and I am able to use the very convenient and civilised facilities.

A nice surprise is bumping in to Tim and Rhona, who I had stayed with on the south coast. They are visiting Rhona's mum who is local, and with some help from the tracker we have coincided. We go for a coffee. I'm so chuffed they detoured to say hello. By the time we finish coffee the wind is fully in – a solid force 6 in the Firth.

That gives me a free rest of day. Turid and co. are in Edinburgh today at the Festival. Not really my thing but what the hell, I decide to jump on the train to go see them.

Scotland's capital is hot and busy. I find the Johnshaven group on The Meadows. Most people aren't doing much but fortunately Turid is hyperactive and takes Camillo and I off to see some challenging art. For Turid, art should provoke: not for her a vase of tulips. Most provocative are the human abattoir photographic prints. Turid is so refreshing, she doesn't just get stuck on the "yuk, disgusting".

Culturally enriched, we grab a take-out curry – vegetarian - and then depart our separate ways. I'm pleased to be leaving the city. Pleased I went too, but a few hours is enough for me.

I meet up with Fiona and Paul back at their place. The forecast is for quite a bit of swell and zero wind tomorrow. Paul has the day off so we hatch a plan to go surfing.

Day 79 – 24th August

Paul lends me a wetsuit and surfboard and we head east in search of waves. I enjoy the drive, and the opportunity to get a visual on the coast to be sailed.

After checking a few points and beaches we suit-up at Pease Bay. I am shocked at how cold the water is. After my third duck dive the wetsuit hood goes up to prevent ice-cream headache. I rarely fall-in when sailing, and when I do am out of the water pretty soon, or so amped on adrenaline that I don't notice the cold. I am not very amped up for the surfing, feel the cold, and don't last long.

There is no doubt that the water on the northern east coast is *much* colder than the water anywhere on the west.

Maybe I'm just slightly under the weather. I can't shift the feeling of cold, so spend the afternoon in bed, curled up in a ball under the duvet.

A few hours later, Paul is in the garden playing with Duncan. He's a nice dad. Duncan's got a good start.

I take an evening stroll up Berwick Law - an isolated crag behind the town. A whale jawbone sculpture at the top is easily outdone by a dramatic sunset that goes on for hours. It's very calming. I leave descent until near dark.

It is a good day for reflection. If tomorrow goes well, I could end up in England. I have an awareness that my journey – a journey that I only ever imagined as having a beginning – is drawing to an end.

Day 80 – 25th August

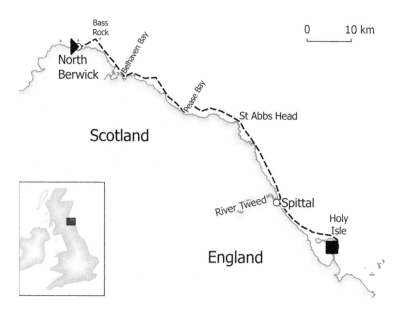

It is a bright and breezy start to the day. Once on the water I need to crank on maximum downhaul to fully depower the sail. I haul the tension on with *Jee-sus - here we go again* resignation. This act is always performed with a mental crossing of fingers that the mast won't snap.

The broad reaching is quick and bumpy. Close in the water is flatter, but the gusts fiercer. When they hit, a surge of power accelerates the board further downwind.

Sailing on the margins of control is like playing Russian Roulette. I could hit a dozy seal, plastic bag, submerged log, or some other flotsam. A miscalculation or bad luck would take me out in spectacular style. And visibility for hazards is poor. My eyes are being bounced around their sockets and jet-washed with salt spray.

I stop in the waters off Bass Rock to take photographs. The rock has been described as one of the wildlife wonders of the world

Sailing past Bass Rock. The white flecks that cover the rock and fill the sky are gannets. Photo: Paul Rigg

and is inhabited by the world's largest northern gannet colony. Birds cover the rock and fill the skies. It is an amazing sight.

My pictures come out reasonably, but a real bonus are the ones that Paul sends later. He has driven down the coast and caught me as I sail under Bass Rock's vertical walls. I am dwarfed. A blip. An incredibly privileged blip.

I anticipate less wind as the coast bends round, and in the meantime try to be gentle on the gear. Even so, I hit what must be the fastest speeds of the expedition. In the flatter water of Belhaven Bay, probably around 25 knots.

Somewhere past Torness Nuclear Power Station, over the course of a mile, the wind moderates from a gusting 6 to a patchy 3. The stress of sailing on the edge is lifted from sailor and equipment.

I put my nose in at Pease Bay and eat lunch afloat. Land on three sides keeps the sea flat. The cheese and ham rolls Paul prepared at breakfast make a good picnic. The sea glistens as if in reward for this morning's job well done.

Non-planing progress along a spectacular coastline then delivers me to St Abbs Head - which is wobbly and difficult to photograph, but not a real challenge. South of here the sea is flat

An alternative angle on Bass Rock. My sail is just visible below the
vertical cliff. Photo: Paul Rigg

and progress genuinely smooth. Twenty kilometres later I cross
the mouth of the River Tweed, and land on English beach at
Spittal.

At the beach café services I have mixed emotions. Sadness at
leaving a Scotland that seemed like it would go on forever.
Incredulity at how far I have come. And fond memories of sailing
here with friends on a wet New Year's Day a few years previous.

Part of me wants to slow down, extend the expedition. But I
know that would be artificial, and greedy. I should sail the
distance it feels right to sail. Today that means I should keep on
going. This is a simple approach and easy to live by. I take
whatever distance comes – there is no too much or too little – I
don't push for miles that aren't there, nor do I pass up those that
are graciously offered. The same applies to any help that comes
my way.

On a more practical note, I know that my gear is getting old and
tired - sooner or later breakages will occur. My task is to occupy
myself with the expedition in hand. Consolidate what I set out to
achieve. I am happy living the life of a nomad windsurfer, but
thoughts of continuing south – to Minorca maybe – are easily
quashed.

A kind onlooker makes a donation to the pancreatic cancer charity. Hearing her accent is a shock. The people here are - without doubt - English. This happens some days: you start off one place, and end up landing into a different dialect.

I push out through the small waves and continue south.

A beach gets wider and wider until it could pass as a desert. It is slightly other worldly sailing along here. The superstructure of a wreck buried in the sand, and the remnants of a washing line style fish trap, are the only features on the flat expanse.

My target for the evening is Holy Isle. There being no water for the inshore passage I sail round the east side, to the squelchy mud of the harbour.

Given its remote location the island is busy with people. Many stride purposely to take in sights before the tide cuts off the island's connection to the mainland, and the visitors' exit. By evening the atmosphere is different – relaxed and peaceful.

I wander around and under the tall arches of the ruined monastery. As evening falls a red sky develops to the west, silhouetting the stonework. A wailing sound penetrates the gloaming, travelling in from somewhere distant. The ghosts of sailors lost come to mind. I walk towards the sound and can just make out a colony of seals on the flooding mud flats.

The detour means I am too late for pub food. Four units and a few bags of crisps later I turn in. Sleep comes easily.

Day 81 – 26th August

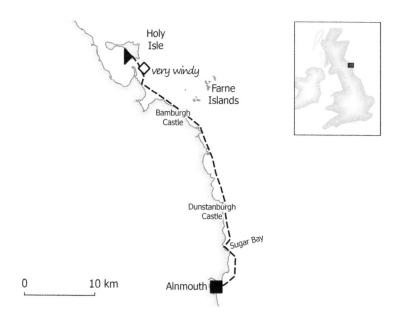

My fleecy hat wasn't in its designated pocket yesterday. And this morning's search through all my gear proves in vain. It is lost – resting place most likely a garage at East Lothian Yacht Club. I consider the hat a safety-critical item and am annoyed at myself for this slip-up.

The forecast is for a breezy cross-offshore wind from the south, and beyond the sheltered harbour there are already Norway-headed whitecaps that make me screw up my face at the thought of sailing. I delay for a while, convince myself that it isn't so windy. More face contortions. Then I head out all the same.

An upwind heading takes me south. The Northumberland coast bends in and soon I'm well offshore. It's thumping windy. I kill power with stacks of downhaul and outhaul but am still uncomfortably overpowered. Wind rattles through the rig and my muscles burn. It's no fun being this exposed. I put a tack in and battle back to the safety of shore.

Half an hour of sailing has left me dripping with sweat. It isn't sensible to push the gear this hard. Sail, mast, boom, daggerboard - they've all come a long way and although I try to be gentle with them they won't last forever. And although I can *try* to stay close in to limit exposure, there is an inevitability to being forced further out than is prudent. That's the nature of sailing a coastline. And, if something were to break on a day like today, there would be no way of clawing myself back to shore.

I'm in England now. Time is on my side. I don't have to take these risks. So I take the opportunity to enjoy the pristine beach where I have landed. It is a glorious day. Crystal clear tubing waves peel along the shore, double overhead for the average sized rabbit. I daydream of being rodent sized, as I imagine every surfer does when presented with scaled-down perfection.

The wind eventually moderates enough to venture back out. I leave the Farne Islands to seaward. I would have liked to have sailed amongst them, but don't want to put myself that far out today. Closer to the mainland, compensation is a view of Bamburgh castle. This north-east coastline is jaw-droppingly beautiful.

Bamburgh Bay with castle in background

Low headlands, reef, and beach punctuate the next 15km to Dunstanburgh castle. Castles stick out: literally, because of the commanding positions they tend to occupy, and in a visual sense too.

These testing conditions are mentally and physically tiring. The shoreline has now become rocky, cliffy, slabby - with a white margin of sea. Hostile, whichever way it is considered. The next 7km are straight into a headwind which blows with added clout. Today's miles are hard earned.

Finally, there is somewhere to put in. A beach, angled north, offers welcome refuge from the building southerly swell. This is Sugar Bay. It is considered something of a secret spot, I hear from a friendly local. Shhh.

It is remarkable how food restores energy. Egg sandwich, Snickers bar, water, general snacking. I'm ready again for battle within the hour. Around the headland is Alnmouth, where I have a Contact - Linda. I messaged her earlier: no reply as yet, but there will definitely be a pub. The thought spurs me to relaunch: one last push!

The next headland looked more significant on the map. In fact, it is a low reef rather than dry land. The wind is moderating towards evening too. I make Alnmouth without incident.

I surf in on a wave and then have a long walk up the beach with my gear. There's often a long walk. I can carry board as one trip, and sail plus barrel as another, and be done in a couple of journeys. Much worse would be hauling a trolley-less boat up the beach, as my inspiration Ron Patterson had to do on his Laser dinghy sail round Britain.

There's no news from Linda, but there is comfortable camping and a choice of pubs. I settle on the Sun Inn, for its optimistic yellow paintwork. Warmth, fish and chips and two pints of Golden Fleece leave me most satisfied with the choice.

It's dark back at my campsite. The grassy car park is also evidently popular with Alnmouth youth. Fortunately, they are easily spooked by the wild-looking crazy guy with a headtorch, and pretty soon it is just me.

Day 82 – 27th August

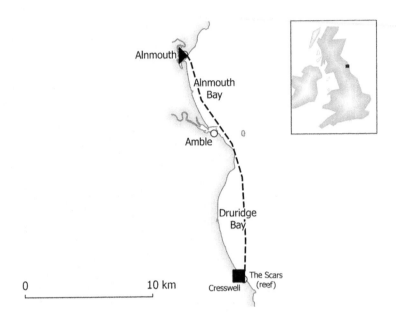

I think about an early start but realise my map is missing. I probably left it at the Sun Inn. I'm fortunate that a cleaner opens up and I can retrieve the map – still in protective splash proof case - from the corner where I had sat.

The day shapes up to be a rerun of yesterday. On the sea, countless flecks of white head east. With a discontent that grows over the coming hours I know the only thing to do is bide my time until the wind drops. When it is a borderline decision to stay put the mind stays restless. Every few minutes I look out to sea and screw up my face.

I do at least manage a blog post. And get up to date with my voice recordings. And it is another glorious day.

By late afternoon the temptation to head out is too great. The wind has moderated a little and I knock off two long crescents of sand either side of a protrusion at Amble. Conditions are still lively but it is good for morale to win a few miles against the run of play.

I land for the evening at Cresswell which is the end of what I consider to be semi-wilderness coast. Beyond here is the industrial north-east. I'm already nostalgic and after neatly parking my board on the beach go exploring the wildlife on a reef exposed by the low tide. I did this as a kid. It is good for the soul. There's a very healthy diversity of rockpool life, and thousands of birds. The sun eventually gets low. I could wander and wonder until dark.

But my meanderings on the reef are cut short. A huddle of people are - between them - carrying my board away. *Oh dear*, I sigh. *I'm being rescued.* I wade across a gulley to the beach, and intercept the good Samaritans before they reach the dunes. Unfortunately, the ringleader has already notified the police. With some firm prompting he makes a second call and the search for a body is called off. They aren't sailing folk these, and I don't question how my kit was supposed to have been washed up by the sea on a day of howling offshore winds. Instead I enlist their help to carry the gear the rest of the way up the beach - no need to dampen their spirits too much.

The misunderstanding is representative. Many non-sailors seem to think that windsurfing is similar to yachting. Or perhaps they *assume it is* when they twig what I'm doing. People often think I'll be sailing at night... sleeping on board... smoking a pipe with a seagull on my shoulder.

Even for people *with* a sailing background, an appreciation is not guaranteed, instant or automatic. The people who do understand are the ones who stop to think. I see it every time now. For a few seconds their eyes roll away to rest on something blank and they become lost in their imagining. On a regular basis I observe the reality dawn on people's faces. I enjoy watching that happen.

I position camp at the highest point of the dunes. A bit sandy, but the view of my reef and the sweep of sand going north is so stunning that it has me forever won. I won't be disturbed, and the

Cresswell reef

clear skies and full moon will illuminate the scene throughout the
night.

I'm cooking dinner when Linda phones, all apologetic at not
having been around the last few days - though without need of
course. There's a nice looking café behind the dunes – The Drift
Café and Bookshop - open from 9am. Linda knows it and I've
already found it too. We decide to meet there for breakfast in the
morning.

I wake a few times during the night, which is clear and moonlit.
How restrictive four walls will seem. How limited the view from
windows: constrained, like snapshots in a book. My window these
last months has been all around - including up and over my
craning head, back down to the water's surface, and often down
to the depths below. And I sense that I haven't been just
observing. I've really been a part of this world that I recall now
so vividly. I know this is a privilege, and perhaps I am a little
melancholic too. Goodbye wild Britain.

Day 83 - 28th August

Linda is inside the café when I arrive. The setup could be a bit *breakfast date*, not that I have experience of breakfast dating. Initial awkwardness put behind us, we chat.

Linda is clearly a kind and thoughtful person, naturally quite introverted, and with a quiet courage. I expect she's struggled a bit at times, and I'm sure she can recognise that I've had a few struggles too.

She is also on the cusp of acting on her dreams. I sense that she has sought me out because she is looking for courage to take her own plunge. I don't remember what Linda's dreams are. That's the least important part anyway. The important part is that she worries about the details. She's looking for a certainty that isn't there.

This is new territory for me - being a wise head – being someone who people listen to. But maybe I do have something to say now. Maybe my experience of taking the plunge and trusting that things will work out is what Linda needs to hear. In my case I pretended to have had a plan – to have painstakingly risk assessed the route, to have gone over every detail in exhaustive preparation. *Did I fuck!* I traced a line on Google Earth and measured a few distances and thought, *yeah - doable.* Every aspect of my luggage has evolved en route, my techniques have evolved en route, every day evolves en route. And when there are difficult days, there are difficult days. And what does that matter, for at the end of every day the same thing happens: the sun goes down. And at the start of the next, up it comes. And despite all the difficulties, the most difficult part of getting this far, the part that I might not have overcome, was making the decision to go ahead with it in the first place.

And in any case, when the time is right - you know the time is right. So there's no reason to worry about that either. Words to this effect, said one worrier to the other.

Linda insists on picking up the tab and we wish each other well on our respective journeys. I like to think both slightly the richer for our crossing of paths.

* * *

The wind is once again cross-offshore from the south, but a little less strong. Most of the time I am well powered up. Only when too far offshore after rounding the headlands am I unpleasantly overpowered.

I pass a curious sculpture embedded in a rock breakwater: an oversized man and woman staring out to sea. The scale is disorientating, but - close up - I decide I quite like it. It certainly puts Newbiggin on the map.

I fail to spot - and fall off upon sailing into - a drift net. This is off Blythe. It's my own fault. I'm too busy taking a picture of the fishing boat to notice its nets. Each part of Britain has its own style of boat. Here they are open with a tarp covered bow, maybe thirty feet long, painted in bold colours, and with a crew of one. Attractive craft. No damage is done and I can extricate myself without problem.

I get thumped by particularly strong offshore winds between Newcastle and Sunderland. It is a relief to get in to Whitburn Bay and put feet onto the safety of land.

The landing is improved further when a vivacious woman bounds over and with baffling but delightful enthusiasm explains how they'd just missed me in Scotland but had met people I'd met in Ullapool and how I must really be in need of a cup of tea. And of course I am. So up we go to a greensward café and I spend a very pleasant hour with Margaret and her in-laws, who also volunteer themselves as Local Contacts for when I get to Norfolk.

I only go 200m before landing again, next to a pair of windsurfers who I have been watching blast up and down. They are the first I've seen since Ireland. I feel less pathetic about my struggles with a 9.5 metre sail when they say they've been out the last three days blasting around with 5.0 metre rigs. Andy and his mate donate a Boost bar and I'm on my way again.

The wind has dropped, but I still get thumped again going round a protrusion of land at Sunderland, and it takes forty minutes to get back in to the shelter of low cliffs. I decide I'm done, and look for somewhere to land. A little harbour at Seaham fits the bill.

Seaham has a history in mining. Shafts extend out under the North Sea for up to three miles. It is strange to think that earlier today I sailed over where men spent their working lives. And sobering too, because many men would have died in accidents or prematurely as a result of work-related ill health. According to Wikipedia, when the pits closed this 'hit the local economy extremely hard, and Seaham sank into a depressed state in the 1980s and 1990s'.

Recent efforts to regenerate Seaham are obvious. One of these is the previously industrial harbour area, which has had money spent on it so that it can now also accommodate yachts. But the shiny facilities are incongruous with other parts of the town. The main street is mostly betting shops, boozers and boarded-up windows. There is little here to suggest hope or opportunity. The harbour gates are shut up and locked at 9pm, presumably a measure to protect against vandalism.

The harbourmaster - also a surfer, and with the open mind of a traveller – has one of Seaham's better jobs. He lends me keys to the shower block and introduces me to Sean, who might have a place for me on his boat. Sean's thirty-a-day habit precedes him out of the little boat's cabin, but I manage to park my clean air preference and still manage a grateful acceptance. Poor old Sean: divorced, destitute and - just a bit - deluded. Life's not going well. He's living on his boat and would like to sail it to Greece. The thing is, I'm not sure he can sail, and he hasn't been out the harbour in months. Work is a few hours a week, and fiddling the system to keep some benefits coming in. We talk a bit and occasionally he gives a wry smile. Look closely and it's easy to see that inside there is a clever man. He needs a few changes to get back on track though.

Sean's diet and smoking make me crave healthy food. I pop to Asda for green and fresh stuff. Oh, and to run an errand for a pack of Lambert and Butler. When I return, for the first time in his life Sean eats humus. He seems to be pleasantly surprised, and manages a few tomatoes too.

Today is a Saturday, and another lifetime's habit means that Sean will go and prop up a few bars tonight. I join him at the first two before retiring early.

Day 84 – 29th August

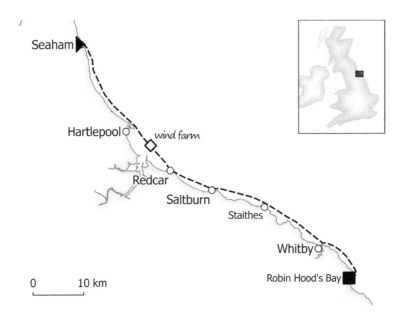

In the morning a mate of Sean's shows up. The friend has a monumentally ugly powerboat that is almost as wide as it is long. The boat's engine is non-functional. Really it is just a floating caravan, but it serves that purpose well and probably won't be expected to do more. The friend is round and jolly and obviously not in financial strife. It is easier to be chipper with a full wallet, of course, but the friend also has a good heart. He asks Sean about work and generally shows concern, and invites us both to a Wetherspoons breakfast.

The harbour gates are closed until near high tide, leaving me with time on my hands. I repair my inflatable camping mattress, which for the last week or so it has been self-deflating during the night. Clothes get washed and are dried on the guardwires of Sean's boat.

An hour later I'm really itching to go but the harbour gates are still closed. There is an alternative route. I carry my gear round to the sand of the outer harbour, say my goodbyes, and escape to the open sea.

Seaham has been an interesting but slightly uncomfortable stop. The town focuses attention on the inequality and divisions in our society. It raises questions. Despite the nice people I meet, there is no denying that parts of it *bring me down*. I am grateful to the town too. Without places like Seaham, it would almost be possible to sail round our Isles and believe they are all National Trust and tea shops.

Conditions on the water are – *hallelujah!* – just perfect. The wind direction is unchanged, but it is gentler - which removes the continual worry of breakage and being carried offshore. I contentedly sail past Hartlepool, through a wind farm, and then stop for an ice-cream at Redcar.

The seaside town amusements remind me of Clacton. The tide is coming-up to high, and myself and numerous beachgoers are squashed onto a narrow fringe of sand, but no-one says hello or shows interest. Confirmation once again that the busier a place is, the less likely are its people to engage.

Further down the coast Saltburn looks pleasant, but is in a nook that is slightly off route, so instead I proceed along a coastline that has changed to cliff. This is now definitely Yorkshire. I'd been a bit concerned about getting past the industry of Teesside and Tyneside, and am surprised that in just a couple of days all that is behind me. The apparently major cities of Sunderland and Newcastle were barely registered.

The water is flat and the sailing easy. I don't stop at Staithes – once home of Captain Cook – but do say hello to fishermen in small boats pulling aboard plenty of fish on rod and line. I wonder a bit about the explorer mentality and conclude that it must be quite a selfish one. Cook twice left wife and kids at home to go off exploring the world on a trip from which he might never return. The second time he didn't return. Spare a thought for Mrs Cook and a life she hadn't been expecting.

A single life for me. A simple and less guilt-ridden existence.

By late afternoon I reach Whitby. It is a fine looking town presided over by the ruins of an abbey. Possibly I should sail into the harbour but I can't see that there will be good camping options within so phone Gregg for some Google Earth input. Gregg blithely sends me on a bit further, disregarding my comments about the wind dying and a tide on the turn. Like an idiot I listen to him.

Getting to and in to Robin Hoods Bay is touch and go. The sea goes glassy and the foul current gains in strength. I curse at Gregg for his advice. For the last hour the wind is desperately light – just occasionally a puff falls off the cliff to lay a few ripples on the water, providing something to work with. Dark isn't far away by the time I make land and make a begrudging mental apology to *that fucking brother of mine.*

Now I am here I am pleased. Tomorrow is forecast as a drifter – probably no sailing – so being somewhere pleasant and relaxing will make for a nicer day. Plus: miles are miles, and you never know when a few extra will help you make the cut further along the journey. Every mile won is valuable.

The village at Robin Hood's Bay is also called Robin Hood's Bay. It is the designated end of Alfred Wainwright's Coast to Coast walk, and a pint of Theakston's Old Peculiar is customary for those who have completed the walk. I figure I've done enough to earn a couple of pints, and yet another plate of fish and chips.

I'm too late to identify a good camping spot and instead end up perched on a narrow sea wall with a two-foot drop one side and a much higher drop the other, on an incline of about 20 degrees. Very poor planning. I feel like a rock climber sleeping on a cliff edge and throughout the night am fearful to move.

Day 85 – 30th August

That really was a poor night's sleep. At least climbers are roped on.

Today there isn't a breath of wind. I don't mind that. When there is no wind and none forecast it takes the pressure off. Let's me catch up with repairs, voice notes and - a favourite of mine - eating.

The Tourist Information here have a good selection of screwdrivers that they are happy to lend for a few hours. That allows a service of the mast track which is back into its previous habit of jamming.

I also use some bits of sticker to reinforce the sail where the monofilm shows signs of wear. The window part that rubs the boom has gone thin and brittle. I should have beefed up the film before departing on the expedition, and don't have enough material to do a thorough job now, but something is better than nothing and hopefully this will get me to Clacton.

There is still not a breath of wind. Fine by me. A nice walk on the beach next. The tide empties out to reveal a multitude of gullies in the seaweed-covered rock. They run for hundreds of metres and are fertile exploring grounds for bank-holidaying families. I people watch and wade through rock pools. Higher up the beach there is a café with a queue at least a hundred strong.

Unusually, for there has been no contact, I receive a text from my ex. It is friendly - caring even - and I take it as confirmation that friends is a good way to be. That was how I understood it at the time, anyway. I reply in a similar tone. I'm clear in my own mind that becoming close again would be a mistake, it wasn't to be, and moving on is best for both of us.

I return to practicalities. There's no way I'm sleeping on that sea wall again. A small group of campers and their tents are next to a picnic bench on the only patch of grass at Robin Hood's Bay. There's room for a sail too, but that would require introducing myself, not my forte...

I rise to the occasion and even end up being offered a cup of tea. Yeah - smashed it!

On the way to get my gear I bump into some fishermen. These are the smartest-dressed fishermen I have ever seen. Neat hair, trousers, shirts - that are both clean and tucked in. It turns out that they are part-timers. Nonetheless, their professional approach has paid dividends because in the boat are buckets brim full of mackerel. The fishermen are friendly, and we talk fish, and they can't possibly eat that many mackerel anyway, so I end up with a bagful to take to my new friends by the picnic bench.

Remarkably, out of this group I am the culinary expert. And their shared spork is hardly going to cook half a dozen mackies. They head off in search of a barbecue and - to my surprise - are successful in their quest. I gut and cook the fish. Ben and his girlfriend are really nice and are far more responsible than Ben's dad. The older man seems never to have emerged from the sixties and is nice too – until he has a bottle of wine inside him, at which point he starts getting on everyone's nerves. To his credit Ben is very kind with him even then. The fish are *so* tasty and I think we all enjoy the evening.

The picnic table allows for a new stick-less sail shelter arrangement. It rains; water pools on the sail and drips. A simple batten flip cures the problem. In blissful comfort I drift off to the gentle patter of rain on sail.

Day 86 – 31st August

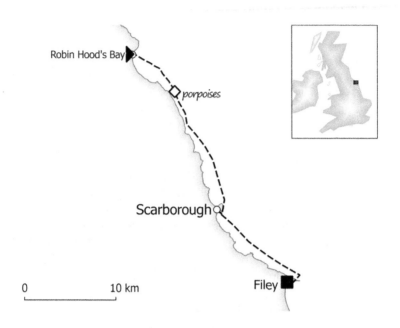

No wind early on. I second breakfast in the Old Post Office and read the papers over a bacon sandwich. Upon return to my picnic table I discover this has now become the admin centre for the finish to an 'Open Adventure' challenge, which I take as my cue to move on.

It is low tide, so two long walks are needed to get myself and kit to the water's edge. I launch between fingers of rock, and row the sail through still air to open water. An hour later, outside the bay, there is the faintest of following breezes and a tide that also carries me south.

It is very tranquil. I enjoy pumping the sail in light winds: find it relaxing. It requires moderate effort but more important is rhythm, and that allows the mind to drift. *Scoop! ...and recover. Scoop! ...and recover.* Very therapeutic. On this particular meditation I am joined by a group of porpoises. Small dorsal fins - a group of probably five. The sound of their breathing alerts me to their presence. And although they hang back there is no doubt that we travel in convoy. I want to stay in sync with them so return to the pumping – looking ahead, but listening behind. The porpoises periodically roll through for a noisy breath, which reassures me that the pace is right, and for a while we are companions.

A combination of tide, wind and effort - but mostly tide – carries me to Scarborough. The town is bigger – and parts of it much grander - than I had imagined. A café on south beach does a pretty good tea and doughnut. Out on the water there are yachts being leant over by a breeze that has come from nowhere. I am tempted back out and enjoy cruising south through the racing fleet, before leaving the yachts and the wind behind.

Next stopping option is Filey. Beyond that is Flamborough Head: the last of the major headlands, looking quite imposing from here. Filey itself has a smaller headland where currents collide and kick up a bit of a sea - enough to persuade me to leave Flamborough for tomorrow. A bit of north swell has also appeared.

Tucked behind Filey headland is a sailing club. There's no one around but the veranda is nicely decked and looks good for camping. I've no contacts here though, so google then phone the Commodore - James - on the scrounge for access to the changing rooms and a hot shower. James initially seems a bit reticent. *Who wouldn't be?* It's an odd call to receive when you are about to sit down to your dinner on a Monday evening. But James agrees to comes down and is friendly and helpful when he arrives to open up.

Rinsed, warmed and dried I head into Filey town. I crave vitamins, so buy salad stuff to eat. Still hungry after that I grab a takeaway: baked potato and coleslaw as second course. Third course is a local ale at the Star Inn.

Facebook informs me that my friend Alex and his wife Rosie have completed their swim of Lake Windermere, in aid of the RNLI and in memory of Alex's dad. Good on you guys.

Day 87 – 1ˢᵗ September

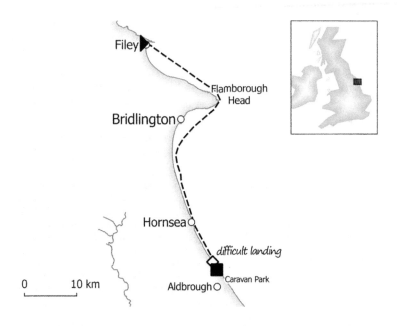

It rains overnight. I'm not very mobile this morning – the muscles across my back are in spasm. A bit of rolling around and stretching-out kind of frees me up.

Over homebrew coffee I look out toward Filey headland and a spikey sea. The white horses rear in unpredictable ways: wind against tide conditions, background swell and colliding currents all contribute to the melee. Flamborough Head will be similar but on a bigger scale. I'll give it a few hours before setting off: round the peninsula on slack tide.

My Uncle Alan calls. He's Yorkshire based, but just back from New Zealand. We chat and agree I'll call later - maybe we'll link up. I get up to date on voice notes before going afloat.

The sail to Flamborough is very pleasant. Broad reaching with rolling waves. 10 knots. Sometimes 12 knots. Surfing. It takes about an hour.

At the headland the sea is initially confused, but subsides to pleasantly flat in the lee. I savour the views on the rounding. Chalk cliffs are indented with little coves. Above them green pastures, a few low white buildings, and a tall and proud lighthouse. Also a few people looking out to sea. The scene brings to mind a *Lego* reconstruction of a headland. Certainly pretty, but not quite awe-inspiring like the West and North Coast headlands. The scale is slightly wrong - the people and the buildings slightly too big.

I know I would have been different had I arrived earlier. Or on another day.

Stronger wind behind the headland allows for a flat water blast to reconnect with the coast south of Bridlington. It is easy sailing. I feel safe. I am complacent. I warn myself against complacency.

Continuing is easy. Stopping is not. A north swell is back with me and the rising tide dumps a shorebreak onto the beaches. I say beaches – really the coastline here is one long beach. Very few features. Very little protection. All along are waves that dig at the steep-shelved shore.

The wind is becoming very light. Somewhere I will have to stop. I consider Hornsea. There are breakwaters at least. I get close for a look. Probably possible, but highly undesirable. Easier to continue.

Fifty minutes later the urgency of getting in somewhere is pressing. No wind – making progress just on tide now. A big, high, spring tide. A tide that will not recede until after dark.

Soon there will be no beach left. Waves at the base of the cliffs tear at sand and clay - devouring the land. Every few seconds the waves take a new chunk. The cliffs bleed red-brown.

I'm now looking for cliff to scramble up. There is a slither of beach. Beyond here the cliffs are too steep and the sea is already against them. This is *the last* bit of beach and it won't be around for much longer. Last chance.

Not quite last chance, but best option. There is another option – to stay out through the night. But in conditions like these… No thanks - I'll take a gamble before that.

So, I investigate, and then back out of, a landing attempt. Within thirty metres of shore, and without wind to move, I am a sitting duck. The waves are not huge, but they are tightly packed and destructive.

I hang back just beyond the impact zone. Any nearer and a wave would catch me. I'd fall, the shorebreak would then pound the kit until everything was broken. I'd likely make it out with superficial wounds, but any rescued gear would be crumpled and worthless.

A dark, brooding cloud approaches from the north. I pin my hopes on it bringing wind. On the edge of rain there is often wind. It becomes gloomy. More gurning of my face. I don't like it. I don't like the thought of no wind, swell, no landing, in the dark.

The cloud brings a few knots of breeze. A puff. But enough to generate an attack. I pump hard for momentum and attempt to time my run with a lull in the sets. Waves roll underneath on the approach and then I am in front of the impact zone. The fin grinds. I jump from the board and haul equipment by tip of mast. Retreating water tugs at my legs. I win a few metres before the next dumper dumps. A few metres more and safety is reached.

I fall back on the beach, panting for breath. Happy - exuberant even - that I've made it. The emotion is short-lived. The sail didn't make it. *Fuck!* There is a big tear from seam to seam across the main panel.

Oh well. That could have been a lot worse.

I accept the setback and get on with resolving it. Next is to haul the gear onto the cliff face, safe from the waves. At the top of the cliff there is a mobile signal, and the heavens open. It chucks it down.

Google Earth shows nice grassy cliffs here, but the reality is more akin to jungle. Gregg says that best bet for civilisation is a caravan park about a mile south. A place called Aldbrough. *Sounds good.*

I phone Uncle Alan. He and cousin Tom are planning on heading over. *Brilliant!* I put in a request for sticky plastic film. Lots of it. We'll meet up tomorrow morning.

I de-rig on the cliff. Everything gets plastered in wet clay. I find the most amazing fossil; the most amazing I have every found:

A damaged sail is a small price to pay for landing through this

hundreds of ammonites in a beautiful teapot-sized rock. A sign that this is part of the plan? I think but don't believe that - but the thought is enough to lift the spirits.

It is a bush-whack through the jungle, past a Ministry of Defence sign that yells:

Danger! Unexploded Ordnance. Keep Out!

That would explain why it's a bit overgrown. When I reach the caravan park it is deserted. The film version of Stephen King's novel - *The Shining* - comes to mind. In the empty car park are some huge puddles: good for cleaning sail and getting clean myself. Rolling around in a carpark puddle, in the dark, adds to this oddly surreal experience. Afterwards, I find a launderette room and use it as a kitchen to prepare some couscous. I do eventually find a bar. I've not seen anyone other than the occasionally-present bartender, and I am the only customer in an enormous room.

The fossil rock

I sleep on a road that finishes as a jagged edge of tarmac. The rest of the road has toppled down the cliff. No sail shelter tonight, and much colder too.

Day 88 – 2nd September

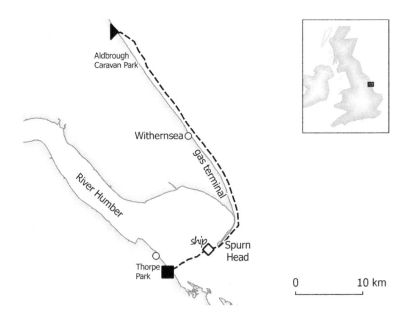

Alan and Tom turn up early, still on New Zealand time. The caravan park diner doesn't open as advertised but Al produces a continental breakfast from the boot of their car. Also in the boot are about fifty rolls of duct tape and sticky backed plastic film – the entire supply from Tesco's York store. Perfect!

For the tape to stick the sail must be dry. There are some picnic benches that will do for a drying line, but I think it polite to ask before draping the sail over these. The caravan sales office is open. The manager listens to my request with a sneer, before turning it down on grounds that it will put off his customers. *Not that there are any customers. Not that they would be put off.* His attitude is sad, and is far more likely to have damaged his day more than mine.

I've no desire to wind him up at all, so dry the sail in a kids' play area instead.

We do a good repair. Surgery goes well. Hundreds of duct tape butterfly stitches on both sides of the sail neatly join the two halves of panel. It should be OK if I exercise sensible post-operative care: keep dry, avoid strenuous activity. A tall order - but this is at least good enough to get me on my way.

We descend the cliff at Aldbrough caravan park, and walk along the beach back to where I made landfall yesterday. Fresh lumps of clay - casualties of last night's attrition – line the upper shore.

Alan and Tom – their rescue mission complete – leave me to re-rig the sail and then head back. Tom in custody of a teapot-sized fossil rock. Thanks Tom.

Military Personnel come to see what I am up to. I explain that I am leaving. They are fine with that. The freshly fallen cliff has revealed ordnance to explode.

The waves at low tide crumble further out and then dribble in to the beach. A light breeze is enough to punch out through them. The first explosion happens just a minute or so later. Smoke rises from adjacent to my launch site. Yesterday's sign had been on the money.

The breeze soon turns feeble, but both tide and wind carry me south. Today is a re-run of yesterday. Nowhere to stop and an incoming tide that will leave me with few landing options. Safety today is the River Humber. I need to make it that far.

Concern is a good motivator and continual pumping helps to maintain a respectable average speed. I am also loathe to let the damaged sail rest in the water where the movement of the waves will undo my repair. The coastline is relentlessly straight. From mid-tide the swell picks up more and I can discard thoughts of stopping on the beach. A few surfers are taking waves at Withernsea. The town itself has a heavily fortified sea wall, but it seems unlikely even that will save it for long.

Mostly the low cliffs have farmland behind. Later in the day a gas terminal provides a welcome alternative backdrop. My fingers ache - I get some tendonitis on the light wind days when the harness can't be used. Important now is the maths: distance (nautical miles) over speed (knots) gives time to destination (hours). Still on target to reach the River Humber before dark. That's fine.

The cliffs descend and transform into Spurn Head – a 5km long spit of sand. I consider walking across the spit to the river on the other side. Consider that would be cheating.

The end of the spit is a complicated bit of water. Sandbars trip up the North Sea swell, there are strong currents, and shipping – some of it stationary, some of it creeping. Tide shoots me over a hump of sand and into the river. After five hours of slop, the water here is *blissfully* flat.

On the other side of the estuary is Lincolnshire. Pumping my way there takes another hour. The movement of shipping is difficult to judge. I cross the bows of something big, not realising that it is under way. I make an apologetic wave to acknowledge my error. On the bridge they are either not impressed or not friendly. Pah! I had it under control anyway…

I head for Thorpe Park, as instructed by my Local Contact Derrick. I'm shattered. Derrick has a flag so I know where to land; and a trolley for the board. Later I am offered a coat hanger with inbuilt electric fan for drying sailing gear. This is a man with *all* the toys.

Derrick also windsurfs, and is chairman of The Seavets - an association of veteran windsurfers. I know quite a few of them from teaching in Menorca and consider them to be friends. It is nice to know that some are following my adventure.

Derrick and wife Ellie offer every comfort. A big Chinese takeaway and a hot shower are particularly restorative. Today I need restoring. The guest room is a very nice camper on the drive. A *very* nice camper on the drive.

Day 89 – 3rd September

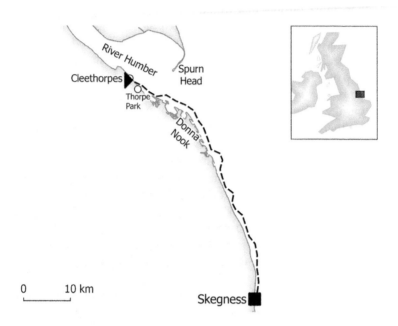

Derrick takes me upriver to a launch site where deep water is easy to access. In my barrel is a Seavets polo-shirt – presented last night in what was a touching gesture. I don't generally have room for such offerings, but decided at the time that I will sail this one back to Clacton. We take a commemorative photo and I set off down the river.

Wind conditions are good, and become excellent. Planing in the footstraps once I reach the outer margins of the estuary. From a navigational perspective it is just a case of follow the coast, but there is a Royal Air Force bombing range in my way too. I have a number to call when I reach the range limit.

Unfortunately, I have made an error with my GPS coordinates. Irritating. It takes ten minutes of squinting and poking at screens to correct my wayward waypoint. The repair to the sail suffers during this time. Bits of it are hanging off.

Fast and fun sailing to Skegness

I phone RAF Donna Nook, and am given the green light to proceed through the range. The sailing is joyously good. A clean cross-offshore wind leaves the water smooth, and a generously spaced groundswell approaches the shore in neat lines. I take wave after wave - riding each until it steepens to a point at which prudence tells me it is time to gybe. It is very fast and very fun. Heading out I sail full speed at waves that jack-up on a sandbar. It would be *so* fun to launch off these. But I know I mustn't stress the gear. At the last moment self-restraint kicks in, and I throttle back to take the ramps more gently. The windsurfing equivalent of sex without orgasm!

Conditions remain good for the whole day, although the wind gradually becomes less strong, and a more familiar general lumpiness returns to the sea. I cover a lot of distance – 59km according to the tracker – but that doesn't count the zigzags. Today - against the tide, short on power – those have been unusually compressed.

The landing at Skegness is easy. I step off the board into the soupiest water of the trip. Thick, brown and shockingly warm.

The sound of seaside-town amusements competing for attention comes from above the beach. This is familiar. Clacton but bigger. I brace myself.

I am fortunate to have received a last minute Local Contact sign-up from here. I think Derrick put the word out. First I call Simon, who calls his son Rob, who is finishing work shortly and will pick me up. I de-rig; enjoy tea and doughnut; try to blank out the wailing of amusements.

Rob is a really nice guy. He is part of the UK Olympic windsurf team youth squad, transitioning to the senior squad. I know a bit about Olympic windsurfing and have done the odd regatta. It is hugely tough. On an ability level someone like Rob could windsurf round Britain the way I nearly have. I tell him as much and he knows that too. He identifies the bigger challenge as the mental one. He is right.

Back at the family home I meet a few more relatives, am fed, and encouraged into the outside hot tub. It doesn't have the character of the Johnshaven version, but it is *hot*. I appreciate the disconnect time. Five hours at sea and then landing in Skegness town centre was a contrast too far.

Day 90 – 4th September

Rob donates his supply of sticky patches for re-repairing the sail. This repair won't last long either, but if I am careful it might just last long enough. Thanks Rob. And fingers crossed.

I look out across The Wash from Skegness beach. This is the last significant crossing. It is only 22km to the other side, but the unknown has me nervous. Today is a windy day with a sizeable northerly swell. The offshore sandbanks will be tripping up the waves. I have visions of being trapped between them, unable to escape from chaotically breaking white water.

I'll leave it for a bit.

I don't venture far, preferring to keep a close eye on my gear. The kiosks do a pretty good tea and doughnut. I know that from yesterday.

A while later I check in with the Beach Patrol. Young kids in a lookout. They are pleasant to talk with and have powerful binoculars. The crisp horizon of rearing white horses makes my mind up. I don't need to push. Time is on my side. Stay put.

I feel it would be an imposition to call on Simon's busy family again, but have an alternative option. A college friend of mine - Ian - has been in touch and has relatives local who I can call on. I vaguely know the relatives from Ian's daughter's christening. I think that is an example of networking. I never knew I could do that.

The gear is a hassle to move back and forth. Perhaps the Beach Patrol crew can look after it? They want to and do their best to help, but are met with an unimaginative and inflexible response from their senior colleague at the other end of the phone. *Nope. Not insured. Wouldn't be covered. Can't do it.*

No bother. The poor kids look forlorn, until they realise I'm *genuinely* not upset, at which point they are back to their smartphones and who's-with-who gossip.

Plan B works. Ian's Auntie June turns up with a trailer. That gets the gear back to theirs. Later I am also reacquainted with Uncle Trevor.

I text Simon and Rob, just to let them know that I am not homeless in Skegness tonight.

A day around the beach kiosks has left me no less tired than a day on the water. Trevor and June are quiet and calm and the amusement arcades are out of earshot. I would skewer my ears to escape that noise.

Day 91 – 5th September

Trevor and I polish off the Telegraph crossword during breakfast. My contribution: a lucky stab at *four across*. Then it is back down to the beach.

Trevor has sailing contacts and introduces me to the RNLI station staff. A mild anxiety prevented me doing that yesterday. Fear of authority? Concern they'd tell me not to cross The Wash? Mental note to self: pull socks up.

The RNLI are friendly: don't chastise, or try to dissuade me from the crossing. In a half-hearted and your-guess-is-as-good-as-mine sort of way they help with the route plan. I'm not wholly reassured.

Sea and weather conditions are similar to yesterday in any case, so no sailing just yet. In the mean-time the RNLI have no insurance problems with me storing my gear at the station.

That leaves me with time to kill in Skegness. Remarkably the aural barrage has worsened. Today, self-proclaimed 'Youtube sensation' *Lenny* overpowers the amusements with his excruciating karaoke. On the seafront there is no escape from the torture. I head into town.

Tired and bored of wandering I settle on a bench with a coffee. An observation is that a majority of people here are obese or chronically obese. The exceptions are mostly elderly males, and the youngest of children who have not yet had obesity forced upon them. Large people queue in shops that sell sugar muck dressed up as food or treats. Some shoppers eat or drink more of the same, even whilst waiting in line. And the kids are on sugar junk too, or whinging to be given more. What a sad scene. Here are significant problems in the making. There is no doubt that many of these people will lead shortened lives that are plagued by health issues. This is an end result of capitalism without conscience. Profit that comes from convincing easy targets to make bad choices. A malfunction of society. Here are the victims. That's my take.

I feel alien here. Want out of Skegness now. Back to the genteel National Trust lands. Back to concern for nature that conveniently averts the gaze from social issues like these. But this is Britain too. To sail past and not see these places would be fraudulent. So I am also content to think and observe. And there is far more to reflect upon here than in the coffee shops of Nationaltrustland.

Back at the beach Lenny is still going strong. Conditions on the water are also unchanged. *Patience Jono. Sailing today is an unnecessary risk. Don't fuck it up.* There's no need to put on a spectacle. I'll go tomorrow. Maybe get to Cromer. Then just follow the curve of the coast to home. Easy, in theory. For the first time of the trip I would like to be finished.

I chat with Gregg who is away adventuring. He's off on another incomplete rounding of the Isle of Wight. This time, walking.

We talk about the finish. Inevitably there will be a few people there. Gregg and Clyde may sail the last day. That would be good. The three of us – low key. That would be good.

We have a provisional finish date - have done for a while really; but it's not easy to judge. Next Saturday as finish day seems achievable and should be convenient. We make it unofficially official.

Trevor and June are not surprised to hear from me, and I head back to theirs for another night.

Day 92 – 6th September

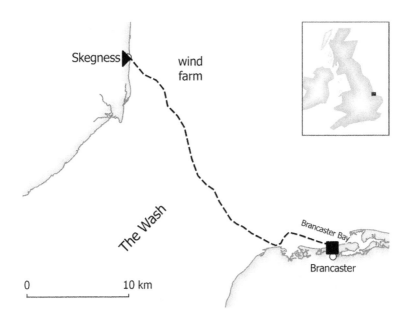

There is a short delay waiting for the RNLI station to open up. I am going to go today. The meagre breeze and residual swell makes for a difficult launch. Getting out unscathed is a big relief.

My course across The Wash will be a zigzag to avoid shallow areas over sandbanks. Accordingly, I head high for the first few miles. Waves break on a sandbank to leeward. The wind is horribly light but – well, I'm no stranger to that now. Stay in deeper water and I'll be fine.

A change of course near a wind farm sets me towards my second waypoint – a buoy which I never find. At some point the Norfolk coast comes into view.

Progress is so slow that I just aim for the nearest bit of land. The breeze is whisper faint. Behind me, the blades of the wind turbines are static. Both the promising forecast and my ambition to reach

A windless Wash

Cromer have proved laughably optimistic. Right now, just reaching land will suit me fine.

At least it is a proper summer's day, good visibility, no real time pressure. Tide and sail-rowing pull me in closer to the coast. Features grow and split until people are discernible on a sandy beach.

The final approach happens quickly. All of a sudden I am close. And although the wind drops to zero I don't care. This is near enough – worst case scenario a swim. That's The Wash ticked off. There is no sense of jubilation after this crossing but it does feel good to be back on track. Back enjoying the adventure. In my mind, the last obstacle now is the north Norfolk coast.

Light wind and swell deter me from landing on the beach. But I do need a break. I sit on the board and sink my teeth into a sweaty cheese roll. Food can taste great sometimes. Less comforting is the sound of my sail being washed by the passing waves. Each ripple does its bit to peel away the tape and sticker repair. When a trickle of breeze returns I resume sailing.

A weak afternoon thermal fills in from the north-east. Upwind sailing now. And I won't get far in this. But some distance I do make and a large building comes into view. Possibly somewhere that might do a cup of tea. And there is a nice sandy beach with an easy landing. Certainly good enough.

The bigger building is a golf club but next to it is a shack style café. I'm there just before closing. Good timing. Here looks like a good place to camp, too. A scattering of beach goers do beach things on the wide expanse of Brancaster Bay sand.

One visitor strolls over: barefoot, and smiling in the afternoon sun. I meet Penny - who is a Local Contact and has offered help on this coastline. She is very willing to help out and has good information for around here, including directions to the nearest pub. Our conversation is easy and pleasant. I decline the offer of a bed on practical grounds as Penny lives some distance away. And after a few rest days, camping is fine for me tonight.

Brancaster is a short walk. I find the pub and enjoy an excellent cod and chips, and an ale or maybe two. I don't manage to pay. Penny had sorted the bill before my arrival. Kindness can have real impact.

A wind picks up during the night, requiring a change of orientation to prevent my shelter blowing away. The ground's a tad lumpy too. It's great to be outside camping again, under the stars of the East Anglian sky.

Day 93 – 7th September

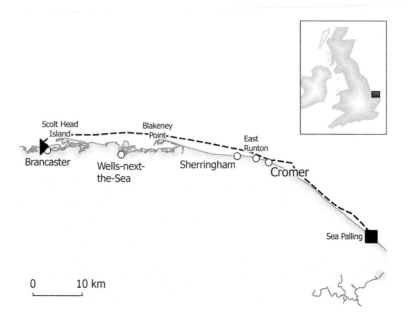

Scolt Head Island
Brancaster
Wells-next-the-Sea
Blakeney Point
Sherringham
East Runton
Cromer
Sea Palling

0   10 km

I get away for an early start on a blustery morning. There's a long hike through shallow water until the depth is sufficient to sail. That gets the blood pumping. I'm in a *let's get the job done* mood.

A few tacks upwind to clear the sand spit off Scolt Head Island. Get far enough offshore to stay out of trouble. The sea is quite corrugated. The cloud base low and grey. Water drips continually from my face: a mixture of salt spray and clean-tasting drizzle.

I reconfigure for reaching mode, and free-off until pointing parallel to the coast. The board accelerates to 20 knots. It spears, slices - occasionally demolishes - the waves in its path. There's not really a gentle way to sail this. I trust the gear, don't hold back.

The north Norfolk coastline is complicated: inlets, estuaries, sandbanks and sand spits. Swell at high tide will make landing difficult. My plan is to be out of here before then.

Sand spits with breaking waves force me further offshore at Wells, then Blakeney. Large channel marker buoys roll drunkenly, suggesting a path in for the intrepid. No takers evident. To leeward I glimpse a coast that is managed, but left to nature. The few villages along here are separated from the sea by marsh and dune.

Cliffs come in to view and a coastline I am familiar with. Sherringham, East Runton and then Cromer. I've time for a quick break before the tide fills too high, so stop on the slightly protected beach behind the pier. That was a great two-and-a-half-hour sail. I am now on home territory.

The Lifeboat Café does decent bacon rolls. The owner is a bit annoyed that I drip on the floor. Sorry, but call yourself Lifeboat Café… I would go outside but it is cold out there.

I search in town for a suitable fleecy hat replacement. None of them have the ideal feature set of *my* fleecy hat. I give up. Tomorrow will be warmer, and I've not far to go. I don't need a fleecy hat now. It dawns on me just how close I am.

A sudden panic. Will the sea be up at my board yet? I rush back to the beach. OK by a few metres. The waves will soon be dumping on the shingle. Time to be gone.

A complicated launch this. I have an audience of fishermen and lifeguards. I sense their eyes on me, anticipating me coming off second best against the surf. I'm in no mood for that. I power out in attack mode. Absolute focus; technique unconventional but functional. Beyond the last wave. A mental clenched fist moment. *Yeees!* A glance back. Cromer already an insignificant feature.

This time I know exactly where I'm going. Sea Palling. The low lying village has rock reef sea defences, and a high tide landing is possible even on a big swell. The coast bends south. Sailing is in downwind zigzags. The sun comes out. The water is green here - good riddance chocolate soup of The Wash. I am euphoric. Conditions are great, and there is nothing compromising about what remains to be sailed.

I sail between two lines of Norwegian granite for an easy landing at Sea Palling. Time for another break. Conditions are also tiring.

The RNLI lifeguards are particularly welcoming and friendly. They make me a cup of coffee in their well-equipped hut. I leave my sweat soaked gear to dry on the balustrade and head to a café behind the dunes in search of more coffee. Overdoing the coffees today.

A man approaches. I immediately recognise him from twenty-three years previous. Bill Short. I met him once at a youth training camp in Weymouth, where he did a talk about something or other. Not that he remembers.

Bill's been sailing up here, and tracker chasing me today. He got a near miss at Cromer but managed some photos just as I was sailing away. On the beach he met a journalist who had also just missed me. That worked out well, as the East Anglian Daily Times now have some pictures to use.

I enjoy the chat with Bill and very much appreciate that he has made the effort to locate me. Better than most he comprehends the finer details and difficulties of the expedition.

Back with the lifeguards I decide to call it a day here. The tide will be high for a few hours yet and I'll have nowhere else to stop. A seal pup rests on the beach. Apparently the young ones get tired and also need an easy landing place, and here does the job for them too.

The lifeguards link me up with an off-duty colleague - Becky - who lives in the village. She is as nice as they say she is (very!) and has a camper on the drive as spare bedroom. Board and sail sleep on the beach.

Day 94 – 8th September

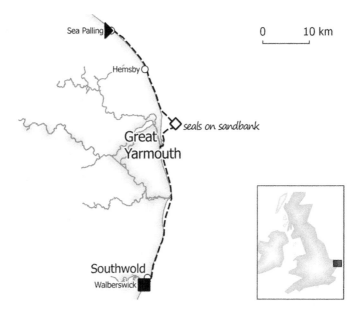

Becky drops me down at the beach. On a ramp that leads through a gap in the dunes are two Coastguard Landrovers, and crews. With a certain dismay, the realisation dawns that they are here for me. I claim the shipwrecked board and the search is called off. I can't quite bring myself to thank the rescuers, who must realise that my neatly beached board is a tsunami-safe distance above the high-tide mark.

I quietly suit up, say goodbye to my lifeguard friends, and slip away.

Sailing inside the reefs is flat and pleasant. Beyond the dashed lines of rock there is a small swell that adds an element of fun to sailing tight to shore where the tide is less foul.

I pass Hemsby, where Margaret's in-laws who had offered help are from. I assume they are back from Sunderland now. No sign of recognition though from the people on the beach.

310

Seals deserting a Great Yarmouth sand bank

Beach, beach and more beach. The occasional slight corner with a spit of sand. Then more beach.

Eventually Great Yarmouth arrives. Rather than sail straight past I head out 3km offshore to a sandbank that has caught my eye. The sandbank has dark features that experience tells me are seals.

A hard edge of sand immediately goes deep, allowing me to sail alongside the offshore shore. There are hundreds of seals. Sand coloured pups and darker, Labrador-faced adults. The seals scatter on my approach, but with no consensus about where safety lies. Most haul themselves downhill into the water; but a minority seek safety on higher sand. I'm pleased that a few bolder individuals stay put. At least I haven't ruined *everyone's* siesta.

A hundred seal pictures to the good, I head back inshore for the cruise past Yarmouth's port. A pair of red ships levitate above the water, jacked up on legs that extend to the seafloor, part of the wind farm construction fleet. A porpoise patrols the harbour entrance.

South Beach. Lunch stop. Standard rations of bacon roll and cup of tea.

The next hour is kind to me. Good wind and double figure speeds. That gets me just short of Southwold. The Suffolk coast is lovely. I like it more than I remember liking it. Having been nearly the whole way round Britain, I quite like my home patch after all. I'd come to take for granted what is on my doorstep. I guess it feels good to be back.

Lighter wind for the final wobble to Walberswick - a beach and a village I know well. Mum and Peter are on the beach. I've often thought about sailing from Clacton to Suffolk. Now I've done it.

I'm not celebrating yet. I'm not quite finished. But we do have a meal and Peter organises a toast of champagne. It is a nice meal, although – bizarrely - a waiter in the pub complains about my bare feet. Yes, that's right. My feet. I don't have shoes on. That's a problem. Tension rises until the waiter is relieved of his duties. The proprietor by way of apology offers a place to store the gear. It works out fine.

Back at Jen and Peter's house I sleep in a bed I have slept in many times before. How odd.

Day 95 – 9th September

I am now ahead of schedule for the programmed Saturday finish.

A staged finish would embarrass me so I want to avoid one of those. But if a few people can come along for the actual finish I am fine with that. Would like that. I am also very happy to hear confirmation that Gregg and Clyde will sail the final day with me. We will sail in convoy.

Timing the run in to the finish is complicated. I need to be in position the day before. We need to be lucky with the weather. We must allow sufficient time to complete the sail, and hope nothing unforeseen slows progress. If all goes to plan, we will sail past Clacton Pier shortly after the advertised finish time of 2pm.

These will be the last judgement calls of windsurfing round Britain. It seems appropriate that the final days finish this way. The endgame, after 3-months of play.

Every day has involved choices. Delicate decisions that could so easily have left me stranded, in need of support - with my dream and target of an unsupported rounding in tatters. Decisions of when to sail - and of routes to take - that tied me in knots inside, occasionally with a pain more than physical. Decisions that have kept me safe, but that have also permitted risk such that I have got this far, to within a few days of my goal.

When to bank the miles, push on, tack, gybe, stay offshore, come in close, cross in front or cross behind. Whether to believe the forecasts, the locals or the developing sky. When to eat, pee, drink. How hard to push the gear, and how hard to push myself.

The notion that I could have been bored on this journey - mentally unoccupied - seems comical. Every move has been weighed up.

For today my judgement call is to let the clock wind down. I don't sail.

The Suffolk coastline, which I have come to appreciate more, and realise there were pockets I did not know.

Day 96 – 10th September

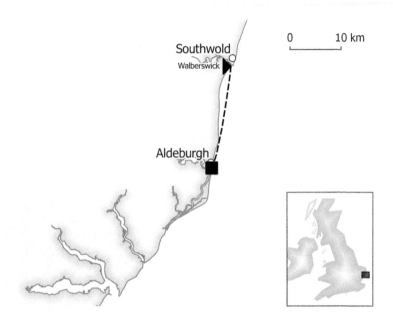

Today I sail 10 miles. That leaves a bit less for tomorrow. A south-easterly force 5 makes for fast progress. I could make Clacton today – conditions are that good – but instead stop at Aldeburgh. I hope I don't come to regret this forced go-slow.

There is a hefty shorebreak on the shingle bank. I won't be getting back out through that anyway. Aldeburgh Yacht Club - situated on the river side of the shingle bank - look after my gear. This is also Wayfarer Fran's local club.[6]

A website update and more getting looked after by Mum fill the rest of the day. Time at the Suffolk retreat is coming to an end. Tomorrow begins the two-day run in to Clacton.

---

[6] Local girl Fran sailed round Britain in a Wayfarer and offered encouragement when I was expedition planning.

Day 97 – 11th September

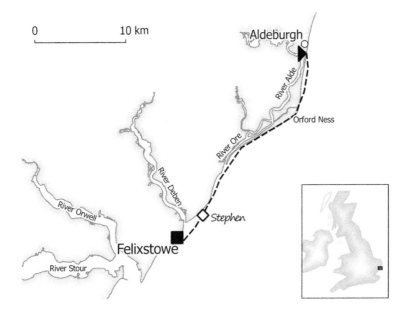

Getting off the beach today won't be easy. Waves break onto the shingle bank every three seconds and the light onshore wind provides no angle for a getaway, or even for a beach start. I study the situation for fifteen minutes before settling on a new strategy: wait for an opportunity - a slight lull in the waves, run and chuck gear, swim it out as fast as possible. More easily explained than executed - my gear is less than chuck-able. I make it out, very satisfied and relieved with how that went.

The sail to Felixstowe is pleasant. The shingle beach is a long and empty peninsula that extends to the mouth of the Alde. A lone lighthouse at Orford Ness is the only feature of note. As I kid I used to find it unnervingly empty and barren along here. The wind always seemed unnaturally cold; and the swirling currents at the mouth of the river Ore scared me too. But that was a long time ago.

There are so many rivers around here I get mixed up which is which. The next one throws up some waves on the sandbars. Trivial stuff that adds a bit of interest. I've still got to clock up the remaining miles, but those left hold no menace.

Half an hour from Felixstowe I spy a windsurfer sailing towards me. We link up, and Stephen Squirrel introduces himself. I'm instantly impressed to hear that he is also a long distance raceboarder. Like me he is carrying an EPIRB radio beacon and GPS. A rare breed we are – but we get to see extraordinary things.

Stephen is part of the Felixstowe Windsurfing Club. Some more of their members are gathered in the carpark by the beach where we land. Campervans and a ring of friendly faces on fold out chairs greet me. Some of the faces I recognise – people I raced against twenty-five years ago. We drink tea and reminisce in the afternoon sunshine.

Club ambassador Mark has agreed to put me up tonight. I am warned that he will try to get me drunk. He tries his best, but I suspect it will be Mark who has a sore head tomorrow.

Day 98 – 12th September

At 10am I depart from Felixstowe beach accompanied by some of the club sailors. They have made more effort than the weather, which is damp and grey. But to my relief there is wind, and those of us on raceboard style boards zigzag upwind at a reassuring pace.

The convoy soon fragments. Only explorer Stephen and I continue across the Felixstowe shipping lanes. We stop on the beach at Dovercourt, for a planned rendezvous with Clyde and Gregg, just in front of Mum's open beach hut. Gregg has bacon and coffee on the go. Clyde runs around getting his gear ready. Both have nervous energy for the upcoming sail. I observe their excitement with curiosity and slight amusement. I would have been this way 3 months ago.

Clyde (left), Gregg (right) and I sailed 'together' for the final leg from Dovercourt

Stephen finishes his bacon butty then heads back. That leaves the dream team – the Isle of Wight nearly men - to finish the job. I genuinely wouldn't want it any other way.

Predictably, our leisurely social sail to Clacton becomes a competitive race as soon as we hit the water. What's more the bastards are quicker than me! Not an inch is given. I sneak past Clyde but Gregg has an obvious speed advantage. I hope he won't have the legs to maintain that pace. Clyde searches for more wind further offshore and makes an unexpected gain. That forces Gregg to cover the inshore line and he obligingly donates a few seconds on every tack, narrowing the gap.

We call a truce just short of Holland Haven; stop on the beach for a breather and re-group. The stage win goes to Gregg. Pleasingly he is also most tired. I pretend to be fresh as a daisy, but if Gregg and Clyde aren't listening would concede that race pace is definitely more tiring. It makes no sense to sail flat out normally, the extra tenth of a knot literally isn't worth the effort.

We throttle back a little for the remaining 5km. A beginner's windsurfer sail comes into view. It turns out to belong to my friend Mark, last seen on Day 14 delivering cake from Portland Bill's rocks. He waves us on and will see us at the finish. The day has turned out grand. Blue skies and bright sunshine.

We sail past the Gunfleet Sailing Club – the modest little club where I learnt to sail that is still held dear. Its flagpole is decorated with every letter of the nautical alphabet. A long time ago I was a sprat in a Topper dinghy here. One of many. Perhaps my journey might be considered memorable by some of the current shoal.

A transformation of Clacton's shoreline has been completed since my departure. Crescent-shaped bays protect the now redundant sea wall. The pleasing curves of new sand reach to the pier.

A crowd becomes visible on Clacton's most famous landmark.

I sail close to the pier. Make sure I don't drop my tacks, or get caught by the fishermen. For the crowd on the end of the rickety structure my finish is an imaginary line extending out to sea. Cheers, hoots and applause compete with the wind as I – and the crowd - cross to the pier's windward side. It seems appropriate to sail in closer to the gathered crowd. I identify some of the faces, and wave. The gesture is reciprocated. Above the throng a Menorcan flag is energetically swirled.

I turn my attention to the sail to the beach. For 98 days, dry land has been the finish that counts. Ahead of the group, I haul my gear onto the sand. A simple arrival, having windsurfed round Britain.

There is no drama, fist punching or surge of emotion. I do not throw myself onto the beach or into the water. I notice a few people: outliers from the crowd. Southend Richard on a breakwater with a camera. Keith? I neatly arrange board and sail – for the first time without the pressure of *not messing up*. I have little awareness for *what* I feel, but am profoundly calm.

Half an hour of photos follow. My dad gleams and is outwardly so proud. My mum is more contained. She barely says a word but there really is no need. I pull her in close to me and we look ahead for the cameras. I know that my happiness is a weight off her shoulders.

Arriving at *my* finish line: the sand of Clacton's Pier Beach. Photo by
Mark London

Rita and Carme - Paco's daughters – have made the journey
over from Menorca. The sisters stay close to each other and are
all smiles. Rita's voice is as husky as ever. A more adult version
of the same Rita. I smile back at the favourite little sister I never
had. Paco would be so proud of his girls, and of me too.

Moira and family have made the trip up from the south coast.
Their support throughout the expedition has been as steadfast as
Dennis himself.

And many more have travelled from near and far to see me in.
Multiple short conversations. Then people break off, allow
someone else a go. Is this fame? I allow a politely waiting
journalist to grab me for a few words. When she has done the
crowd has dissolved.

* * *

We sail back to my Dad's house - jumping the waves and falling
at the corners the whole way. The accumulated tension drains
from my body.

The damaged sail falls apart upon de-rig. Like a butterfly's wings at the end of summer.

* * *

There is a buffet reception at the Gunfleet. A quick shower and I show my face. No speech from me, but a proper opportunity to chat with friends. "Will there be a book?" they ask. Maybe.

* * *

I am emotionally controlled for the finish. Relieved primarily, briefly joyful on the sail home, but nothing overwhelming. Powerful emotions do follow, including very real reliving of experiences, but these take months to emerge. They surfaced frequently in the writing of this book.

* * *

I finish my second beer and – public duties concluded - slip away. These are the first moments I have to reflect. Calm and serene as the night around me. I slow-pedal the seafront route home.

1 year on

For a while I was content. I would walk and look out to sea and from most parts of the UK coastline I could look out and think "I sailed past there". I felt privilege. For all the things I saw and the experiences I lived. My gaze would be distant, my attention too. The daydreaming phase lasted months.

* * *

My desire to windsurf round Britain tore me apart. Suppressed, it contributed to an inner sense of failure. Then, at a time in my life when I needed it most, if offered me a lifeline. In my world in which enthusiasm had become a distant memory, here – at last – was something that I wanted to do.

I never set out to write a book. Never thought I had a book in me. Never thought I'd have a story worth telling. The voice notes I recorded during the expedition were a *just in case*. An insurance policy against regret in hindsight.

When people told me I should write, I shrugged off the suggestions. It was only when I was already a long way round Britain that I began to think I might have something to say.

It was a few months after finishing before I *could* write. I had been so focussed on completing the expedition, that the psychological aspects were still raw and unprocessed. The emotions that re-surfaced were overwhelmingly powerful. And - just as with the real expedition - it was the getting started that was most difficult.

When I found my rhythm, the emotions first experienced windsurfing round Britain came flooding back. The headlands were ordeals that drained me. Land's End left me in pieces. The crossings that filled me with indecision and sometimes torment were re-anticipated and feared. And I also re-experienced gratitude, awe and appreciation. I would write each day in one sitting, and the majority of days would shatter me. Every milestone on the journey was a milestone in the book. From an emotional perspective I sailed round Britain twice.

The progression to adventurer and to writer followed similar paths.

In the early days of the expedition - and of writing - I was neither adventurer - nor writer. When press or passers-by referred to me as an adventurer, I would cringe inside. And when I wrote, if I dared think of myself as a writer, those pretentions would embarrass me.

But that changed - in both cases - when I reached as far as north-west Scotland. At that stage I had become an adventurer. And having written to that point, I felt capable as a chronicler of the experience.

And when I rounded Duncansby Head, and started the journey south, for the first time there was a conviction that I would finish this thing. I would succeed in windsurfing round Britain. Likewise, when I closed my laptop at the end of writing day sixty-three, for the first time I knew that I would finish this book.

And just as windsurfing round Britain was a fascinating and hugely rewarding experience, writing about it has been too.

* * *

An account of this type is by nature somewhat autobiographical. There may be some expectation that I touch on how my experience has changed me. I have tried to hint at these things.

I am freer. Having windsurfed round Britain I no longer want to do it. And that is most liberating. The relief from the constant pressure I put myself under during the expedition to *not mess up* is also a weight off my shoulders.

I hope that a bolstering of self-esteem can be detected. A shrugging-off of a sense of failure. A reinforced ability to see other human beings as other human beings. An acceptance of me as me, and a contentedness with how I am. Be that or not a little bit different.

Other changes might be subtler, or only have become apparent more recently, or just need some more explanation. All have been hugely positive.

I am far more likely to engage with people. The people who engage are the people who seem to get more out of life and be happier, I have observed. Sign me up please.

In situations that might be considered emotionally uncomfortable I am more in control. This is certainly helpful, though I am far from a finished article.

I have a strengthened conviction that just *keeping going* is enough. It doesn't matter what or where the goal is: keep plugging away and things will work out. Faced with something big, or difficult - that is helpful. At one difficult time during my teenage years my dad gave me a book - *The Shepherd*, by Frederick Forsyth. The message that I took from the short story is that *something will get you home*. It is a powerfully calming message - one that I repeated to myself during the expedition when struggling to get to shore, or around an island, headland, or beyond a section of cliffs. And also whilst writing this book. Focus on what you can influence, do that well, do it for hours, days or – months. The rest will work itself out.

I considered Shepherds – of a spiritual nature - on this journey. But I wasn't really looking, so didn't really find.

I finally let go of a relationship that although ended I had struggled to move on from. That is positive too.

Sometimes I think that I worried myself round Britain. That doesn't sound like an adventurer to me. But other times I fit the loner and roamer profile remarkably well. Labels: more trouble than they are worth. A label I will accept is that of being lucky. For all that has gone well in my life and all that has gone wrong I am hugely grateful.

In some ways I might consider myself *cured* - of my obsession to windsurf round Britain. But that would imply that there was something wrong with me for wanting to pursue it in the first place. I don't believe that. Not now. There were negative psychological consequences from suppressing, or being too fearful, to take on the challenge, but its ultimate realisation has led only to positive outcomes. That the obsession remained dormant and undisclosed for so long may – of course - speak of me in other ways.

The cascade effects of insights learned are still unfolding. Windsurfing round Britain released a bottleneck in my personal development. I'm happier than I've ever been in myself. And at least a bit wiser too. A good start.

* * *

Windsurfing round Britain was an adventure decades in the making. My next adventure – a book – I never saw coming. With end of expedition in sight, it came into focus and became my new goal. I've just some maps to draw now.

There is another map. On the kitchen wall. I put it there last week. My eyes move to the coastlines and I wonder about *the real sea* off those. About landing options, exposure and cold.

I didn't want that fear again. I was clear about that. But those memories are fading. The map intrudes again: beckons my focus to exclusion of all else. My mind wanders to the wild and empty solitude - to a world I have neither desire nor will to resist. And I know my greatest fear is that of regret.

I was always going back. The realisation excites and terrifies in equal measure.

Blog entries

Gregg and I both contributed blog articles. These are available online at: www.windsurfroundbritain.co.uk/blog

Below is an excerpt from the final blog entry.

"I set out from Clacton 98 days ago and turned right. I kept on sailing every day I could. I had the best 3 months of my life. I arrived back where I'd started from, with a hole where my dream had been.

"I'm sad to have finished, slightly proud and definitely relieved to have completed this adventure the way I intended: without requiring on water assistance. I could have blown that on the long journey south. My mantra to myself on the home leg was always to minimize exposure, but in strong offshore winds there is a certain amount of exposure you just can't avoid. Especially during those most exposed times, even simple acts such as flipping battens after a tack were made with an exaggerated care. I did everything I could to prevent breakages, and luck was on my side.

"It is nice to have been considered newsworthy, and charity donations have received a boost as a result of press coverage. The attention has felt like a bit of weather coming through. Like the weather, the attention soon passes. I'm really more comfortable in the post-attention sector anyway.

"I have hundreds - nah, thousands - of thankyous to make. To name each and every person who has helped me along the way is a near impossible task and certainly not one to attempt in this post. Perhaps there will be a book that will do a better job of acknowledging the support that made my windsurf round Britain such an enjoyable, and goodness-of-humanity affirming, experience.

More adventures

At the time of going to publication Jono is preparing to solo windsurf the mainland coastline of western Europe, from Russia to Russia. He estimates the 15000km journey will take two years to complete.

More details about that expedition – including how to get involved – can be found at
http://windsurfroundeurope.eu

Stay in touch

For occasional updates of adventures and publications please subscribe to Jono's newsletter at
http://jonodunnett.com/newsletter/signup

If there's a round Europe book, you'll be the first to know…